HOTEL MANAGEMENT: CURRENT ISSUES & PRACTICES

Hotel Management

Current Issues & Practices

H.C. Chaturvedi

AKANSHA PUBLISHING HOUSE
NEW DELHI - 110 002 (INDIA)

AKANSHA PUBLISHING HOUSE
4649/21-B, Ansari Road
Daryaganj, New Delhi - 110002
Phones - 23263193, 9811582579
Email: ektabooks@yahoo.com

Hotel Management: Current Issues & Practices

First Published, 2006

ISBN 81-8370-066-7

PRINTED IN INDIA

Published by M.P. Misra for Akansha Publishing House, New Delhi - 110 002 and Printed at Capital Offset Press, Delhi.

Contents

Preface

> "A sense of the value of time—that is, of the best way to divide one's time into one's various activities—is an essential preliminary to efficient work, it is the only method of avoiding hurry.
>
> —*Arnold Bennet*

Basically, hotel is an institution or building in which meals, lodging and other services are provided for the travelling people, i.e., the guests. It also provides facilities like room services, valet, laundry services, sundry shop, airline ticketing, tour reservation, transport, banking and communication services. The wide range of business activities of a hotel can be grouped as—providing accommodation; supplying food and beverages; transportation, recreational and entertainment facilities; and other activities incidental to business. A hotel is a fixed immobile installation.

With the globalisation of economies and growth of tourism all over the world, hotel industry have come to prominence and now hotel and catering industry is one of the largest employers in many developed or developing countries. As such emerged the demand of professionally trained manpower and skilled labour. Thus came in the Hotel Management. Hotel Management as a professional course is much popular and most sought-after career these days.

This book compiles vital information on some salient aspects of hotel management. Amidst plenty of literature, this book is unique, which portrays various issues in the shape of well researched articles, penned by leading experts, both academics as well as professionals in the field.

These include—Introduction to Hotel Industry; Work and Hotel Industry: A Sociological Perspective; Developing Graduate Managers for Hotel Industry; Hotel Industry and International Labor Markets; Controller: A Career for Hotel Management; Hotel Industry and Human Resource management; New Operations Management Curriculum: Change, Opportunity; Performance Management; Hotel Operations Management; Food, Beverage and Accommodation; Hotel Managers in Emerging Locations; Hospitality and Tourism Academic Research: Clusters and Gaps; The future of Hotel and Catering Work; and Staff Management in Hotel Industry; etc. A glossary of relevant terms and an exhaustive bibliography are its added features.

Admittedly, the liberal borrowing from one quarter or other, made this effort come to present shape. As such entire credit goes to the original contributors, whose works we have heavily drawn upon. We owe a deep sense of gratitude to them all. Different professionals from various hotels and industry, libraries etc., deserve our appreciation for their inspiration, help and assistance. Finally, we thank our publishers for bringing out this book in superb way.

—HCC

1

Introduction to Hotel Industry

The world turns aside to let any man pass who knows where he is going. The ability to make up your mind inspires self-confidence, it gives you inner power, and it commands the respect of your fellow men.

—*David Starr Jordan*

India has had a great legacy of hospitality. 'Guest is God' is the typical Indian tradition. Its history goes back when the necessity and urge to travel for food or animals led to the setting up of places where rest and food by the travellers could be obtained. The people of India have travelled long distances either for pilgrimage, or for trade purposes. There were no hotels in the ancient times and the needs of the travellers for food and accommodation were mostly met by the house-holders, which are still existent in the interior areas of the country. For facilitating travel is North, South, East and West parts of the country, kings and rulers took the responsibility themselves. They built Dharmshalas, constructed roads, planted trees and arranged drinking water nearby.

Developments in the means of transportation and communication have resulted in the establishment of accommodation in the major cities of the country. However, as far as the modern lodging facilities are concerned the credit goes to the Britishers.

By the early 18th century plenty of taverns with fashionable names like Georg's, Parsei George, Victory hotel and luxurious Hope Hall were in existence in the country. David Prince in 1778, could find the hotel accommodation in India. David Prince who visited India stayed at Macfarland Hotel, Mumbai which was a luxurious and expensive hotel. Victory hotel and Albion hotel were perhaps the first to acquire the name 'Hotel in India'. However, these early hotels were owned as well as used only by the Britishers. The credit for opening the first western style hotel goes to Pallongee Pertonjee in 1840, when he started the 'British Hotel' in Mumbai. He is known as the pioneer of the western style hotels in India, for his reputation and efficient management. Subsequently, Auckland hotel was also started in Kolkata in 1843, which was renamed in 1858 as 'Great Eastern Hotel'. The first large scale hotel in India was opened in 1871 by Mr. John by Mr. John Wakson named 'Esplanade Hotel'. The hotel industry then grew rapidly and by the end of 19th century there were a number of hotels in India. Remarkably 20th century was a turning point in the history of the hotel industry in India. It is in this century that we find the real growth and development of the accommodation sector. Ownership has changed from sole proprietors to corporate and big business owners and new enterpreneurs entered in the field of accommodation sector. In 1902 there was a significant event in the history of hotel business when the Indian Hotel Company was incorporated on 1st of April 1902 in Mumbai with the authorised capital of Rs. 30 lakh. In 1904, J.N. Tata opened the Taj Mahal Hotel in Mumbai. Thereafter a number of other hotels were opened such as Ajanta, New Woodland, Grand Hotel, Associated Hotels of India Ltd., East India Hotels Ltd., Oberoi Hotels, Cecil Hotel, Wild Flower Hall etc.

Further, for the first time in India it was pointed out by the Sargent committee (1945) that they were facing a serious problem of accommodation. After Independence, many more private sector and public sector entrepreneurs entered into hotel business such as Indian Tobacco Company Ltd., Air India, Hotel Corporation of India Ltd., India Tourism Development Corporation and the Clarks Group of Hotels.

Since globalization and liberalisation, the International hotel chains have registered there presence in India. A Park Royal Hotel in New Delhi has recently been opened under the banner of South Pacific Hotel Corporation (SPHC). Presently, in India, the accommodation capacity of 80,000 rooms is slated to go up by 100,000 and the target of 1,30,000 rooms by 2010 AD is likely to be met.

Classification of Hotels

Basically, hotel is an institution or a building in which lodging, meals and other services are provided for the travelling people. In addition, it also provides amenities and facilities like room services, laundry services, valet, sundry shops, auto rentals, airline ticketing, tour reservation, transport, banking and postal services etc. Thus, it is said that "a hotel is a world within a world with its own peculiar movements and fashions." A hotel has a wide range of business activities which can be grouped into four categories:

- — Providing accommodation
- — Supplying Food and Beverage
- — Having transportation, recreational and entertainment facilities,
- — Other activities incidental to business.

A hotel is a fixed immobile installation. Its products i.e., acommodation + Food + Beverage and other services can not move to the tourists. It has an open and unique system because customers/tourists enter the hotel boundary, consume the products within it and return with intengible product while the other industries or plants never permit the consumers to enter its boundary and consume the product within its boundary, inspite they return with a tangible product. Therefore, a number of factors are acting together which put a great demand on the hotels for its products. The main are:

— Increasing population
— Rapid urbanisation and growth of cities.
— Broader parameters of tourism.
— Proliferation of economic transactions, intraction, sports and recreational facilities.
— Proximity to other large towns and accessibility.

No doubt, the classification of hotels within the industry is a complicated task. Hotels are of various types depending on the factors like the natue and types of facilities offered. The classification in a real sense means that which separates accommodation into different categories or classes for example hotels, motels, tourist lodges, resorts, heritage hotels, youth hostels, inns, Yatri Niwas, holiday camps and so forth. It presents information about accommodation which enables the travel companies, travel agents, tour operators and tourists to reserve accommodation as and when it is required. Lodging establishments are classified on the following basis.

A. *Physical Characteristics*

— Hotels
— Motels
— Resorts
— Roatel
— Floating hotels
— Conventional hotels
— All-suite hotels
— Condotel
— Heritage hotels.

B. *Tarriff Pattern*

— American Plan
— European Plan

— Continental Plan
— Modified American Plan.

C. Size

—	Small Hotel	—	25 Rooms or less
—	Average Hotel	—	25 to 90 Rooms
—	Above Average	—	90 to 250 Rooms
—	Large Hotel	—	250 and above Rooms.

D. Price level

— Luxury hotels
— Executive/First class hotels
— Tourist Class hotels
— Budget hotels

E. Geographic location

— Mountain Hotel
— Hill Resorts
— Beach Resorts/Hotels
— Forest Hotels/Resorts
— Farm Houses.

F. Facilities and degree of comfort

— 5 star deluxe hotels
— 5 star hotels
— 4 star hotels
— 3 star hotels
— 2 star hotels
— 2 star hotels.

Apartment Hotel Classification

Since Hotel sector is an important segment of tourism industry, and is growing at a very high rate. Due to this many NNCs and other industrial organisations are entering into this vital sector of Indian tourism industry. These companies are building hotels and other accommodation to cater the growing demands of visitors. In these days apartment hotels are becoming more popular among the business travellers, families, conferences, events, and holiday travellers. Thus, with the aim of providing standardised, world class quality and services to the tourists, Department of Tourism, Govt. of India has introduced a voluntary scheme for classification of fully operational apartment hotels in the categories of 5 Star Deluxe, 5 Star, 4, Star and 3 Star.

Classification Committee

The Classification Committee for apartment hotel consists of the following:

- Chairman (HRACC) or his representative.
- Representatives from FHRAI, HAI, IATO, TAAI, IHM, Director (T).
- Member Secretary.
- Any other member of State Govt.

In case of any classification with the decision of HRACC the Hotels may appeal to Secretary (T) Govt. of India, for review and reconsideration with 30 days.

Classification of Apartment Hotels

Department of Tourism, government of India has issued terms, condition and guidelines for approval and classification of apartment hotels vide its letter No. 3 - TH.1(2)/2002 dated 4th March 2004. The terms and conditions can be modified and changed at any time. Project approval is valid for 5 years. Project approvals of the Department of Tourism Govt. of India cease 3 months from the date that hotel becomes operational. On the other hand, classification for newly operational hotels must be sought within 3 months of completion of approved hotels projects. Classification is valid for five years.

Hotel Room Types, Location, Bedding and Rates

Notably, selecting the right type of accommodation for the right person at the right time and place is one of the most important decisions to be taken by a tour planner. Type of room, location, bedding type and room rates are the prime factors in most of the requests, whether it is business man who does not want to waste time in getting his appointments or holiday travellers who want to get away from the hub of life or others who need accommodation. Thus, the tour planner must understand the nature of the room, its type, location, bedding and rate for a particular client.

Type of Room

However today, due to the rapid growth and diversification in hotel industry, several hotels provide different types of rooms and different rates are charged from the clients. The following basic-room-categories are widely used:

— *Deluxe Room*--It contains extra amenities such as refrigerator, stock of beverages and a minibar. The bedding in a deluxe room usually consists of one or two queen beds or one king bed. It has a prominent location and the highest comfort.

— *Suit*--It consists of separate living and sleeping areas, with cooking facilities. A bedroom suite may have one, two or three bedrooms in addition to a living room or a parlor and a full kitchen. It has also been noticed that some suites also have conference rooms.

— *Superior Room*--A superior room may have the same comforts and furnishings as in a deluxe room but it has a less desirable location or a smaller bedding. Usually, the location is on the ground floor. The rate and bedding depend on the property as in case

GUIDELINES FOR APPROVAL OF APARTMENT HOTELS

General	*Star*	*Category*	*Comments*
24 hour lifts for buildings higher than ground plus two floors	N	N	Mandatory for new hotels. Local laws may require a relaxation of this condition.
Parking	N	N	One parking space per unit should be provided.
Guest room Minimum 10 lettable rooms. All rooms with outside window/ventilation.	N	N	
Minimum floor area Studio including sleeping, living, bathing, cooking and dining - sqft.	250	251-350	
Minimum floor area 1 bedroom including sleeping, living, bathing, cooking and dining - sqft.	500	500-650	Living, During, bedroom and kitchen areas are separate with doors.
Minimum floor area 2 bedrooms including sleeping, livings, bathing, cooking and dining-sqft.	760	950	Living, Dining, bedroom and kitchen areas are separate with doors.
Minimum floor area 3 bedrooms including sleeping, living, bathing, cooking, and dining-sqft.	1000	1250	Living, Dining, bedroom and kitchen areas are separate with doors.
Dining area	N	N	Separate dining table and chairs to accommodate maximum bedding.

General	Star	Category	Comments
Air - Conditioning	N	N	Air-conditioning/hearing depends on climatic conditions and architecture, Room tamp, should be betwen 20 and 28 Degrees C. for 4*, 5* Deluxe between 20 and 24 degrees C. For 3 star minimum 50% of the apartments should be air-conditioned.
Iron with iron board	N	N	
A 15 amp earthed power socket	N	N	
Television	N	N	
Internet Connection	D	N	For 3 star and 4 star internet facility be made available in the Business Centre.
Telephone in the room	N	N	
Ward robe with minimum 12 cloths hangers per bedding	N	N	
Shelves or drawer space	N	N	
Bathrooms No. of dedicated (private) bathrooms - studio	1	1	
No. of dedicated (private) bathrooms - 1 Bedroom	1	1½	Half bath toilet and wash basin.
No. of dedicated (private) bathrooms - 2 Bedroom	2	2½	

General	*Star*	*Category*	*Comments*
No. of dedicated (private) bathrooms - 2 Bedroom	2	2½	
No. of dedicated (private) bathrooms - 2 Bedroom	2	3½	
Minimum Size of Bathroom in square feet	36	40	
Western WC toilet to have a seat, lid, toilet Paper	N	N	
Floors and walls to have non - porous surface	N	N	
Water saving taps/shower	N	N	
Kitchens/Kitchenettes			
Kitchenettes for Studios	N	N	Screened area-- two burner stove top, no open flame, Microwave oven or OTG, Fridge (165 Ltr.) utensils, crockery and cutlery, Tea/Coffee maker, sink, exhaust fan.
Kitchens for 1 bedroom and larger	N	N	Dedicated kitchen - 4 burner stove, Microwave oven, Tea/coffee maker, full size fridge, sink, exhaust fan, utensils, cutlery, crockery.
Washing Machines/dryers	D	D	Arrangements be made available for laundry/ dry cleaning services.
Public Areas			
A lounge or seating in the lobby area	N	N	
Reception facility manned 24 hours	N	N	

General	*Star*	*Category*	*Comments*
Heating and cooling t be provided in enclosed public rooms	N	N	Temperatures to be between 20 - 28 degrees celcius
Lounge or seating in the lobby area	N	N	
Dining room serving break - fast	N	N	
Garbage room (wet and dry)	N	N	
Room for left luggage facilities	N	N	
Health Fitness facilities	N		Necessary for 4 star and above, desirabel for 3 - star
Guest Service			
Utility Shop	N	N	
Acceptance of common credit cards	N	N	
A public telephone on premises, Unit charges made known.	N	N	
Wake - up call service on request.	N	N	
Messages for guests to be recorded and delivered.	N	N	
Name, address and tel. no. of doctors with front desk.	N	N	
Assistance with luggage on request	N	N	

General	*Star*	*Category*	*Comments*
Stamps and mailing facilities	N	N	
Left luggage facilities	N	N	
Fax and Photocopy service	N	N	
Business Centre	N	N	This should be a dedicated area. In resort destinations, tourist and pilgrimage centres this may be relaxed.
Safekeeping facilities available	N	N	
Smoke detectors	N	N	These can be battery operated
Fire and emergency procedure notices displayed in rooms behind door	N	N	
Fire exit sign on guest floors with emergency power	N	N	
Public liability insurance	D	D	
Swimming Pool	N		This can be related for hill destinations. Necessary for 4 - star and desirable for 3 - star.
Indore Games Activity Rook	N	N	
Outdoor Games Like Tennis, Badminton	D	N	

of international hotel chains the bedding and rate will be higher as compared to other properties. Bedding usually consists of one or two double beds or queen beds, or one king bed.

— *Standard Room*--It consists of one or two double beds; one queen bed or two twin beds. Rooms in this category usually do not have a view and may be located in the least convenient section of the hotel.

— *Economic/Budget Room*--This tyupe of room is usually used by the budget class tourists and might be given at low discounted rates. Budget rooms are smaller than other rooms in a hotel and also has a smaller bedding.

— *Bedding types*--Besides the room category, the tour planner also had to understand the types of beds because some people want to stay in those hotels where they can find bedding according to their desire/ need.

The main bedding types are:

— *King Bed*--In king beds, one will find the largest mattress size i.e. 76 inches wide by 80 inches long. These type of beds are provided only in suites or deluxe rooms.

— *Queen Bed*--It is about 60 inches wide by 80 inches long. A room with queen beds may have either one or two beds.

— *Standard Double Bed*--A standard double bed in 54 inches wide by 75 inches long and is usually provided in standard and economy rooms. A room may have either one or two beds.

4. *Twin Bed*--It is about 39 inches wide by 75 inches long and is designed for one adult. In most, of the cases a room equipped with twin beds has two beds.

Rates of Room

As a general practice, in almost all hotel properties, the rate of various rooms are based on room location such as pool side, ocean view, beach front, market front, ground level and suitability to the handicap. One more thing should also be clarified before a room is booked i.e., the taxes. Various states, countries or cities impose taxes on hotel rooms. Such taxes may be called room tax, hotel tax or bed lodging or value added tax, etc. The ranged tax is from 2 per cent to 20 per cent. Generally, the room rate excludes these type of taxes. But what actually is a room rate?

No doubt, room size, location, type and rate vary significantly from one property to another and often within the same hotel. The price charged from the traveller by a hotel for the right to occupy a room is known as room rate, which is based on the season i.e., a peak or a lean season. Mostly in peak season the hotels charge a high rate whereas in a lean season low rate is charged. However, the following room rates are mostly followed in hotel industry:

1. *Group Rates* — It is a discounted rate based on the purpose of a pre-set quantity of rooms. For example when rooms/accommodation is required for the attendees of convention, conference or a meeting, the hotel charge a discounted rate because it increases the sale of rooms during that period or it provides a consistent cash flow.
2. *Rack Rates* — It is a standard rate charged by a hotel from the guests. Basically, it depends on the room category and bedding type rooms sold to an invidual at the rack rates are called transient rates.
3. *Package Rates* — Many hotel chains offer a complete package of hotel products. It means hotels provide/ offer accommodation and other components in a package such as a new year's eve package or a

tennis resort that offers a package rate that includes tennis court fee as well as accommodation in a seasonal package.

4. *Wholesale Rate* — It is also known a tour rate. It is given to wholesalers or tour operators who buy the rooms in bulk. In some hotel properties, it is a fixed rate, while in others it is negotiated by the tour planners. Usually the tour planners fix this rate for a specific period, say one night or peak or lean season, before the client itinerary is made.
5. *Special Rate* — It is known as promotional rate and is offered to corporate clients, government employees, travel professionals, military personnel and repeat customers.
6. *Run of the House Rate* — If, for some reasons, a hotel management cannot guarantee a particular room type, a special rate may be offered for the best room that is available at the time of check-in. For example, rooms that are sold by hotels at tour rate are based on the run of the house.
7. *Family Rates* — Some hotels provide free accommodation to the children with parents, under a specified age. However, additional rates are charged if extra facilities are provided to the children.

Evaluating these facts we find that the selection of accommodation is very important in tour planning, whether it is a simple booking for one night or for a full tour. But sometimes it can be one of the most difficult decision—area in travel planning due to the limited number of hotels, and the lack of hotel ratings that are good and factually due, which can be depended upon for unbiased opinion. Unless the tour planner himself has a personal knowledge about the hotels, he cannot rely on the claims in the borchure and the current hotel-rating-lists available in the market.

The hotel brochure presents the most attractive pictures and the most glowing descriptions. Hotel ratings vary according to the system used at a particular destination/ country. Almost every country has of a different hotel classification system and the hotel rating is based in the classification of property. Thus, a uniform system of hotel rating would benefit the entire travel industry and would simplify the tour planner's job in selecting a hotel and in providing exact information in the tour itinerary.

Reservation Procedure

Empirical evidences show different tourists require different types of accommodation for example American tourists want private baths; German, Australian, English, French, Italian and even the Indian outbound tourists have their own requirements concerning the accommodation. It has also observed that this requirement is different for business travellers, corporate travellers and others. Generally, tours are sold on a two person per room basis, that is usually referred to in the industry as twin-in-sharing. However, those wishing to have a single room are charged a single room supplement. Therefore, tour planner/ manager must strike a balance in obtaining quality accommodations at a price that is affordable so that the largest market can be solicited for participation in the tour.

During the 'Fam Trip' the tour planner must identify the requirements of various lodging properties for tours that he is going to organise.

By 'Hotel reservation' means an advance request for accommodation. The reservation is the most important function of hotel management which consists of receiving, documenting and analysing room requests. It is also known as selling accommodations. Mostly hotels perform this function through sales representatives, own's reservation offices in different locations, travel agents, airlines, cruise companies and tour operators. Before the reservation of accommodations, the tour planners and hotel managements enter into a contract. Practically, the negotiation for the price or room rate is based on two types of contracts between the tour planner and the hotel management. These are:

Generally, the request for reservation for a Foreign Independent Tour (FIT) or Group tour should be in writing, either in the letter from or on a pre-printed reservation form and it should be sent as far as possible in advance. However, for individual domestic tours or Group domestic tours, telephone is the quickest and the most efficient method of making request for hotel reservations. Some tour operators have devised their own types of hotel request forms and print it locally. The request forms are usually in different parts, may be in three to five parts. An original and two duplicate copies are sent to the hotel. The hotel management then return one of the duplicate copy with either their confirmation their refused on the request. The third copy is replaced in the client's file. The other copies are used in 'commission due' and book keeping purposes.

On the basis of this information a tour operator purchases rooms in bulk, negotiates prices or rates, confirms and makes it sure that the accommodation is according to his itinerary planning. However, the success of hotel reservation lies in good relationship, communication and understanding between hotel management and tour management. It is the tour planner's responsibility to forward exact information on each booking and it is the hotel management's responsibility to keep the tour planner or tour manager informed on the current or proposed developments which may effect the decision in hotel selection. It is also the hotel management's responsibility to honor confirmed reservations made by the tour planner. Today, many tour companies are using Computer Reservation

Systems (CRS) for the reservation of accommodations. This system can be used either in producing a list of participating hotels in a specified city or to indicate the room types and rates that are available in each hotel property for a specified period. The property description containing information about facilities, reservation policies, room options, credit cards, hotel vouchers, and acceptance, can be obtained through a computer.

The computerised reservation systems in the hotel industry were first used by Sheraton Group of hotels in 1956. These were further developed and refined by Holiday Inn in 1960 and since then this system have gone through a generations of refinements. Today, all most every hotel and hotel chains have their own computerised reservation system. This has helped the tour companies in the quick reservation and confirmation of thier accommodations. Another dimensions of information technology is 'Internet' which has changed the entire structure of travel industry distribution in the world.

Procedure for Payment

Whether the room are purchased in bulk or a single room is booked for one night, the tour operator has to make payments on behalf of his clients. Therefore, a client/group of tourists does not pay the dues to the hotel management for the use of accommodation and services. He simply shows the hotel voucher or any other document issued by the tour company. The document is issued by the tour company for hotels, starting that the individual/ group has already paid for it and is entitled to use certain types of rooms and services. The document serves, both, as a reservation/confirmation voucher as well as a receipt for the money collected by the travel/tour company. The hotel voucher has three parts, the top part is for the client and the bottom part is sent by the hotel to recover the payment from the tour company.

Conventionally, the tour companies are entitled for commision on reservation. The rate of commission vary from property to property, city to city or country to country. In many cases, tour operators collect money from the client for the accommodation in advance and send to the appropriate hotel the collected amount by deducting the commission from it. This is usually done in the case of Foreign hotels. In the case of travel agents, the commission is the main source of income, whereas in the case for a tour operator, the commission hardly matters, as he is more concerned with his profit or loss because he has purchased the accommodation in bulk.

The payment for the reservation is made by the tour operator in different ways like—partial payment and full payment.

The mode of payment is based on the contract between the tour company and the hotel management. However, in case of foreign hotels or overseas hotels, the payment is made periodically as per the agreement with the currency control officials.

It would be advisable, if the group is not escorted by a staff member of the tour company, to select a member from the group to act as a liaison between the hotel management and the group members. The group should also be advised that each individual of the group must pay those charges which are not included in the price of the tour.

Currently, hotel industry is getting momentum not only in India but at global level. The World Tourism Organisation (WTO) has estimated that there will be more than 20 million rooms world wide in the accommodation sector by the end of this century. The world's inventory of rooms will also increase by 4 per cent annually.

Since 1990, many Indian and Foreign companies are entering in this fastest growing industry. The Government is also motivating the private entrepreneurs to enter into this venture by giving them various financial and non-financial incentives because they can contribute much towards Indian economy such as: Employment generation; Foreign exchange; Balance of payment; Rural development; Development of transportation and communication; and High standard of living.

REFERENCES

Foster, I.D. (1994). *Introduction to Travel and Tourism*, Macmillan, New York.

Holloway, C. (1994). *The Business of Tourism,* Pitman, London.

Poynter, J.M. (1993). *Tour Design, Marketing and Management,* Prentice Hall, New York.

Seth, P.N. (1997). *Successful Tourism Management,* Vol. II Sterling Publication (P) Ltd., New Delhi.

Vale, P. (1995). *The Business of Tour Operations*, Pitman, London.

2

Work and Hotel Industry: A Sociological Perspecive

> Every man is to be respected as an absolute end in himself; and it is a crime against the dignity that belongs to him as a human being, to use him as a mere means for some external purpose.."'
>
> —*Immanuel Kant*

As per latest estimation, the hotel and catering industry is one of the largest employers in the Britain and many other developed (and, increasingly, less developed) countries. Some 10 per cent of the British workforce are engaged in hotel and catering employment, representing somewhere between two and two and a half million persons. The 'hospitality industry', as it is now commonly referred to, is the most important element in the wider tourism sector. Economists frequently point to its heterogeneous nature: the industry comprises units ranging from the most humble cafe to the largest luxury hotel owned by a multinational corporation. Hospitality industry employers stress the caring people-oriented nature of hotels and catering, generating a glamorous mystique that is all too easily reinforced by images in popular media (Wood, 1990a). Further, the industry is often presented as a paragon of conservative virtues. Low barriers to entry mean that, in theory at least, the hotel and catering sector is fertile ground for the small-time entrepreneur. Similarly, a view is promulgated of career development in the industry as open and meritocratic: even the kitchen pan washer can rise to become general manager of the hotel with hard work and dedication.

Supporting these powerful images is an educational system that for post-school students separates out courses in hotel and catering management from those in general business studies, encouraging an insularity that is characteristic of the industry as a whole. This insularity manifests itself in a variety of ways, most commonly in pleas from those connected with it for the industry to be regarded as unique and 'special', requiring specialist skills and training, a special attitude of mind and body, specialist professional associations and, above all, special academic understanding.

Those engaged in the hotel and catering industry at all levels have elevated special pleading to a fine art but the mythologies that surround the industry cannot disguise the true nature of much hospitality industry employment, of low wages and poor working conditions, of exploitation and minimal job security, of monotonous yet demanding work, of degrading and low status occupations. Evidence for all of these is to be found in a substantial body of published research concerned with the nature of hotel and catering employment. Broadly speaking, this literature can be divided into five categories:

1. a number of sociological studies of work and employment in hotels and catering the majority of which are concerned with workplace relations;
2. a body of quasi-sociological research addressed to one or other of the hospitality industry's labour 'problems', for example labour turnover and the adoption of flexible working strategies in hotel and catering organisations;
3. a literature combining sociological, economic and social policy concerns and centring on the nature of hotel and catering labour markets (Henderson, 1965; Witz and Wilson, 1982; Alpert, 1986; Crompton and Sanderson, 1990);
4. a variety of mainly official reports by government and other organisations on the condition of labour

in the industry and the nature of labour problems in hotels and catering; and

5. similar reports published by campaign and pressure groups, most notably in Britain, the Low Pay Unit network.

The casual researcher would be hard pushed to find mention of this material in the many textbooks devoted to personnel management in hotels and catering. These manuals, purporting to apply 'human resource management' techniques to the hospitality industry are for the most pan 'how to do it' manuals which often verge on the anodyne. Their content bears little relevance to either the realities of work experience in the industry or actual labour management practices. Most are written without reference to hard research data, exhibiting instead a tendency to offer prescriptive and generalised solutions to personnel issues (Mars, Bryant and Mitchell, 1979: 128).

This book draws across the range of studies of hotel and catering work though the main objective is to construct, in the broadest sense, a sociological account of employment in the hospitality industry. This presents an immediate problem for, despite the existence of a small literature, within the mainstream of sociological studies of work and industry more generally, hotels and catering along with other service industries have attracted little research attention compared to manufacturing. This reflects wider societal attitudes towards service industries which vary from the indifferent to the outrightly hostile. A commentator in the *Guardian* newspaper (2 July 1987) observed of economic trends that 'we are left with the distinctive feeling that the country is being seduced by the short-term palliatives of the candy-floss tourist economy'. Attitudes like these undoubtedly have some grounding in hard economic and social analysis but they are also the product of a deeply ingrained snobbery that characterises British social institutions. The academic establishment is not immune to such prejudices and amongst industrial sociologists it is difficult to find a satisfactory explanation for the general neglect of service employment. As Crompton (1989: 129) in a review of Gabriel's *Working Lives in Catering* (1988) puts it: 'Much of the empirical research and theorising current in the Sociology of Work is derived from what are now outdated studies of predominantly male, predominantly white production workers'.

Crompton's strictures identify only one of the problems attendant on any discussion of the sociology of work. Internal debates about the scope and methods of industrial sociology and the use of a range of terms to describe what appear to be roughly similar areas of concern are two further barriers to clarity. Detailed examination of both the historical development of industrial sociology as a field of study and the preoccupations of its major sub-disciplines fall outside the scope of this discussion. However, some brief sketch is necessary in order to demonstrate those connections that do exist between the mainstream of industrial sociology and existing sociological analyses of hotel and catering work.

Infact, the origins of industrial sociology lie in the attempts of the classical sociologists Marx, Weber and Durkheim to assess the impact of industrialisation on society within more general theories of social development. It is the work of F. W. Taylor, however, that is generally accepted as marking the beginnings of a specialist sociology of work. His development of 'scientific management' (Taylorism) entailed the application of supposedly scientific techniques to the analysis of employment for the purposes of controlling and quantifying labour and resources in order to eliminate industrial inefficiency, inefficiency perceived as deriving both from workers' attempts to control and limit output in order to maximise rewards and the ignorance of managements as to the nature of the productive process. If not quite the original 'time and motion' man, Taylor proposed strategies based on the acquisition of workers' knowledge and its vesting in separate and specialist managerial functions combined with systems of reward that would appeal to employees' self-interest. In short, with sufficient encouragement, money could buy anything including the acquiescence of the greedy worker.

Much of Taylor's theory of scientific management was derived from close observation of work at plant level and the tradition of 'plant sociology' with its emphasis on workplace behaviour was continued under the auspices of those researchers committed to a human relations perspective. Rose (1975) has remarked that Taylor and other early industrial sociologists were not, in point of fact, sociologists at all, and early social scientific interest in industry was more to do with improving management and productivity than with intellectual inquiry. To some degree, the human relations perspective was perhaps the first 'movement' in the study of industrial sociology to strive for credibility in both respects. In many ways a reaction against Taylorism, the human relations movement emphasised a vastly different view of human nature based on the idea of people's need for sociability, a need regarded as being constrained by then prevailing modes of factory work organisation. The best known studies of the human relations movement are the 'Hawthorn experiments' conducted for the Western Electric Company. After the Second World War, human relations, like Taylorism, fell into disrepute, criticised for favouring managerial problematics and priorities and neglecting conflict and the wider socio-economic and political context in which work was performed. It was around this time that the sociological study of work began to become more obviously fragmented into specialisms. Plant studies continued to dominate, though now the focus shifted to the role of technology in determining work experiences, workplace behaviour and organisational form to the extent that the British Tavistock Institute 'developed' the concept of socio-technical systems, most clearly associated with the work of Joan Woodward (1958, 1965) who claimed to have found that management style and formal work organisation were determined for the most part by technology. This post-war offshoot from human relations constituted in the most general sense the beginnings of organisational sociology.

Throughout the 1950s and 1960s the neo-human relations school was also concerned with the relationship between work, the individual and the organisation. Exponents of this approach continue even now to enjoy enormous popularity amongst writers of 'behavioural science' textbooks for management students, despite the fact that much of the work associated with the neo-human relations school has been discredited (if ever it were creditable). Rose (1975) calls this group 'organisational psycho-technologists'.

Watson (1980) is altogether less charitable:

> A psychologistic concern with some notion of 'human nature' as the basis for understanding human aspects of work is clearly seen in what is proving to be one of the most influential contributions of social scientists to managerial thinking to date. This is the work of those writers frequently seen as composing a neo-Human Relations school and whom I like to label *behavioural science entrepreneurs.* These writers include some of the best known names among modern management writers, including McGregor, Likert, Argyris, Gellerman, Blake, Herzberg and Reddin [to this list one may add with some qualification the name of Maslow whose work inspired many of those in this list]. I refer to them as entrepreneurs because their work is designed to sell, whether in the form of books, management seminars, training films or consultancies. Like the task-splitting scientific management with whom they so passionately take issue, their work is reductionist, partial,

> evangelistic and sociologically highly inadequate on the explanatory level with its underplaying of structural, situational, cultural, political and economic factors. It is ultimately simplistic but by a judicious mixing of simplistic assumptions and pseudo-scientific jargon it has made itself highly marketable.
>
> (Watson, 1980: 38)

The second approach that complemented the emergent sociology of organisations was the sociology of occupations, the origins of which Rose (1975) traces to the early 1940s and the work of Chicago sociologist E.C. Hughes. Many introductory texts on the sociology of work and industry accord the sociology of occupations little attention (Watson, 1988 and Salaman, 1986) and Rose (1975) dismisses the area thus:

> While most of those who have claimed the title of industrial sociologist have traditionally been concerned primarily with behaviour in the work-place, the occupational sociologist has explored such matters as the subjective consequences of work for the individual, its meaning to him, its effect on his attitudes and relationships in other social contexts, and the tactics which members of an occupation adopt to increase their rewards, security and prestige.... Generally speaking, however, occupational sociology can be regarded as complementary to traditional industrial sociology.
>
> (Rose, 1975: 18)

This dismissiveness presents something of a difficulty here since many sociological studies of work in hotels and catering are within the broad tradition of occupational sociology, a point that will be elaborated upon later in the chapter.

Diversification of sociological interest in work in the post-war period makes it possible to speak of distinct sub-disciplines or thematic orientations, but it is necessary to appreciate that such distinctions disguise overlapping concerns and are thus necessarily artificial. Having said this, the two final 'strands'--industrial relations and labour process approaches--represent slight deviations from this norm.

The industrial relations approach is exceptionally difficult to define in terms of scope and interest, maintaining at one level an extremely formal interest in the mechanisms of the relationships between capital and organised labour--most notably collective bargaining, trade union organisation and behaviour, and the relationship between trade unions and employer organisations in terms of the maintenance of stability and control in industry. At another level, more radical perspectives have eschewed this institutional approach in favour of the analysis of industrial conflict in terms of irreconcilable class interests and class conflict and the dislocation of trade unions' behaviour and activity from the (supposed) real interests of their members (Hyman, 1975). Whilst there are clear overlaps of interest between industrial relations and other branches of the sociology of work and industry, the links are, in some areas at least, arguably weaker than those that exist between other sub-disciplines. The same cannot be said of labour process approaches.

In 1974, Harry Braverman's *Labor and Monopoly Capital* offered a trenchant reassertion of the Marxist analysis of work that sought to eliminate what the author viewed as the artificial complexities erected by sociologists in an effort to understand the nature of work, and reassert a view of work as degraded as a result of the application of Taylorist techniques to labour processes. The extent to which the labour process approach has dominated recent sociology of work cannot be underestimated. Despite accusations of 'Bravermania' (Salaman, 1986: 24), as debates have developed, a much richer vein of analysis that draws on many of the other traditions in industrial sociology has been tapped--on organisational and occupational control and resistance to work degradation and deskilling--whilst at the same time extending the scope of sociological analysis to take into consideration, in a more explicit way, economic factors influencing labour and work.

Catering Work and Hotel

The foregoing discussion is necessarily skeletal and professional industrial sociologists will readily note its inadequacies and omissions. The important point is that the preoccupations of mainstream industrial sociology have left the analysis of hotel and catering work relatively untouched. The earliest systematic study of hotel and catering labour was W.F. Whyte's *Human Relations in the Restaurant Industry* (1948) which was firmly rooted in the human relations tradition. It was followed a year later by an article on similar themes in the *American Journal of Sociology* (Whyte, 1949). From the general perspective of organisational sociology, Bowey (1976) attempted to apply a form of action theory to the analysis of restaurants and Shamir (1978) examined the implication of contingency theories of organisation for an understanding of hotel work. Industrial relations approaches have generated a small number of case studies of trade union activity in hotels and catering (Horowitz, 1960; Chopping. 1977; Wood and Pedlar, 1978) and the labour process debate has also made its mark, though only on a limited scale.

Despite being undertaken from different theoretical and methodological standpoints, many of these studies are loosely bound together in terms of certain shared concepts, ideas and assumptions. There is little theoretical synergy however. Indeed, if the sociological study of hotel and catering work to date has any defining feature it is the triumph of empiricism over theory, of data collection and description over systematic attempts to relate data to wider theoretical issues in the sociology of work and to the experiences of labour in other industries. The empirical base is a very narrow one at that but has come to form the bedrock of an orthodox perspective on hospitality employment, a 'dominant research paradigm' (Lennon and Wood, 1989). This orthodoxy tends to depict hotel and catering employment as a special analytic case and is accepting of the industry's own self-perception of itself as 'unique', as a closed industrial and social system sustained and influenced by its own structures and procedures to the near exclusion of the effects of exogenous factors.

Many operational and labour problems are seen as deriving from the singular service nature of hotel and catering operations. Whyte (1948) recognised and to some extent attempted correction of this view by drawing attention to both the production and service elements of restaurant operations, an observation subsequently reiterated more famously and in more general terms by Levitt (1972):

> Purveyors of service think that they and their problems are fundamentally different from other businesses and their problems. They feel that service is people-intensive, while the rest of the economy is capital intensive. But these distinctions are largely spurious. There are no such things as service industries. There are only industries where service components are greater or less than those of other industries.

To many, the observations of Whyte (1948) and Levitt (1972) may appear blindingly obvious but the assumptions described by the latter continue to enjoy substantial currency. One consequence of approaching the hospitality industry as a 'special case' has been a tendency to adopt a 'problem-solving' approach to hotel and catering work that treats the principal features of industry employment as immutable. From this position, many of the industry's labour problems are seen as emanating from, what are usually presented as, antediluvian management practices amenable to improvement through alterations to organisational design and management style. As might be anticipated, there are elements of this approach in the human relations work of Whyte (1948). In a somewhat exaggerated response to *Human Relations in the Restaurant Industry,* Rose (1988: 162), with dismissive clinical disapprobation, remarks that the book is 'a popularly written work with much advice to restaurant managers on keeping employees happy, containing little systematic theorising'. Rose has a point. Whyte suggested, *inter alia,* that conflict between food production and service staff might be reduced if management introduced communication devices that eliminated face-to-face contact. For Whyte, face-to-face contact allowed the pressure under which food service staff were placed to be articulated in hostility to food preparers and others, a hostility compounded by the possibilities for wider conflict based on status differences. Both themes are returned to later in the text Whyte's 'problem solving' orientation is evident in several other pieces of advice to managers as Rose suggests, and other writers have been similarly eager to present their theoretical predilections as possessing the potential for problem solving. For example, Bowey (1976: 15) in her study of restaurants sets out to:

> test the validity of William Foot Whyte's interpretations and analyses of the behaviour of the employees in restaurants (Whyte, 1948). During this investigation it became clear that the inadequacies of Foot Whyte's work were due to the shortcomings of the 'Human Relations' theory which he used. It did not afford a sufficiently accurate model of behaviour in organisations for adequate interpretations to be made of that behaviour. The aim of this book is to present a model of behaviour in organisations, which can be used by research sociologists (organisation theorists) and by practising managers for diagnostic organisational analysis.

In describing certain sociological perspectives on hotel and catering work as constituting an orthodoxy, it is not the intention to suggest that these perspectives are in any way invalid. Piecemeal and limited development of research in the field has made it to some degree inevitable that certain key studies have assumed special importance as a basis for informing other commentaries on hotel and catering employment. The orthodox view does, however, present an incomplete and occasionally distorted perspective on hospitality industry employment, placing undue stress on internal workplace processes and neglecting the wider social and economic context in which work is performed (cf. Gabriel, 1988). Indeed, there is a noticeable tendency in much research to present hotel and catering employment as an atypical intellectual curiosity, obscuring the very real drudgery faced every day by many of the industry's employees. For the most part, the orthodox view has grown out of a very narrow occupation-based approach to the study of hospitality industry employment.

Even writers like Whyte (1948) and Bowey (1976) who have ostensibly been concerned with broader theoretical issues have ultimately directed their attention towards the relationship between occupational groups in the industry. At the wider theoretical and empirical level, sociologists of occupations have been concerned with six inter-related issues.

The First of these is *occupational recruitment and socialisation* by which, through the interaction of both formal and informal procedures (including education, certification and modes of recruitment), an occupational set creates and recreates itself.

Studies of occupational careers have elaborated the scope for progress and development within particular occupational sets, including analyses of hierarchical career structures and the nature of work careers in occupations where the scope for upward movement is limited by the social and technical components of the occupational set-class, economic position, skill, gender and so forth.

Thirdly, studies of *occupational strategies and professionalisation* have examined, *inter alia,* the processes whereby occupational solidarity is encouraged via some form of professionalisation.

These processes need not be confined to occupations conventionally understood as professions: attempts to emulate the procedures and practices of the professions have filtered through to other occupational groups involving, in varying degrees, attempts to exercise some 'form of control over occupational recruitment and career structure. Clearly, there are many occupational sets who can proceed only so far down the road towards professionalisation by arguing that they possess particular competencies. This points towards the fourth area of interest of occupational sociologists, and that is the extent to which occupations are *socially constructed and reproduced.* To a large degree, the distinctiveness of any occupational set relies on the extent to which the claims of members of that set for such distinctiveness can be justified to the wider society and other occupational groups with whom they engage in the workplace. Occupations are therefore dynamic, subject to pressures of both internal and external change. This can be seen, fifthly, in the nature of occupational cultures and ideologies, which provide a system of values that bind occupation members together and serve to legitimate their collective and individual interests. Shared ideologies provide a source of strength for bargaining over power, privileges and rewards particularly if they are linked to concepts of professionalism predicated on the possession of scarce skills and knowledge. Finally in this catalogue is the study of *occupational communities* that embraces two areas of enquiry-communities at work and work within communities. The former is concerned with growth of community in particular occupations. People share a social and cultural network of values but do not usually live together though they may share similar work and leisure interests. The study of work within communities is represented by a much more distinctive sociological literature usually focused on a discrete geographical area where a particular form of work or occupation is the dominant form of labour. The most famous example of this kind of study is *Coal is Our Life* by Dennis, Henriques and Slaughter (1956) but there are others such as Tunstall's (1969) study of fishermen. Rarely in the study of hotel and catering work are these areas of interest explored in any systematic way.

Notable exceptions would include Chivers' study of chefs and cooks (Chivers, 1971, 1973). Saunders study of the social stigma of occupations, with particular emphasis on the role of kitchen porters in the catering industry (Saunders, 1981a), and Shamir's analysis of hotels as workplace communities (Shamir, 1981). The vast majority of what may be termed 'mainstream' *sociological* studies of hospitality industry occupations have been of food (and drink) service staff. Put crudely, many elements in what has been described here as the orthodox approach to the study of hotel and catering employment derive from studies of waiting-on-table, and the experience of food service staff and their relationships with other workers (notably chefs and cooks), have been generalised to the workforce as a whole (e.g. Mars, 1973; Bowey, 1976; Butler and Snizek, 1976; Howe, 1977; Mars; Bryant and Mitchell, 1979; Butler and Skipper, 1981; Mars and Nicod, 1981, 1984). The majority of these studies differ from the work of writers like Chivers, Saunders and Shamir and others in an important methodological sense. The bulk of studies on non-food service staff have utilised what may be termed in the broadest sense a survey/questionnaire/interview style of methodology.

Research on food service staff in contrast has almost invariably entailed some (usually extensive) element of ethnographic research involving participant observation. In some cases this reflects the social anthropological training of the researchers concerned, as in the case of Mars and Nicod who, in their examination of waiting-on-table, claim that 'the methods anthropologists use to study, say, the New Guinea Highlanders are also ideally suited to a study of the "tribe" of waiters at work in Western hotels' (1984: 2). The extravagant confidence of this claim is highly suspect.

The principal tool of the social anthropologist is ethnography. Participant observation usually involves living or working alongside the group under study either openly or, more commonly, covertly so that the subjects under scrutiny are unaware of the researcher's status. The latter is generally justified in terms of the naturalistic data that may be collected. In contrast, in making evident to a community under scrutiny that they are being studied by the ethnographer, the activities of subjects may be affected and altered thereby reducing the reliability of experiential evidence. A problem with ethnographic technique in general and participant observation in particular concerns the possibility of the researcher 'going native', becoming so much a part of the fabric of the research situation as to be unable to adequately discriminate 'relevant' from less relevant data. Some researchers have in fact suggested that 'going native' is to some extent a necessary and integral part of competent ethnography.

Collins (1984) argues that for sociologists of science researching scientific controversies in which the emergence of a new piece of knowledge is at stake, technical and cultural immersion--what he calls participant comprehension--is a vital aspect of adequate understanding without which the researcher is unlikely to penetrate fully to the social processes entailed in scientific debate. This may well be fair comment but it obscures the danger that in 'going native' researchers' analyses will tend toward the insular. Ethnography, almost by definition, is concerned with the behaviour of discrete groups of people in a given social setting or settings. The charge of insularity could no doubt be levelled against many sociological studies of occupations but it is one that has especial salience for the analysis of hotel and catering work. Ethnographic studies of food service personnel have tended to focus attention upon the 'soft underbelly' of work processes in that occupational group, particularly in respect of concentrating upon the efforts of waiting staff to secure tips, and the extent to which they engage in acts of petty (and not so petty) theft. The study of workplace relations and conflict in hotels and catering is almost entirely based on evidence of the conflict between food service personnel. This leads conflict to be regarded as a pathological expression of industry 'culture' rather than a response, at least in part, to the more general social and economic disadvantage faced by many employees. To cap it all, the culture of the industry is seen as encouraging large numbers of 'marginal workers' to enter the ranks of the workforce--not primarily marginal in their relationship to labour markets, that is in the context in which they sell their labour, but in the sense of being socially-psychologically disposed to 'enjoying' the kinds of work experience offered by the hospitality industry. An appreciation of these three concepts--the marginality of the workforce, the nature of remuneration in the industry, and the nature of conflict--is fundamental to a wider understanding of employment in hotels and catering.

In nutshell, it is necessary to reiterate that the core of sociological literature that represents the orthodoxy described above is small. Its influence is much wider and echoes of the 'dominant paradigm' will be found throughout the text. This is unavoidable: it is only possible to work with that material which is available. However, with all the major topics examined below, an attempt has been made to 'explode' discussion, to relate what is known about hotel and catering work to wider issues in industrial sociology. This effort to broaden discussion is on a small scale, confined, for example, to examining trends in industrial conflict and the rote of trade unions in the hospitality industry and trends towards deskilling and 'flexible working'. Indeed, the structure of the text is deliberately programmatic in order that it may fulfil its primary purpose as a reference point/sourcebook.

Any attempt at synthesising an account of hotel and catering work is necessarily schematic, if only because the available source material is limited and patchy in its coverage of the industry. Many studies of hotel employment are of chain-owned hotels and/or those operating in the middle and luxury markets. In contrast, many studies of restaurants are of relatively small, often independent owned units. In both cases, individual research reports have tended to focus on a small number of units and, in many cases, single establishments. In short, there is a problem of representativeness not only in the findings of individual studies but in the relationship the types of establishment bear to other establishments and sectors in the industry. For example, there are few studies of work in non-commercial catering services. Further, any survey of the literature reveals there have been few investigative incursions by sociologists into the world of high-technology, high-capital food provision--the world of fast food and advanced process catering. Indeed, most research has focused on 'traditional' forms of hospitality operating, detracting from the extent to which the growth of the hotel and catering industry in recent years has been predicated on high levels of capital investment in fabric and technology.

Hotels are certainly not immune to these processes.

Many hotel customers would be surprised and probably irked to find that their *haute cuisine* meal began life in a food processing factory, was committed to a foil dish or plastic bag and then transported to the hotel where, with a suitable delay after being ordered (to give the appearance of meticulous preparation), it was regenerated in one or other kind of oven along with half a dozen identical packages before being presented for consumption. Customers would be further surprised to see that the hotel kitchen was not that much bigger than a large school classroom and possibly shocked, if their attention was drawn to these things, to be given a bill at the end of their meal reflecting prices based on the cost of preparation of fresh ingredients. A further problem of representativeness arises from the fact that much data on hotel and catering work derives from occupational studies.

The experience of individuals and occupational groups cannot be viewed independently of organisational structures. Yet, one of the biggest weaknesses in current understandings of the hospitality industry is the absence of comparative studies of how organisational and occupational structures are mediated at unit level as a result of the particular market circumstances of individual establishments. It is common to assume that occupational structure in the hotel and catering industry corresponds to organisational structure, each department in the organisation corresponding to an occupation, for example housekeeping (cleaners), front of house (receptionists), kitchen (chefs and cooks) and so on. To a very large degree this is an accurate view but account needs to be taken of the ways in which departmental organisation differs from or coincides with organisation according to functional and cost-centre criteria. For example, department activities tend to be aggregated and subsumed under higher-order organisational categories such as food and beverage (food and wet in some operations) and accommodation.

A corollary of this is that the existence of a particular organisational structure does not necessarily imply that that structure is the basis for systems of organisational control. Shamir (1978) demonstrates this in his use of the distinction between mechanistic and organic organisations originated by Bums and Stalker (1961). Mechanistic organisations are characterised by high levels of bureaucracy, extensive specialisation and division of labour and hierarchical structures of control. Organic organisations are characterised by less pronounced bureaucracy, more flexible task performance, lateral communication and less rigid rules and systems of control.

The essence of pungency theories is that the success of a particular organisation is contingent upon it choosing a structure most suited to its environment. Shamir shows that hotels tend to exhibit a formal mechanistic structure behind which lies an organic informal structure characterised by informal and lateral communication, an ability to transfer labour resources across departments, and the maintenance of a reserve of labour in the form of five-in staff. Further, the relative autonomy of hotel departments appears to vary greatly and hotels appear to be centralised and devolved at one and the same time, some departments coming under central control, others being allowed a degree of autonomy.

Shamir additionally argues that most large hotels appear to lack any formal integrating mechanisms for the control of organisational elements short of co-ordinating managers with responsibility for several departments. He concludes that traditional hotels resolve the conflict between the demands of bureaucracy and of hospitality by preserving a mechanistic facade whilst practising organic styles of organisational control. The general point here is that organisational structure can have a profound effect on the experience of work, whether this be individual or collective experience. Whilst the literature on hotel and catering work provides many instances of how organisation impinges upon this experience, there is little in the way of systematic analysis and thus there are limitations in what may be regarded as 'typical' organisational influences on the performance of work. Whilst representativeness is a problem, it is to some degree counteracted by a relatively high measure of agreement as to the principal features of hotel and catering work though, as indicated in the previous section, the interpretive scope of many studies is somewhat limited.

Having said this Lowe (1988), on the basis of detailed examination of the independent small-hotel sector in Scotland, has cast both implicit and explicit doubts upon the extent to which research findings from studies of large hotels can be generalised. Lowe found relatively reasonable working conditions and a moderately content workforce, experiences arising in part from the role of the hotel and catering industry within the surrounding community and the economy of the local area. Lowe and many others have drawn attention to the ever more complex diversity of the industry and every effort has been made in what follows to specify what type of operation is being discussed. Cross-sectoral and intra-sectoral variations serve as a reminder of the dangers in drawing far-reaching conclusions from limited data. This should not, however, serve to detract from general trends and repeated observations of the conditions and experiences of hotel and catering labour.

For many employees--probably the majority--labouring in hotels and catering is a last ditch option characterised by exploitative and conflictual relationships. The wider social emphasis on service work as servitude, as inferior to manufacturing work, does little for the morale of the industry's employees and, indeed, permits employers to maintain terms and conditions of employment that in many respects are still medieval in character. The frequently patronising approach of academic analysts to services in general and hotels and catering in particular plays its part in obscuring the extent to which work in hotels and catering differs little in kind and quality from similar work in manufacturing.?'

3

Developing Graduate Managers for Hotel Industry

> Hospitality is a wonderful thing. Concern for the pleasure and comfort of a guest is an extremely admirable trait. However, I think the Eskimos carry it a little too far. As for example, when a man traveling alone stops for a period at the house of a friend, the host offers to share his wife with his guest. The offer usually is accepted. A refusal might be considered insulting. As women are somewhat scarce in the Arctic, wife-sharing is not unusual. At times, three or four Eskimos share a wife. They all live together. The men do the housework.
>
> —*E.V. Durling, King Features Syndicate*

The final part of the study organises views of the meeting into three different graduate scenarios. This was undertaken through the use of scenario planning tools. Scenario planning is "a tool for ordering one's perceptions about alternative future environments in which decisions might be played out" (Schwartz, 1991). Scenarios can be viewed as possible futures or contingencies and in essence can be defined literally as the script for a play. They are not meant to predict the future and indeed are valued by those who believe it impossible to predict the future. Instead scenarios allow managers to stretch their thinking and widen the range of alternatives considered (Porter, 1985). The process of scenario planning generally involves the development of three or four diverse plots and associated narratives, each of which illustrates the possible playing out of major forces driving change within a system, the interrelationship of these driving forces, and critical uncertainties in the environment (Wack, 1985). Under Van der Heijden's (1996) typology these are external, value-free scenarios. They are based on an analysis of present forces and their likely evolution. It should be stressed that these scenarios were developed by the authors from the recorded views but not with the active involvement of those attending the event.

Driving Forces

Hotel and tourism management education has played to very different conditions over the past 30 years. The nature of economy has changed drastically, as has the role of HE and individual students and their career ambitions.

International Perspective of Economies

Global economic restructuring and freedom of trade impact on national economic success. Components of change include a decline in the importance of primary and manufacturing sectors juxtaposed with growth in financial and other services and an increasing internationalisation of trade. Advanced economies transform themselves into ones that are service-based and information technology geared and recognise the emergence of a knowledge society where the basic resource is no longer capital, or natural resources or labour, but knowledge, and in which knowledge workers will play a central role (Drucker, 1993). In this economic environment much activity is consumer-driven. For suppliers this has important implications for cost, quality of service and customer focus. The ability to respond positively to these changes by public and private sectors is considered important both for organisation and economic prosperity (OECD, 1998; Campbell, 1999).

Structure of the Industry

The role of tourism and hospitality in the economy is now well documented. Tourism and the cultural industries contribute £75 billion to the UK economy, with significant foreign exchange earnings. However, suppliers do not represent a homogenous group, with similar characteristics and operations. There is a breadth and diversity over the sectors. The industry is fragmented though there has been a trend towards consolidation of larger companies, particularly in hospitality. However, the roles of micro-businesses and small medium-sized enterprises remain very important. The role of graduate managers is relatively limited in quantitative terms, compared to total industry employees. The Hospitality Training Foundation (2002) quotes the ONS Labour Force Survey recording 4.9 per cent of employees in the hospitality sector as possessing degrees.

The Image

Studies over the recent past have identified that the hospitality sector suffers from a poor image: for example some recent research in Scotland (VisitScotland/George Street Research, 2002) showed that while a career in tourism is generally considered interesting (87 per cent) and challenging (81 per cent) it is also perceived as offering long working hours (56 per cent), repetitive work (51 per cent) and low pay (54 per cent). Conversely, the survey found that a majority of their respondents stated they did not have a good understanding of the range of jobs and career opportunities available.

Increasing Uptake of higher education

An important recent change has been the increase in students studying at universities. Over the period 1990/1991 to 2001/2002, *Social Trends Edition 34* shows that students on undergraduate degrees have increased from 538, 000 to 782, 000 (+45 per cent) (National Statistics, 2004). This has changed the nature of the student population, with a greater emphasis made on vocational degrees. The Scottish Executive (2003) have stressed the need to focus on the changing requirements of learners and to be responsive to the demands of employers, whilst at the same time maintaining the value of the student experience and their retention from entry to qualification.

The Competitive Position of Tourism and Hospitality Degree Programmes

The Learning Teaching Support Network (Hospitality,

Leisure, Sport and Tourism) (2004) published data provided by the University and College Admission Service to show that there has been a decline in demand for hospitality and tourism programmes. Over the period 1996-2003, programmes with the term "hospitality" in the title experienced a decline of 34 pr cent (to 2, 742), while demand for those with "tourism" decreased by 3, 174 (32 per cent) to 6, 754. However, because of their high popularity these declines have not been matched by a decrease of students joining Universities. For hospitality those joining increased by 49 per cent over the period. For tourism there was a 12 per cent increase (to 1, 583 and 3, 334 respectively). Thus the ratio of acceptances to applicants has decreased from 1:3.34 (1996) to 1:2.02 in hospitality and for tourism courses from 1:3.94 to 1:1.73. The Hospitality Training Foundation indicated that around 3, 500 students graduate with hotel and catering degrees each year (1998-2000).

With increasing student numbers and changing government funding policies there has been a marked change in the nature of student experience. Through student loans this includes having to shoulder increasing financial burdens during their periods of study. Many more students than in the past take on part-time job commitments, working during term time as well as holidays. This can create real problems for students who have to juggle paying jobs and academic work priorities. In addition it may result in significant numbers of students entering employment carrying loan burdens arising from their undergraduate studies.

Trends in Continuing Professional Development

Definitions of continuing professional development (CPD) vary across professions though there is some consensus on its key features. The Institute of Continuing Professional Development (ICPD)—launched in the UK in

1998 to raise the effectiveness of professionals by establishing new CPD standards - defines it as:

> ... the systematic maintenance, improvement and broadening of knowledge and the development of personal qualities necessary for the education of professional and technical duties throughout the practitioner's working life.

Or:

> ... the process by which a professional person maintains the quality and relevance of professional services throughout his/her working life.

Others, such as the UK's Chartered Institute of Personnel and Development (CIPD), see the focus more as the individual's responsibility, so define CPD as a "constant updating of professional knowledge throughout one's working life by means of systematic, on-going, self-directed learning". This focus on the individual runs counter to a perception, perhaps more widely held in the past, that CPD has been vocational/professional focused and might therefore appear to have been employer-driven and concentrated on short term upskilling of the workforce (Shaw and Green, 1999) and even regarded as an optional extra (Guest, 2000).

Fowler (1996) suggests four main categories of activities or events from which CPD evolves:

- work-based activities (e.g. membership of project teams, investigating or advising on a new or difficult task);
- courses, seminars and conferences;
- self-directed and informal learning (e.g. planned reading, technology-based training approaches); and
- personal activities outside work (e.g. acting as a school governor, carrying out voluntary work).

Additionally, there is debate as to whether CPD should be optional or mandatory. A mandatory approach runs the risk of professional bodies making CPD seem like a product forced on their membership (Guest, 2000). "O'Rourke's Paradox of CPD" (O'Rourke, 2000) asks how self-directed learning combines with ensuring people chose appropriate and useful courses. In fact, he identifies those who come forward for voluntary CPD as likely to be the more informed and motivated clinicians:

Trying to rope in the others by making the process compulsory may destroy the motivation of the self-starters, without inducing it in the sluggards. Compulsion may simply produce "bolshieness, " or doughy resistance in the "can't learn, won't learn" hard-core (O'Rourke, 2000). HCIMA intends that CPD will be mandatory from June 2004 but indicate that the extended CV method being piloted is user-friendly, maximising the benefits of CPD recording and minimising its drawbacks (Rossiter, 2004).

Applications

Globalisation and the rise of services in economies heighten the role of labour, and management, as a key competitive resource. Against a changing customer-driven environment, hospitality and tourism suffer from a poor public image and lack of career knowledge. Whilst the UK undergraduate population has grown, demand for undergraduate places has declined and, though numbers enrolled in hospitality and tourism have not yet been affected, changing demographics and economic demand of the undergraduate experience may yet create a negative impact on the modest numbers of annual hospitality and tourism management graduates. Meanwhile, there is recognition that undergraduate study is the start of the individual's management learning where work experience is supplemented by CPD.

Destination Application

Tourism is a varied industry with many stakeholders. Stakeholders grow successful business links if the destination builds and shares a strong aspirational vision. For example, VisitScotland has set itself a target of increasing its tourism by 50 per cent over the next decade.

The vigour of the vision must be led and be underpinned by individuals who have an integrated view of the industry, perceive people (customers and staff) as key, and develop successful partnerships between sectors. The destination's customer base must be understood. Customer segments and trends, national and international, should be appreciated in a context of a global marketplace. Competitiveness is important to Scotland and the UK, which are not low-cost destinations and need to compete on marketing and high quality. The vision should bind together its location, transportation, culture and history, venues, hospitality and service quality.

Higher Education Application

It is important for vocational areas to consider employability skills and the extent to which these could be embedded in work-based learning. Questions on the balance between generic business skills and sector specific skills in the curriculum require consideration as well as the amount future and current managers should engage in sector-specific professional development. New opportunities offered by information technology could facilitate major changes in delivery of education, though major change requires substantial investment. New ways of getting academia and industry to work together at national and local levels are also important, for example in work-based learning.

Views advanced in the round table discussion are summarised under three main headings.

Course design and the skills base:

— Courses should consider the inclusion of foreign languages as a compulsory element of the curriculum.

— There was general agreement that soft skills (e.g. IT skills, communication, team working, problem solving, numeracy, motivational skills, literacy) should be provided as a priority. HE should find innovative means of giving students opportunities to acquire these soft skills especially in relation to people care and management skills.

— Language competences would greatly supported if students were given the opportunity to undertake full year placements in hotels and other tourism businesses abroad (e.g. Continental Europe).

— Teaching should embrace work-related contexts where possible, e.g. high quality case studies which apply general business skills within hospitality and tourism

— Universities and colleges should use semester/term-time work experience of students as an educational opportunity and bring work-based experiences to enrich student learning.

— Greater clarity is required in HE and industry in relation to the balance between vocational/sector needs and academic requirements. It is important that all stakeholders appreciate that both are critical to produce high value, successful tourism.

— It may be valuable for HE to undertake selection interviews as part of the recruitment process for programmes in hospitality and tourism. Interviews should aim to find the applicants who demonstrate the capacity to develop people skills.

— Greater emphasis could be given on training for a graduate's first job destination. Employers report that they need to top-up graduate skills, mainly in practical skills.

— Universities could focus on producing the top-level management staff for tourism and hospitality. Students with a less academic orientation could focus on training for front-line and operational jobs.

— With an ageing population it is important to recognise that older tourists have special needs. Perhaps the sector can learn from the approaches of other service industries to address the needs of the "grey market".

Stakeholders Outside Academia

— It is important that public sector initiatives are monitored, relative to their role in management education and development. Taking over from the Hospitality Training Foundation in 2004 will be the Sector Skills Council for Hospitality, Leisure, Travel and Tourism (now established as People First) both as an agency to support the industry but also to work with to ensure positive change in attitudes and measures to increase the quality of management and management education

— Staff investment is important for sectors to demonstrate its appreciation of staff as its key resource. This means investing in staff rewards, incentives, development and working conditions to create a culture where the workforce values high quality customer care.

Student and Graduate Attitudes

— It is critical that students appreciate that there is a strong practical element to their studies and future careers.

— Students and new graduates should approach the industry with a positive image of its opportunities and working conditions. Currently some work experience (casual or formal requirements) gained during studies colours student views negatively through a combination of various factors including extensive work demands, low wages and relatively poor working conditions. This does little to encourage the best graduates to work in the sector.

— Attitudes can be as important as the knowledge gained in studies. People management and customer care attitudes are particularly important.

— Graduates should understand that they will enter a sector dominated by small businesses and owner-businesses. These often possess a culture of long hours and hard physical and mental work.

Conclusion

Apparently most of the round table discussion centred on how HE could prepare individuals for future management. While views were diverse there was a noteworthy emphasis from many discussants on the importance of providing individuals with appropriate attitudes and aspirations to guide their career trajectories and industry vision. Thus the role of HE must be more than just to provide a skills base. The role of industry at undergraduate level was less clear and a number of initiatives for co-operation were suggested, while it was recognised that employers could help reverse negative public images of the sector by addressing issues of rewards and incentives.

There was consensus on the provision of management expertise and on developing positive industry employment attitudes (generally and during the students' undergraduate learning). There was further agreement that HE and industry should act as partners and recognition by employers that learning is continuous and requires their investment. These issues provided a baseline for the three scenarios which were developed post the event and which are presented below. The authors do not claim they were articulated in the manner presented, though every attempt is made to remain true to the spirit of the contributions. However, the authors' views are likely to influence the scenarios to an extent. The intention of producing three scenarios is not to provide a definitive statement on graduateness. Scenarios are value free (i.e. none is preferable to another) and are not intended to be mutually exclusive. Each scenario gathers characteristics under three headings: individual graduate characteristics; the role of HE; and industry roles. Thus their focus is on the inputs and outcomes of the undergraduate experience.

1. The professional developer scenario emphasises an operations specialist with contemporary expertise and a strong customer focus. HE concentrates on operations management with high levels of contemporary relevance and technological expertise. Employers invest to ensure that HE has the knowledge (and, where appropriate resources) to provide relevance to the current environment. Undergraduates are highly sensitised to industry conditions. Their operational direction requires little immediate on-the-job training. However, the need to develop generic management skills will be important to ensure career development (unless industry wishes to keep graduates in essentially technical-type positions).
2. The management platform for a portfolio strategist is a stronger orientation in generic management. HE concentrates on developing people management skills and customer focus orientations. Graduates see hospitality and tourism management as sharing much with other sectors. They are mentally flexible across functions and hierarchies. Industry needs to invest in quality work-based learning opportunities for students and induction into operations and industry-specific technologies at the first employment

stage. These graduates aim to develop a range of expertise which suits their preferences as well as employer/industry needs. While industry leaning, and likely to join hospitality and tourism on graduation, these individuals are happy to work wherever their skills are valued.

3. Finally, Pragmatic mavericks form the third scenario. They have a grounding in hospitality and/or tourism, but their academic education is mainly led by entrepreneurial and value-added business approaches. Operations "how to" expertise receives little formal attention, most of this being obtained in vacation employment or industry placements. The pragmatic maverick has a highly developed set of personal skills as well as business development expertise. She or he follows a CDP agenda which reflects their personal perceptions of the benefits obtained. Their desire for a career in hospitality responds to employment packages that suit their preferred lifestyles: they may wish to work in large or small organisations, inside or outside hospitality and tourism. A variant to this profile of a pragmatist with industry leanings was also suggested. This is a non-hospitality/tourism graduate who enters employment, initially on a short-term basis. Because they enjoy working in the industry they decide to explore these career opportunities. However, it was suggested, poor work conditions or career prospects usually mean that they (pragmatic "tourists") enjoy only a short visit before exiting the industry.

Here it is apt to note that the development of managers is a key human resources concern to the future health of hospitality and tourism sectors, increasingly affected by globalisation and competitiveness, is hardly a novel conclusion. Neither astounding is the view that appropriate skills sets should be appropriate for future needs. What the review did reveal was the perception that generic management skills were very important, though there was a strong feeling that these should be applied sensitively to the vocational settings. The desirability of close liaison between industry and HE was emphasised. This was expressed in broader terms than the reiterating requirements of high quality work experience and career advice.

If the current public sector focus on lifelong learning enables long-term and fundamental issues which affect both attitudes and skills development, graduates as a group and HR for the sector are likely be better placed to make a contribution to the health of this important part of society. Given the bonds between major stakeholders and potential synergies arising from joint initiatives, there is a clear message for greater co-operation and partnerships amongst all players. A call for collaboration is, once again, nothing new, though difficult to enact in a fragmented industry. It could be argued that some public sector initiatives (e.g. Tourism Training Scotland), whilst designed to bring players together, have lacked the strategic power to concentrate on long-term issues of management development.

REFERENCES

Airey, D., Johnson, S. (1999), "The content of tourism degree courses in the UK", *Tourism Management*, Vol. 20 pp. 229-35.

Fowler, A. (1996), "How to manage your own CPD", *People Management*, No.October, pp. 54-6.

Guest, D. (2000), "Human resource management at work", CIPD, available at: www.cipd.co.uk.

Higher Education Funding Council for England (2001), *Getting Ahead: Graduate Careers in Hospitality Management (HEFCE 01/30 May Report)*, Council for Hospitality Management Education/HEFCE, Bristol.

Impact Skills Network (2002), "An assessment of skills needs in tourism and cultural industries: Skills dialogues", July, available at www.impactskillbase.org.uk.

Jameson, S.M., Holden, R. (2000), "'Graduateness' who cares? Graduate identity in small hospitality firms", *Education and Training*, Vol. 42 No.4/5, pp. 264-71.

Kelley-Paterson, D., George, C. (2001), "Securing graduate commitment: an exploration of the comparative expectations of place students, graduate recruits and human resources managers within the hospitality, leisure and tourism industries", *Hospitality Management*, Vol. 20 pp. 311-23.

Kriegl, U. (2000), "International hospitality management. identifying important skills and effective training", *Cornell Hotel and Restaurant Administration Quarterly*, Vol. 41 No.2, pp. 64-71.

Learning and Teaching Support Network (2004), "Accepted students and applicants 1996-2003 in hospitality, leisure, sport and tourism", based on data provided by UCAS. Learning and Teaching Support Network, available at: www.hlst.ltsn.ac.uk/resources/ucas.pdf.

National Statistics (2004), *Social Trends 34 - a Portrait of British Society*, National Statistics, London.

O'Rourke, A. (2000), "Continuing professional development: too little ... too much ... too late", the Wisdom Centre, The Wisdom Virtual Conference in Clinical Governance, available at: www.wisdomnet.co.uk.

OECD (1998), *Human Capital Investment: An International Comparison*, Centre for Educational Research and Innovation, OECD, Paris.

Porter, M.E. (1985), *Competitive Advantage: Creating and Sustaining Superior Performance*, Collier Macmillan, London.

Sadler-Smith, E., Allinson, W., Hayes, J. (2000), "Learning preferences and cognitive style some implications for continuing professional development", *Management Learning*, Vol. 31 No.2, pp. 239-56.

Schwartz, P. (1991), *The Art of the Long View*, Doubleday, New York, NY.

Scottish Executive (2003), *Life Through Learning; Learning Through Life: The Lifelong Learning Strategy for Scotland*, Scottish Executive, Edinburgh.

Shah, A., Pell, K., Brooke, P. (2004), "Beyond first destinations. Graduate employment survey", *Active Learning in Higher Education*, Vol. 5 No.1, pp. 9-26.

Shaw, M., Green, H. (1999), "Continuous professional development: emerging trends in the UK", *Quality Assurance in Education*, Vol. 7 No.3, pp. 169-77.

Van der Heijden, K. (1996), *Scenarios - The Art of Strategic Management*, John Wiley & Sons, Chichester.

VisitScotland/George Street Research Ltd (2002), *Stakeholder Opinion Research: Baseline Survey Report*, George Street Research Ltd, Edinburgh.

Wack, P. (1985), "Scenarios: shooting the rapids", *Harvard Business Review*, Vol. 63 No.6, pp. 139-50.

4

Hotel Industry and International Labor Markets

He who has imagination without learning, has wings and no feet.

—*Barthelemy Catherine Jourbert*

The nature and statistics of the hotel employment as an aspect of the hospitality industry are discussed in this study. The term "labor market" refers to the supply of workers looking for jobs and the jobs available in a given area. When jobs are plentiful, employers obviously have a harder time finding the people they want, and workers are more particular about the jobs they will accept. When jobs are scarce, workers will settle for less and employers have a better choice.

In the hospitality industry, it is not difficult to find articles regarding the labor shortage issue. The literature suggests that the hospitality industries of the developed world are experiencing labor shortages and can expect to face greater shortages in the future (Lockwood and Guernier, 1990). Where growth forecasts are generally optimistic, as in the UK and the USA, the issue of fulfilling the industry's labor needs to sustain such growth has become serious (Belous, 1989).

The labor shortage issue is receiving the attention of many people in the industry. As the hospitality industry continues to grow more rapidly, it will face the critical question of whether there is a way to achieve a balance between supply and demand in labor. To help answer this question and give a solution, it is necessary to review the nature, characteristics, and trends of the hospitality employment and worldwide population distributions.

Hotel Employment

The hotel is a business unit that is both labor and capital intensive. In order to meet the needs of the guest, the hotel must employ many people, often on an around-the-clock basis. The hotel offers opportunities for work for many employees who do not possess the education or skills for other jobs. Also, the hotel is often the first job for many just beginning their transition into the world of work. Thus, the hotel fulfills an important societal role in many communities.

As per an estimate, the industry employs in excess of 11,194,418 people worldwide and represents approximately 5 per cent of the world's total travel and tourism workforce (WTTC, 1995). By far the largest concentration of employment is in the Americas (the Caribbean, Central America, North America, and South America), where over 4,061,966 individuals earn their living in this industry. This compares with the EFTA (European Free Trade Association) countries, which are estimated to employ 1,873,722 people. While there are more hotels on the European continent than in North America, in Europe many hotels are primarily small family-owned and managed businesses.

There is approximately one employee for every hotel room in the world. This simple one-to-one ratio validates the important employment role of this industry, not only in job creation, but also in providing gainful employment opportunities for those seeking entry into the job market (Olsen and Choi, 1995).

The hospitality industry is diverse in terms of both the types of jobs it offers and the nature of the individual it requires. The spectrum of occupations range from the unskilled porter to the highly-skilled manager. The majority of staff employed in the industry is unskilled, of course. These include many food and bar service staff, uniformed staff, and domestics. The hospitality industry is, in fact, now the largest employer of unskilled labor in many countries. Semi-skilled laborers include those people with professional foodservice skills, clerical and commercial staff, some cooking staff, and some maintenance staff (Hornsey and Dann, 1984).

In 1994, there were more than 5 billion people in the world; these people were very unevenly distributed (de Souza and Stutz, 1994). Recent statistics show that Europe (511 million) and Russia (149 million), along with the other republics of the Soviet Union (135 million), were home to about 16 per cent; Africa (654 million) to 12 per cent; Latin America (453 million) to 8 per cent; North America (283 million) to 5 per cent; and Oceania (28 million) to less than 1 per cent of the world's population (WTTC, 1995). Given such large variations among continents, it is not surprising that national population figures show even more variability. Ten out of the world's nearly 200 countries account for two-thirds of the world's people.

The ten most populous countries. Five countries - China, India, the USA, Indonesia, and Brazil - contain half of the world's population. Approximately 21 per cent of all people live in China, 16 per cent in India, 5 per cent in the USA, and 3 per cent each in Indonesia and Brazil. Six of the top ten countries in population size - China, India, Indonesia, Japan, Bangladesh, and Pakistan - are in Asia. Only three of the ten most populous nations are considered to be developed (the USA, Russia, and Japan).

If we look into the population distribution by region, it becomes apparent that most people are concentrated in a few parts of the world. Four major areas of dense settlement are East Asia, South Asia, Europe, and the eastern USA and Canada. In addition, there are minor clusters in Southeast Asia, Africa, Latin America, and along the US Pacific coast.

The United Nations projects world population at 6.1 billion in 2000 and 8.5 billion in 2050. Almost all of this increase will occur in the developing countries. The largest absolute increase is projected for Asia, reflecting its huge population base. Future population growth will further accentuate the uneven distribution of the world's population.

Unemployed Highly Skilled and Educated Labor

Education and training are often the keys to employment, but in developing countries many remain unemployed despite, or because of, their high level of education. In Asian countries, the least educated often have the lowest recorded unemployment rates, since a majority are involved in subsistence activities such as farming. Unemployment in the selected countries by educational level. In India, while the unemployment rate in 1989 for people with no education was 2 per cent, that for those with secondary education was 9 per cent, and for university graduates 12 per cent. In Bangladesh, about 40 per cent of people with a master's degree are either unemployed or underemployed. In Thailand during 1973-1983, unemployment rates among university graduates ranged from 20 per cent to 35 per cent. In Africa, too, secondary school graduates are more likely to be unemployed than those with less education.

Graduate unemployment, not yet as high as in some Asian countries, is expected to rise in the years ahead with cuts in recruitment to government service, where many graduates would previously have expected automatic employment. The current worry regarding the labor shortage can be solved by using these unevenly distributed labor forces throughout the world. The labor shortage in the international market, and in the hospitality industry particularly, means that there is a shortage of skilled labor, not unskilled labor forces.

Migration of Labor in the Hotel Industry

Evidently, most people move for economic reasons in general; they move to take better-paying jobs or to search for jobs in new area (WTTC, 1995). Others move to fulfill personal dreams. Whatever the motive, migrants generally seek better lives. The causes of migration in the hospitality industry can be divided into "push-and pull" factors. Push factors in the hospitality industry would include poor wages, long or unsociable hours, highly individualized job functions, strong competition, sexual discrimination, awkward shifts, and lack of respect from the public. Pull factors include flexible hours, opportunities for females and minorities, opportunities to learn a skill, and so on. It is generally believed that labor emigration from a country can give rise to several potential benefits. For instance, it can relieve unemployment and under-employment, it can be a source of foreign exchange, it can lead to the acquisition of skills, and, in general, it can improve material welfare by increasing per capita national income.

The potential benefits of labor immigration can also be considerable. For instance, it can allow hospitality firms to realize economies of scale, it can prevent wage inflation in an industry experiencing labor shortages, it can facilitate investment by ensuring that new capacity can be adequately staffed, and generally, it makes available labor services without the need to finance the formation of the human capital.

Skilled and Educated Immigrants

Only skilled and educated workers are the targets of labor immigration by the hospitality business administrators, and only those skilled and educated laborers are welcomed in the world labor markets. The skilled and educated immigrants contribute their human capital to the economy so that they create job opportunities for other workers.

In this case, the positive impacts of the immigrants on the host countries are achieved. A recent study analyzed the impact of immigrants on native workers' earnings and employment (Sorensen *et al.*, 1992). Changes in earnings as a function of increases in immigrant population were estimated for 33 metropolitan statistical areas (MSAs) in the USA. The study found that if highly-skilled and educated immigrants are brought in as worker-preference immigrants, they can be productive and will create job opportunities for other people who want to have a job in the domestic market. It is believed, then, that only skilled and educated immigrants are welcomed in the international labor markets because they add value.

Till recently, labor for the hospitality industry was recruited primarily on a local basis regardless of geographical location. However, a new trend is developing. The US workforce as an example, immigrants are increasingly joining the workforce. In 1985, the immigrant men and women represented only 7 percent of the total US labor force. However, this group is expected to represent 22 percent of the total US labor force within only a few years. Unfortunately, the number of people migrating in the international hospitality industry worldwide at this time is not available. An alternative method that can measure the size of the immigrant workforce in the hospitality industry is that of analyzing the immigrant figures in the entire service industry in the world.

The economically active, foreign-born population (EAP) of Canada, the USA and France. France and the USA are included because those are major tourist countries in the world (Pearce, 1995). Canada is included for comparison. In 1990, the foreign-born labor forces in the service industry represented 37.7 per cent (1,932,316) of the total economically active foreign-born population (EAP) of the USA. Approximately 455,261 (41.6 per cent of the EAP) foreign-born labor forces worked in the France's services industry in 1990. Also, significant number of foreign-born labor forces (about 29.8 per cent of the EAP) involved in the Canada's service industry in 1991. Interestingly, most of immigrant workers in Canada and France are young (15 to 24 age group) and the gender pattern of immigrant workers in France (world's top destination country) is quite different from that of Canada. The table shows that young immigrants are increasingly joining the workforce in the service industry. More male workers immigrated to Canada than to France. This pattern, however, is completely reversed for female immigrants. In fact, female service workers who immigrated to France represent more than 30 per cent of EAP in all age groups.

Migration is a complex phenomenon that raises many questions. Why do people move? What factors influence the intensity of a migratory flow? What are the effects of migration on the hospitality industry? What are the patterns of migration? And what are the immigrant laws in different labor markets?

This study employed data for the economically active foreign-born population working in the service industry. It would be possible to provide more useful information were data on the hospitality industry available. Migration has demographic, social, and economic effects, due especially to the fact that migrants tend to be young adults and often the more ambitious and better-educated members of a society. Not only are there legal matters to migration, but families tend to be socially and culturally rooted in their country of birth, and such attachments are difficult to overcome. Immigration can also be costly. Some of the most skilled and educated members of the population of Third World countries migrate to developed countries. Each year, the income transferred through the "brain drain" to the USA amounts to billions of dollars, although billions of dollars are also sent back home in the form of remittances to family members who stayed behind. Stahl (1986) conducted a study regarding international labor migration as it affects the countries that constitute the Association of Southeast Asian Nations—Brunei, Indonesia, Malaysia, the Philippines, Singapore and Thailand. The study tried to establish how international labor migrated in the ASEAN countries and to evaluate its importance to their economies. Stahl concluded that the benefits of international migration accrue disproportionately to the labor importing countries. In some cases, the country of emigration may justifiably demand compensation against the losses it incurs (even when these fall short of the gains to the receiving country), especially when it has spent resources to train the migrating specialists.

Summing Up

The world population is actually growing, and there are abundant highly educated and skilled laborers in the world. Education and training are often put forward as the keys to employment, but in developing countries many remain unemployed despite, or because of, their high level of education. Recruiting those skilled but unemployed labor forces in one part of the word would provide a solution for skilled labor shortage in the other part of the world. It is believed that the unevenly distributed population in the world is the main reason for labor shortage in particular regions.

Immigration has played a vital role in supplying the developed world's hospitality industry's labor market, and to some extent this can be expected to continue. But, it is not clear whether international migration in the hospitality industry serves as a positive or negative factor for specific economies. Empirical work needs to be done on this question. Attempts should also be made to assess the consequences of labor migration in the hospitality industry for the world economy as a whole.

Obviously the international migration in the hospitality industry will increase dramatically in the near future along with the advance of information technologies. Increasingly, the use of information technologies is seen as an accelerator for these labor markets. With the advanced information technologies, the labor demand and supply become more globally accessible, and individuals and organizations will find their needs more effectively and efficiently. The trend will be supported by the unevenly distributed population in the world, the unemployment of highly educated and skilled labor in the world, the high labor demand in the hospitality industry along with the growth of the industry, and the economic and other benefits of the migration to the entire world.

REFERENCES

de Souza, A.R, Stutz, F.P (1994), *The World Economy: Resource, Location, Trade, and Development*, Macmillan College Publishing Company, New York, NY.

Hassmiller, B. (2000), "Compensation and benefits survey 2000", *The Bottomline*, Vol. 15 No.7, pp. 6-25.

Hornsey, T.M.J., Dann, D.T (1984), *Manpower Management in the Hotel and Catering Industry*, Batsford Academic and Educational, London.

Moore, R.W., Stefanelli, J. (1989), "Power and the hotel controller's role", *Hospitality Education & Research Journal*, Vol. 13 No.1, pp. 1-12.

Lockwood, P, Guerrier, Y (1990), "Labor shortages in the international hotel industry", *Travel and Tourism Analyst*, Vol. 6 pp.17-35.

Olsen, M.D, Choi, J.G (1995), "The scale of the international hotel industry - a statistical analysis", *Into the New Millennium: A White Paper on the Global Hospitality Industry*, The International Hotel Association, Paris, pp.15-26.

Pearce, D (1995), *Tourism Today: A Geographical Analysis*, 2nd ed., John Wiley & Sons, New York, NY.

Sorensen, E, Frank, D, Ku, L, Zimmermann, W. (1992), *Immigrant Categories and the US Job Market: Do They Make a Difference?*, Urban Institute Press, Washington, DC., Urban Institute Report 92-1.

Stahl, C.W (1986), *International Labor Migration: A Study of the ASEAN Countries*, The Center for Migration Studies of New York, New York, NY.

5

Controller: A Career for Hotel Management

Leisure is what you make it. It may be your greatest blessing or your greatest curse. You determine its quality, and its quality determines you. In the old era, the job determined the worker. In the new, leisure determine the man.

—*Walter B. Pitkin*

When asked what career paths hospitality students would take upon graduation, a good number may say food and beverage and others may choose the rooms department. There may also be some who would like to make catering or sales and marketing their career choices, while others may choose human resources. However, only once in a while would one hear from a student in a hospitality program who would like to become a controller in a hotel, club, restaurant or other hospitality concerns. There exists this stereotype that the career of a controller is quite dull and that there is not much human involvement on a daily basis; and as a controller, one would simply sit in front of a computer and work with piles and piles of papers and numbers.

Admitedly, reality, controllers play a very important role both in the daily operations and strategic directions of a hospitality organization. Controllers are part of the executive committee. They are department heads who supervised their own crew. They work closely with all other departments to provide them with the proper financial picture and they assist these department heads in developing their budgets. Most importantly, they are the right-hand confidants of the general managers. Research has shown that hotel controllers are able to exercise a significant amount of power due to their central role in the hotel's information network and in the decision-making process (Moore and Stefanelli, 1989). While some hospitality companies may turn to the traditional business schools for their future accountants or controllers, more and more hospitality corporations are hiring hospitality students, since these students have a deeper understanding of the nuances of the hospitality business. In addition, many hospitality programs, especially those with more of a management focus, require 12-15 credit hours of accounting, cost control, and finance courses with the option of taking a minor in accounting from the business college.

This track of courses is about 10 per cent or in some cases, over 10 per cent of the entire curriculum, and it provides students the best of both worlds - hospitality and accounting. The career of being a controller in the hospitality industry is also a reflection of the best of both worlds. As a controller, one is still in the hospitality business, working in the same environment as his or her hospitality colleagues. However, when compared to colleagues in other operating departments such as rooms or food and beverage, the work hours of a controller are more regular. There might be an occasional weekend that a controller needs to be on property for inventory valuation or finalizing the annual budget. But, there is no shift work and one is not required to stay late because there is a big dinner function booked at the hotel, just to have to return the next morning because there is a 1, 000 person breakfast meeting.

As such, it is pertinent that hospitality students understand that the controller career option is available to them, that it is a most viable career path, and being a controller, just like any other department head positions, can be the path towards the position of a general manager. Indeed, many controllers have taken that next step since they are intimately knowledgeable about the financial performance of each department in the hotel, club, or hospitality operation. From the financial data, one can begin to ascertain the strengths and weakness of each department.

The purpose of this study, is four-fold:

— To provide a characteristic profile of a controller in the hospitality industry; specifically their place of employment, gender, age, years worked in the industry, education, and certification.
— To provide a financial profile of a controller in the hospitality industry; specifically the annual salary and bonuses.
— To ascertain if statistically significant differences exist between the characteristic and financial profiles of the two major segments of the hospitality industry: hotels and clubs.
— To ascertain if statistically significant differences exist between the characteristic and financial profiles of male and female respondents.

Hopefully, through the findings of this research, professors, counselors, and students will be more open to the possibility of being a controller and viewing it as viable career path.

Given the above purposes, the characteristic profile and the financial profile of a controller were determined. The data were then also tested for the following hypotheses.

H1. There is no statistically significant difference between the characteristic profiles of hotel and club controllers.

H2. There is no statistically significant difference between the financial profiles of hotel and club controllers.

H3. There is no statistically significant difference between the characteristic profiles of male and female controllers.

H4. There is no statistically significant difference between the financial profiles of male and female controllers.

Geller and Schmidgall (1984) provided one of the first profiles on hotel controllers. They discovered that hotel controllers were well educated with 72 per cent of those surveyed having at least a bachelor's degree. In addition to being knowledgeable in accounting and financial matters, hotel controllers also had to possess knowledge in personnel management and electronic data processing, a forerunner to the more commonly used term of computer technology. As for professional certifications, very few had such designations. Only 13 per cent of the respondents reported that they were Certified Public Accountant (CPA) and even less, 8 per cent, reported that they were Certified Hospitality Accountant Executive (CHAE). Eighty-two percent of the hotel controllers were part of the executive committee of their property. Controllers at larger properties were more likely to be on a bonus plan with bonuses based on salary (59 per cent) or sales (29 per cent). Sometimes the bonuses were linked to performance or gross operating profit.

A follow-up study was done by Geller *et al.* (1990) to see if the profile had changed and a slightly different profile of hotel controllers emerged. There was a noticeable increase in the number of hotel controllers that had majored in hospitality management. This was viewed as a favorable shift in that hotel companies recognized the value of hospitality management training and operations experience in the controller's position. There was also a significant change in the number of hotel controllers with the designation of CHAE. Instead of 8 per cent in 1984, this percentage more than doubled in about five years, with 17 per cent of the respondents holding the designation of CHAE.

The percentage of hotel controllers that reported having

to be knowledgeable in computers rose to 96.6 per cent (it was 70 per cent in the 1984 study). The 1990 study goes further than the earlier study by actually breaking down this statistic a bit further and discovered that 87 per cent of the respondents were responsible for the computer systems used for the accounting function and 58 per cent were also responsible for the front-office computers and reservation system. Another point that was made clearer in this later study was that the most common basis for bonuses was whether the organization met its profit objectives. An additional item that was added to the 1990 study was the career goals and aspirations of the hotel controllers. The majority of them surveyed were desirous to move to a higher-level financial position (25.3 per cent) or that of a general-management position (27.3 per cent).

Gender and Compensation

A more in-depth analysis of hotel controllers based on gender was done by Ghiselli and Chen (1997). In comparison to the two earlier studies (Geller and Schmidgall, 1984; Geller *et al.*, 1990), almost 90 per cent of the respondents held a bachelor degree. This indicates that a bachelor degree may have become a necessity or requirement for the hotel controller position. Professional certifications have also seen increases with 23.1 per cent having the CHAE and 17.7 per cent with the CPA designation. The majority of controllers (92.3 per cent) had six or more years of accounting experience, which was viewed as a significant increase over previous studies.

Overall, 37.2 per cent of the hotel controllers had been in their current position for five or more years. However, nearly half of the female controllers had only been in their current position for less than a year, while 19.4 per cent of the male controllers were in the same situation.

Ghiselli and Chen were surprised at this finding because of the length of accounting experience reported by respondents. They felt this may have indicated considerable movement or turnover in the profession. Further results from this study show that there was a significant difference in the hotel controller salaries of males and females, with male salaries being higher. Some of this may be due to the high percentage of female controllers being in their current position for less than one year.

However, even if the length of time in the current position, size of hotel, or type of ownership are compared at each level for male and female hotel controllers, the male controller was paid more than the female controller in a majority of circumstances. Some other interesting findings included the fact that base salaries have continued to drift upward but that there were a large number of salaries at the lower end. The authors felt this may be due to bonuses or pay incentives becoming a larger component of wage agreements. As for the necessary skills and knowledge needed by hotel controllers, in comparison to previous studies, the ranking of computer skills went down.

Other research has examined the value of professional designations such as the CHAE. In a survey of CHAE holders (Damitio and Schmidgall, 2001), there was some evidence to indicate that they had higher base salaries than non-holders. Asked specifically about this, almost 58 attributed some monetary value to their CHAE. The longer the respondent held the CHAE designation, the more likely were they to place higher value in it ($5, 000 or more). In a related question, over 61 per cent found the CHAE designation to be somewhat helpful to extremely helpful in getting or changing employment. There are also non-financial benefits to the CHAE such as acknowledging one's commitment to professionalism, identifying one who possesses technical expertise, and representing a basic level of competency in both operations and management skills.

In contrast to the CPA designation, the majority of the respondents felt the CPA was better than, or at least as valuable as, the CHAE. All of this aside, 97 per cent of the respondents would encourage or strongly encourage other hospitality financial and accounting professionals to reach the CHAE designation.

Controllers' Skill Set

The skills and education required to by a controller has changed over the years. Drawing evidence from several competency studies done on the accounting profession, a team of researchers have developed a list of knowledge, skills, and abilities required for all accountants (Palmer *et al.*, 2004). One of the trends identified by these researchers is that there are "some skills that are becoming more important than some of the accounting knowledge normally included in accounting curriculum." In addition to accounting and financial knowledge, they would add communication skills, interpersonal skills, general business knowledge, problem-solving skills, information technology, personal attitudes and capabilities, and computer skills.

The data was collected as part of a biennium survey performed by the Hospitality Financial Technology Professionals (HFTP) Research Institute at the University of Houston. The survey focuses on the compensation and benefits, as well as, the job characteristics and demographics of the HFTP membership. The association of HFTP is the predecessor of the International Association of Hospitality Accountants (IAHA) founded in 1952. The IAHA was the organization surveyed in many of the previous studies already citied. Based in Austin, Texas, HFTP is the professional association for financial and technology personnel working in hotels, resorts, clubs, casinos, restaurants and other hospitality-related businesses. The association provides continuing education and networking opportunities to more than 4, 000 members around the world, and produces the premiere hospitality technology shows HITEC and ONHTEC. HFTP also administers the examination and awards the certification for the CHAE and the Certified Hospitality Technology Professional (CHTP) designations.

Prior to the HFTP Research Institute doing the survey in 2002, the 2000 compensation and benefits survey was commissioned by HFTP and carried out by an independent research firm. The reported results (Hassmiller, 2000) will be referenced as part of the analysis. In 2002, a random sample of the HFTP membership was used (Countryman and DeFranco, 2002). Eight hundred and sixty-one HFTP members were randomly selected to participate in the survey. A stratified sample was used to insure that appropriate portions of the HFTP membership were surveyed. Those not involved directly in the hospitality industry such as educators and vendors were also excluded, even though they are members of HFTP. This survey was mailed to participants and they were asked to return the completed surveys in the postage paid envelope provided. Out of the 861 surveys mailed out, 272 were returned for a response rate of 31.7 per cent.

In 2004, an online or web survey was used (Countryman *et al.*, 2004). This allowed for the entire membership of HFTP to be surveyed or at least those that opted to receive e-mail correspondence from HFTP. Seven hundred and eighteen responded to the 3, 149 e-mails sent out, this is a response rate of 22.8 per cent. The e-mail directed respondents to a web survey.

It is to be noted, participants of the 2002 survey were asked to project their salary and bonus for that year since the survey was done during the middle of the year. Participants of the 2004 survey reported actual salaries and bonuses for 2002 and were asked to project them for 2004. Because of the overlap in surveys for the year 2002, therefore, only actual numbers for 2002, which were collected from the 2004 survey, were used in regards to salaries and bonuses reported in 2002. Unlike some of the early studies mentioned in the literature review, this research chose to focus on those who just have the title of controller and does not include corporate controllers or division/area controllers. The Statistical Package for the Social Sciences (SPSS) was used for the data analysis. Means and frequencies were computed for the various profiles. *T*-tests and chi-square tests were used to determine if statistically significant differences existed between different profiles. *T*-tests were used to test for significant difference between means and chi-square tests were used for the frequencies.

A brief overview of the controllers who completed the survey in 2002 and 2004. As for industry segment, the two top categories are hotels and clubs. These two segments are investigated later as part of this research. Both the 2002 and 2004 surveys were fairly evenly split between female and male controllers with there being slightly more male controllers in each survey. The differences between female and male controllers, especially in regards to salary, are also examined later in this research.

Most controllers are older than 35 years old. The average number of years of experience in finance and accounting is higher (2002: 18 years and 2004: 20 years) than the average number of years of experience in the hospitality field (2002: 14 years and 2004: 16 years). This means that many of the controllers started in other fields before moving to the hospitality industry. As for the length of time in their current position of controller, it averages 6.4 years (2004 survey). This is slightly higher than the 5.28 years reported in 2002. Overall, the 2004 respondents had an average of a little over 11 years as a controller, up from the 9.43 years reported in 2002. Forty percent of the respondents in 2002 and 2004 worked as a controller for a different company or organization prior to their current position as controller.

Other prior positions mentioned by respondents included assistant controller (2002: 16.4 per cent and 2004: 18.9 per cent), accounting/finance manager (2002: 8.2 per cent and 2004: 10.3 per cent), and staff accountant (2004: 7.3 per cent). The average length of time spent in that prior position was a little over five years according to both studies.

The majority of controllers have at least a bachelor or 4-year degree. There are also a noticeable number of controllers who have done some graduate work or earned a Master degree. Beside education, there are a higher percentage of controllers with the CHAE and CHTP designations. There were a few other interesting characteristics. Controllers spend the majority of their time (2002: 82 per cent and 2004: 65 per cent) working on finance and accounting issues. However, they also spend a lot of time on technology (2002: 18 per cent and 2004: 13 per cent). As for the lower percentages reported in 2004, the later survey was more in-depth and controllers were asked to be more specific in their time allocations. In addition to finance, accounting, and technology, controllers also deal with administrative and human resource issues.

On average, controllers work about 48 hours a week. A little over 67 per cent (2004) of them were members of the executive committee. This is up from the 59.3 per cent reported in 2002. A majority of the controllers (2002: 62 per cent and 2004: 59.2 per cent) supervised 2-5 full time employees, followed by 6-10 full time employees (2002: 19.7 per cent and 2004: 17.7 per cent). However, not all of these employees may be accounting or finance personnel. Almost 73 per cent (both in the 2002 and 2004 surveys) of the respondents indicated that they were responsible for the information technology employees as well. Even though this is an additional responsibility for the controller from a supervisory perspective, most IT departments (2004: 81.5 per cent) had only one full time employee, with even less reported in 2002 (21.6 per cent had no IT employees and 63.1 per cent only had one full time IT employee).

Financial Profile

The average salary for the controllers who completed the surveys. Salaries continue to rise over the years. This is consistent with the earlier profiles. As for bonuses, several of the controllers received bonuses. Approximately 67-76 per cent of the controllers received bonuses over the five years examined. The average bonus for each year as reported by the controllers. Criteria for bonuses include slightly more objective criteria (2002: 53.9 per cent and 2004: 55.3 per cent) than subjective criteria (2002: 44.74 per cent and 2004: 44.3 per cent). However, subjective criteria still plays a significant role in the determination of bonuses. The percentage of respondents who indicated that these various elements were used in their bonus determination. There is some evidence that those with certifications do enjoy a slightly better total compensation package. Those with a CPA appear to make the most. This may be due to the fact that the CPA designation has a longer history and is recognized in all public accounting while the CHAE is strictly for the hospitality industry.

Clubs vs Hotels

In terms of *H1* and *H2*, *t*-tests and chi-square tests were performed to determine if statistically significant difference exist between the characteristics profiles of hotel and club controllers and between the financial profiles of hotel and club controllers. Regarding characteristics, there is statistical significance between the gender of controllers in that both 2002 and 2004, there are more female controllers in the club industry than the hotel industry (2002: 58.1 per cent female club controllers, 30.3 per cent female hotel controllers vs 41.9 per cent male club controllers, 69.7 per cent male hotel controllers; Ç^{2}=7.392, sig.$<$0.05 and 2004:

75 per cent female club controllers, 24.3 per cent female hotel controllers vs 50.5 per cent male club controllers, 49.5 per cent male hotel controllers; Ç^2=14.221, sig.<0.05). In addition, there was some indication that club controllers are more likely to have the CPA designation than hotel controllers. In 2002, the difference is statistically significant at the $p<0.05$ level and in 2004, it is statistically significant at the $p<0.10$ level (2002: 26.1 per cent of club controllers vs 2.9 per cent of hotel controllers; Ç^2=8.350, sig.<0.05 and 2004: 19 per cent of club controllers vs 10.6 per cent of hotel controllers; Ç^2=3.531, sig.<0.10).

However, other than gender and certification, there were no significant differences in age, educational level, or industry specific certification designations among club and hotel controllers. While there was no significant difference between club and hotel controllers for the number of years of accounting/finance experience, there was a statistically significant difference in both surveys (2002 and 2004) in regards to hospitality experience. Hotel controllers had on average more years of experience in the hospitality field than club controllers (2002: hotel controllers with 18 years vs club controllers with 11 years; t=4.298, sig.<0.001 and 2004: hotel controllers with 20 years vs club controllers with 13 years; t=6.889, sig.<0.001).

Financially, the hotel industry pays better than the club industry and these differences are at least statistically significant at the $p<0.10$ level, and even more so when considering just the bonuses (significant at the <0.001 level). However, club controllers (2002: 46.30 hours and 2004: 46.11 hours) work slightly less hours per week than hotel controllers (2002: 51.25 hours and 2004: 49.86 hours).

Male vs Female

T-tests and chi-square tests were performed on the profile data for male and female controllers in regards to *H3* and *H4* to determine if statistically significant differences exist between their respective characteristic profiles and financial profiles. As was already mentioned, there are more female controllers in the club industry than the hotel industry. Beyond these specific industries and consistent with the earlier findings, there are more female controllers working for club management companies and there are more male controllers working for hotel management companies and resorts. These differences are statistically different according to the 2004 survey (Ç^2=28.684, sig.<0.001). There were not enough controllers in each of these additional categories in the 2002 survey to test for statistically significant differences but the observed numbers are consistent with the findings from the 2004 survey. As for age, there were no statistical differences found among female and male controllers. However, there were some statistical differences found in regards to education (2002: Ç^2=13.065, sig.<0.05 and 2004: Ç^2=19.660, sig.<0.05). It appears that more male controllers have a Bachelor (4-year college degree) or Master degree. In addition to education, more male controllers have the CHAE designation (2004: 25.4 per cent female vs 74.6 per cent male; Ç^2=15.206, sig.<0.001). Once again, because of the limited number of respondents in the 2002 survey, no statistical differences could be found. However, the numbers are consistent with 2004 results.

On examining the number of years of work experience in the current position or the amount of finance/accounting experience, there were no statistically significant differences between females and males. If there is no difference, it is logical to deduce that there should not be a difference in compensation between male and female controllers. However, such is not the case.

In most cases, the male controller on average makes $10, 000 more than a female controller. With the inclusion of a broader spectrum of controllers from the hospitality field and not just hotels, this provides further evidence to the results discovered by Ghiselli and Chen (1997) that male hotel controllers make more than female hotel controllers. This does not only apply to the basic salary but is also true for bonuses.

Male controllers receive larger bonuses than female controllers. However, more females than males work in the club segment and vice-versa for the hotel segment. As shown above there is evidence to show that the hotel segment pays more than the club segment. Despite this, further analysis within the hotel segment and the club segment separately indicates that male controllers still make more money than female controllers even within each segment.

Summing Up

It is apparent that being a controller is a most viable career path. The average salary in 2000 was about $60, 000. Together with a bonus of over $8, 500, a $68, 500 compensation package is a very good number. This does not even include benefits, which can run anywhere from 25 to 40 per cent of the base salary. For the 2004 projected salary, the total is over $80, 000. Even though the female counterparts make less and the difference is statistically significant, a $10, 000 difference still leaves a $70, 000 package. With an average benefits level of 30 per cent, this makes the total over $90, 000. As the literature also suggest, controllers do more things than simply sitting at a computer. Technology and the management of human resources are important skills for controllers to master. This makes the career of a controller more varied and interesting. Therefore, students who have preconceived ideas of the monotonous life of a controller may want to give this career another serious consideration. As the results also suggest, controllers in the hospitality industry are coming from other fields or have been involved in other fields besides hospitality. Possible explanations may include a lack of supply of controllers in the hospitality field, a lack of awareness of the hospitality field until later in their career, or leaving the hospitality field for a period of time but decided to return.

Regardless, if such is the case, if one begins his or her career in the accounting department, one may attain the position of controller a lot faster as there is a need of competent individuals. If one wants to become a controller, is the hotel industry better than the club industry or vice versa? As the results suggested, the hotel industry pays better than the club industry, especially when considering just the bonuses. However, club controllers do work slightly fewer hours per week than hotel controllers. Thus, if a student is looking for financial rewards, perhaps the hotel segment is the answer. It is also important to know that though both hotels and clubs are part of the hospitality industry, working in a hotel is not the same as working in a club. Hotels operate 24/7 whereas most clubs do not and they are usually closed on Mondays. In a hotel, one deals with an ever changing guest profile with some repeat/ frequent guests while in clubs, one deals with a set of members.

While there are some differences in the characteristic profiles of female and male controllers, these minor differences may not be enough to explain the differences in the financial profiles. And, while the last research hypothesis is rejected, the industry needs to create better pay equity between the genders so that it can attract more hospitality students into this career.

REFERENCES

Damitio, J.W., Schmidgall, R.S. (2001), "The value of professional certifications for hospitality financial experts", *Cornell Hotel & Restaurant Administration Quarterly*, Vol. 42 No.1, pp. 66-70.

Geller, A.N., Ilvento, C.L., Schmidgall, R.S. (1990), "The hotel controller", *Cornell Hotel & Restaurant Administration Quarterly*, Vol. 31 No.3, pp. 91-7.

Geller, A.N., Schmidgall, R.S. (1984), "The hotel controller: more than a bookkeeper", *Cornell Hotel & Restaurant Administration Quarterly*, Vol. 25 No.2, pp. 16-22.

Ghiselli, R.F., Chen, B.Y. (1997), "Male and female hotel controllers in the '90s", *FIU Hospitality Review*, Vol. 15 No.2, pp. 35-46.

Hassmiller, B. (2000), "Compensation and benefits survey 2000", *The Bottomline*, Vol. 15 No.7, pp. 6-25.

Moore, R.W., Stefanelli, J. (1989), "Power and the hotel controller's role", *Hospitality Education & Research Journal*, Vol. 13 No.1, pp. 1-12.

6

Hotel Industry and Human Resource Management

> Nature never hurries: atom by atom, little by little, she achieves her work. The lesson one learns in fishing, yachting, or planting, is the manners of Nature; patience with the delays of wind and sun, delays of the seasons, bad weather, excess or lack of water.
>
> —*Ralph Waldo Emerson*

The delivery of quality products and services, within international tourism and hospitality, reflects an increasing focus on intangibles and the role of what can be styled the "human factor". Companies struggle to create clear distinction and consumer recognition of added value on the basis of physical product differentiation (Balmer and Baum, 1993) except within a relatively limited band of the market. Airline brand relaunches (new first- and business-class products) and the executive floor products, within the hotel sector, represent a small proportion of the global market and trends in this direction are counter-balanced by the growing strength of budget or economy products (hotels and no-frills airlines) in Europe and North America, catering for both the leisure and business customer.

There is considerable evidence to support the notion that there has been a merging of the tourism experience, in physical product terms, across the range of designated quality levels. The introduction of "Business First" products by airlines offers consumers what is claimed to be a first-class environment for business-class price, while budget to mid-range hotel rooms offer a range of facilities which are not significantly different from some products in the four-star range.

This trend is one which has, in part, created the need to focus on service delivery as an alternative differentiator in the marketplace. The Marriott empowerment series of advertisements is a good example of recognition of this focus by a major hospitality corporation. A "people" focus, within tourism and hospitality, is by no means new and successful organizations such as Disney, British Airways, Singapore Airlines, Marriott and Ritz Carlton have developed strong reputations for their recognition of the role which their staff play in meeting customer expectations within their sector. As a consequence, this is an area which has been studied and analysed in considerable depth, and the literature represents a significant collection of empirical research, good practice case-studies and rather polemical "how to wow the customer" pieces. The focus of such work is at the level of the firm and much of it builds on the work of major corporations such as those identified above. Best practice, in the area, appears to recognize that quality service delivery is not the outcome of an isolated service enhancement training programme, but has to do with change in organizational culture from top down and is a complex process which impacts on all areas of the organization and its systems (Mahesh, 1994).

It is also a process which is rather more commonly taken aboard within the context of larger organizations. Small to medium-sized enterprises (SMEs), which have the advantage of simple internal communication systems, face other challenges reflective of their resource structures, expertise and nature of their workforce. There is little doubt that consumer experience of "human value added" through service is varied within and between the hospitality sectors of most countries. In part, this is a reflection of the eclectic nature of customer expectations which may demand very different things from the same service delivery situation. It is also a factor of the number of human interactions (moments of truth) which most customers experience within any one hospitality purchase--these may or may not be within the one organization and thus the ability to "control" the customer's experience may not lie within the organization, which suffers through lost business. In many respects, a customer's assessment of hospitality will be based on the total destination experience. This study develops the argument that human resource management is more than a strategic and operational concern for companies competing within the hospitality marketplace. It considers human resource management as a strategic dimension within the wider enhancement of quality and market positioning of tourism at the level of organizations, specific destinations, regions within countries or whole nations. The main thesis advanced is that the tourism and hospitality industry, from the perspective of all its stakeholders (public sector, private sector, visitors and host community), benefits from the close integration of human resource, labour market and education policies, with those policies relating to, and impacting on, the tourism and hospitality sector. This study is developed by reporting key findings from two research projects which address aspects of the relationship between these two areas of policy.

The first is concerned with the identification of key future policy priorities for human resource development in tourism and hospitality, while the second addresses the structures and policy formulation environment necessary for creation of effective linkages between tourism and hospitality, on the one hand, and education, training and development on the other.

Policy Issues

The tourism and hospitality sector, in all locations, has a close relationship with the labour market environment from which it draws its skills and consequently depends on its workforce for the delivery of service and product standards to meet existing and anticipated demand from its visitor marketplace. This relationship is, on the one hand, one of dependency in that the make-up of the local workforce (or that which can be introduced into the local environment) has a direct influence on the standards and character of the tourist offering which can be prepared and presented to visitors--if local art and craft skills are not developed within the education system or at community level, it will not be possible to offer this dimension to visitors. On the other hand, tourism and hospitality, for many communities, provides a major and growing sector of the economy and, with it, employment opportunities which other traditional and declining sectors of the economy may not provide. This is true in an industrial, urban context where cities such as Glasgow (now the second most visited urban centre in the UK) have developed tourism in the wake of the decline of its traditional heavy industrial sector. It is an equally valid scenario in locations where the exploitation of natural resources no longer provides the same level of employment opportunity as it did in the past--the decline of the North Atlantic fishery has seen island locations, such as the Faroes, Iceland, Greenland and Newfoundland, focus on tourism as part of wider economic diversification strategies. As one of the studies reported in this article illustrates, the two-way relationship between tourism and hospitality, and human resource development and management is not always recognized in a holistic and policy-focused manner by public or private sector concerns.

Baum identified a number of what were described as "universal themes": issues which literature and practical experience identified as the major human resource concerns faced by tourism and hospitality at both a practical, operational level and in the context of wider strategic and policy-oriented discussion. These were:

- For many sub-sectors in tourism and hospitality, and in most developed countries, the negative employment image of the sector is a major issue and barrier to the recruitment and retention of quality and well educated employees (Choy, 1995). Wood (1995) argues that "both industry employees and wider society view hotel and catering labour as relatively low status, mainly because of the personal service nature of the work involved". This poor image is the result of a cocktail of historic and contemporary factors--the origin of hospitality work within domestic service and its consequent associations with servility; links, in some countries, between hospitality employment and colonial legacy; widespread use of expatriate labour in many developing countries, creating the perception that the sector is one offering only limited opportunity for promotion and progression; widespread exposure to work in the sector as a first working experience, resulting in generalized assessment based on limited exposure (see Baum, 1995); and the reality of anti-social working conditions and casualized remuneration. In some respects, the negatively-held perceptions are not wholly justified by the reality of work for major airlines, international hotel groups, theme parks or within heritage organizations. In other regards, the perceptions are a mirror of the reality of work within an industrial sector dominated by small and medium-sized enterprises (SMEs) and the impact of irregular demand. The effect of these perceptions is to impose a barrier to employment and employment choice among school and college leavers, parents and career guidance teachers which has been very difficult to counter. However, the situation, in some developing countries, is rather different in that international tourism offers a high status and secure employment environment when compared to alternatives in both the primary and manufacturing sectors.

- Demography and the shrinking employment pool resulting in labour and specific skills shortages. This is primarily a developed country phenomenon found in Western Europe, North America and "tiger economy" countries of the Far East. However, labour shortage is also a concern elsewhere when it is recognized that the specific skills which tourism demands (technical, cultural, communications) may be in short supply within many, less developed destination areas (see Baum, 1996). Demographic and other forms of structural change within the labour market demand responses which take tourism recruitment beyond its traditional youth pool into consideration of mature worker alternatives (those returning to work; seeking a career change; retirees) and this, in turn, has major implications for relative remuneration, working conditions, employment security and related issues.
- As already indicated, the rewards and benefits structure of the tourism and hospitality industries can act as a barrier to the recruitment and retention of quality employees. This is a concern of particular focus within hospitality (see Wood, 1997) but perceptions regarding working conditions, hours and pay extend more generally across the tourism-related service sector. There is a clear and unavoidable reality, within tourism and hospitality, that the demand cycle is anti-social and falls out with "normal" nine-to-five working parameters. Aircraft fly at night, hotel guests expect services at weekends and theme parks reach peak demand during public holidays. In terms of remuneration, the sector faces challenges in common with other labour-intensive service areas and in many countries has seen pressures for increased productivity alongside deskilling in many areas of work. At a policy level, the sector is influenced

greatly by legislative intervention, for example European initiatives with respect to minimum wage levels, duration of the working week and unsociable working times.

- In some contexts, cultural and traditional perceptions may also militate against the recruitment of the best able and qualified recruits into the tourism and hospitality sector. Religious barriers, for example, may exclude some groups from participation, notably women.
- Notwithstanding national and sub-sectoral diversity within tourism and hospitality, a combination of reality and perceptions gives an overall negative gloss to the image of many areas of the industry. As we have already suggested, this acts as a major barrier to the recruitment of quality personnel into work in the area. Many entrants to work in the sector do so with expectations of impermanence--this reflects reality in terms of the demand cycle (seasonality and fluctuations as a result of instability within the business cycle in general) whereby longer-term and sustained opportunities are not available to those who take employment in hotels, as resort couriers or ski instructors. It is also reflective of short-termism within many tourism and hospitality businesses which may be unwilling to seek long-term commitment in return for reciprocal long-term investment in the recruit. As a consequence, many entrants to the sector do so with assumptions of impermanence--this is work to be undertaken on the way to somewhere else, a first exposure to the demands of the workforce but one to be shed when better opportunities arise elsewhere in the economy. Furthermore, as Riley (1996) shows, the sector is one of unconstrained access to most of its working positions and one which, therefore, benefits from

unrestrained recruitment to most of its positions but, conversely, also suffers because the skills it engenders in its workforce are in considerable demand within other areas of the service economy. Thus, while entry is open, so is the opportunity to move out elsewhere, both within tourism and hospitality, and to other employment areas. Staff turnover, therefore, can be very high, especially in tight and competitive labour markets, and is a major inhibitor for organizations and destinations seeking to achieve overall enhancement of service and product quality.

- Contrary trends, however, also raise important issues with respect to recruitment and retention. The combined impact of technology and product substitution in the workplace; centralization of key management functions (finance, information analysis, marketing); standardization of product and service delivery; and delayering of management structures in many developed tourism economies means that opportunities for meaningful and developmental careers in skilled craft or managerial areas have been reduced. Reduced opportunity, in turn, impacts on perceptions of the sector and the likelihood of young people, in particular, opting for tourism/hospitality as their career choice.
- A changing tourism and hospitality industry environment is, in a sense, complemented but also complicated by changing social expectations of work (Linney and Teare, 1991) and an increasingly diverse profile of employees (Christensen, 1993). Diversity provides the opportunity to create new working environments and conditions, but demands comprehensive review of traditional practice. A good example of this is the present reluctance of many employees to accept split-shift working and the consequent need for employers to reorganize their work environment accordingly.

- A key issue, relating to recruitment, is that of specific skills shortages in key technical and some managerial areas. In part, this is an extension of the concerns addressed above--image, conditions, remuneration--but is also linked to a reluctance, within some industry sectors and businesses, to invest in the skills development of their key personnel. The Irish tourism industry, throughout a period of sustained growth from the mid-1980s onwards, has experienced acute shortages of key technical personnel, particularly chefs, despite levels of national unemployment considerably above the European Union average (Walsh, 1993).
- Education, training and development, for tourism and hospitality is also, in part, a recruitment issue in that providers of educational and training programmes, particularly within the college and university sector, are influenced by the same perceptual factors as the industry itself. Recruitment standards to vocational programmes for the sector are lower than those to equivalent courses in related professional areas, for example business. Tourism studies are, in a sense, somewhat different from hospitality in this respect in that vocational outcomes are less clearly defined and graduate choice is likely to be rather more eclectic. There are clear opportunities to use such educational programmes in a rather more general education sense rather than facing clear vocational channelling (Baum, 1996). Ritchie (1993) argues that one key issue is a lack of tourism sector consensus as to the need for sector-specific educational provision. Commitment to ongoing career development of existing employees, within tourism and hospitality, varies greatly and is influenced by the sub-sector and the size of the enterprise (Cooper, 1993). The presence of career development opportunities, however, is likely to

exert a considerable influence on the retention of ambitious employees, with potential, within the sector.

- Human resource development is, frequently, addressed as a reactive concern within tourism and hospitality, and rarely in a proactive and planned sense. Product and market shifts and developments may be the target of strategic analysis and preparation, but it is not common, within the sector, to find enterprises or wider destination communities putting in place recruitment, education and training in support of such change, whether quantitative (in the sense of increased arrivals numbers) or qualitative (in the sense of new market segments) in advance.
- Recognition remains relatively limited that human resource development is an important contributor to the delivery of quality products and service, within tourism and hospitality, and that this, in turn, impacts on the level of both new and repeat business achieved by businesses and destinations. This situation has altered significantly in recent years and the business advantage achieved, through a people focus, by companies such as British Airways, Singapore Airlines, Marriott and Ritz Carlton, has been an important contributory factor. However, many small businesses do not have the resources or skills to focus on their human capital. Given that tourism destinations have images that are only as strong as their weakest link, it is important to strive to ensure that the visitor's experience is positive throughout the full range of contact with the providers of goods and services.

The foregoing discussion represent a complex and interrelated series of issues and concerns which have greater or lesser applicability according to the specific corporate or destination context. What is clear is that these issues feature in an assessment of human resources, within tourism and hospitality, wherever such analysis is undertaken, and that the response to them is frequently fragmented and limited by lack of co-ordination and policy direction.

Human Resource Demands of the Tourism and Hotel Industry

To develop a qualitative methodology, through a consensus model approach, for determining gaps between the output of education and training delivery systems and the current and future needs of employers. Inherent in the premise is a falsifiable theory: there is no relationship between education and training system outputs and the delivery of quality service (Spivack, 1997, p. 7).

This study brings together two areas of applied policy development which impact significantly on the development of a wider and cogent policy framework for human resource development within tourism and hospitality: first, that of quality service attainment as central to a successful tourism and hospitality sector, and, second, that there is a role which public education and training can play in achieving such quality. Spivack's study consisted of two components, employing similar methodologies but working with distinct groups in order to verify the approach and to test outcomes in different contexts. The first global survey was based on a sample drawn from international tourism interests, from both the public and private sector, and representing a wide range of sub-sectoral interests and geographical regions. The second component involved a localized study, employing a similar approach and located in a region of Spain. Modified Delphi methods were used for both components, recognizing both the benefits that this approach brings to a qualitative study but also its clear limitations (Witt and Moutinho, 1989). Its advantages include the potential breadth of the study, its internal anonymity the manner in which it permits reflection time for participants and the ability of the approach to tackle complex issues in a balanced manner. Problems relate to the sampling process--the rationale for Delphi is that it draws on expert contributors, but there can be difficulties in defining and identifying appropriate expertise; in maintaining response levels over a number of survey rounds; and in the time commitment demanded of participants.

The global study commenced with 100 participants, drawn on a controlled formula basis from both sectoral and geographical populations to ensure minimum representation within each category. The criteria used for inclusion of participants required that panellists exhibit some or all of the following:

— hold upper-level management positions within their field;
— serve in leadership positions in professional associations related to their field;
— demonstrate familiarity with many different career levels within their sector;
— demonstrate leadership and decision-making skills;
— articulate trends impacting their industry;
— possess familiarity with tourism education and training in their world region.

Sample selection was based on access to various databases and directories of international tourism. While there must be clear limitations to this process, the final sample met representation criteria in terms of both sectoral and geographical considerations. Communication was by mail and fax. The response rate to the two rounds of the study showed expected levels of drop-out so that the first round was completed by 66 per cent of the 100-member sample and the second round by 44, representing a 44 per cent participation rate from the original sample.

The local study, based on the Castilla-La Mancha region of Spain, employed the same approach but saw some significant modifications to suit local conditions. Participation criteria were modified to reflect the different level of responsibility of tourism sector leaders at a regional level and, as a result, included rather more members with direct line management responsibility for enterprises or tourism agencies. Geographical considerations related to representation of the five provinces within the region, while the sectors were modified to reflect the structure of the local industry. The sample was 160 and the three rounds of the survey were conducted: first, by face-to-face personal interview; second, using a telephone survey based on a questionnaire resulting from analysis of the first-round outcomes; and, finally, through panel workshops in each of the five provinces, requiring panellists to prioritize the outcome issues relevant to their specific area and to develop regional action plans.

The results of the two studies identified a number of key gaps with respect to the human resource requirements, as articulated by the respondents (both public and private sector) and the skills and knowledge of those recruited into the tourism sector, whether from specialist vocational programmes or through the general education process. The main area of deficiency related to what Baum (1990) describes as soft competences within the sector, those relating to communication (with customers, colleagues and in various languages other than the mother tongue), information (technology-derived, but also analysis and interpretation) and service (marketing-related, understanding customer needs), all of which are attributes which are generic to the sector and, indeed, to services in general. By contrast, technical ability deficiencies were identified as far less significant within both surveys--there is growing recognition that the diminishing technical demands of the sector (as identified above) can readily be met within the workplace by larger employers, provided soft competences and attitude dimensions are in place.

However, the skills requirements of SMEs remains an issue and it is noteworthy that the local study gave a rather less clear-cut endorsement of this assessment than did the global survey representing larger organizations and interests. In policy terms, this central finding affirms previous research at a more localized level and within the context of specific sub-sectors and suggests the need for review of public education and training provision for the tourism and hospitality sector in terms of curriculum and, indeed, wider focus and purpose. The global study also gives an indication of future education and training priorities for tourism and hospitality. Spivack (1997) reports a number of what she calls "skills development issues" derived from anticipated changes within the tourism and hospitality sector, and which the panel consensus process prioritized as central to education and training needs in the future. These were, in rank order:

— will need to develop more skills in human resource management, particularly in knowing how to build an enthusiastic workforce.

— continued internationalization of business, all levels of management will need more training, especially in interpersonal and multicultural skills.

— awareness and conservation techniques will become an essential part of tourism education at all levels.

— expansion of franchises among transnational firms will accelerate the need for international-level quality of service and skill standards.

— health issues, such as AIDS, that relate to the delivery of tourist products and services will become an essential part of tourism education at all levels.

— will need to learn more high-level management skills such as forecasting and strategic planning.

The local study did not generate significantly different responses from those presented above, with the main emphasis on the growing importancc of environmental awareness, business acumen and the enhanced role of enterprises in the education and training of the workforce. On the basis of this assessment, the study also considered and prioritized key training issues for the future. At an education and training level (Spivack, 1997), these were:

— the future, industry will itself assume increasing responsibility for in-house training of employees at all levels, and rely less on formal education.
— of tourism and hospitality management will need to strengthen their curriculum content that deals with business administration skills.
— will need more training to direct a growing contract-based, part-time and possibly job-sharing workforce.
— continued technological change, alternative methods of training and education (such as distance learning, multimedia interactive training, etc.) will markedly replace traditional education.
— with formal education in tourism and hospitality management studies generally perform better than colleagues who lack such education.
— will increasingly encourage and pay for continuing education for their employees to ensure employee commitment and retention.
— employee exchange programmes at all levels of employment will become commonplace.

With respect to wider personnel issues, a number of priorities were also identified (Spivack, 1997):

— will favour hiring employees who have a combination of on-the-job training and formal education.
— standards, rather than other criteria, will increasingly determine employee compensation and benefits.

— that have been traditionally been under-represented at management levels in the tourism workforce, such as women, will have a greater role in the future.

— family lifestyles will require companies to incorporate practices such as work-at-home employees (the virtual office) that lead to a more flexible workforce.

— will be required to adjust their expectations regarding promotion time-frames, entry-level positions and pay.

— downsizing will slow the advancement of employees within their own organizations.

— increase the quality of service and better compete in the marketplace, employee incentives, for example, stock options, will become standard for companies.

If the human resource environment predicted by Spivack's study is taken to be a reasonable prognosis for the future, there are significant implications for both tourism enterprises and the wider communities within which they exist. What is implied is the need for a significant mind-shift by those providing leadership within the tourism sector, both public and private, but it also points clearly to the need for changes, at a policy and practice level, within the environment controlled by the wider public sector, both tourism-related and that within the provenience of education, training, employment or other labour market authorities.

Policy Dimensions of Tourism and the Labour Market

Practically, tourism education, training and development within the firm and beyond as part of public or private institutional provision, is relatively mature in most developed countries and is an evolving area of activity to communities and countries for which tourism and hospitality activity is rather more new. There is, however, ongoing and, at times, acrimonious debate between providers of tourism and hospitality education and those who see themselves as clients of the system, the industry itself, regarding the relevance, level and focus of education and training (Amoah and Baum, 1997; National Liaison Group for Higher Education in Tourism, 1995). One of the difficulties for tourism and hospitality education is that it is expected to dance to the tune of a fragmented and heterogeneous sector where there are few commonly defined needs at a technical or knowledge level. The requirements of major airlines, hotel companies or heritage sites are diverse in themselves but are also significantly different from the needs of SMEs across the sector. The sector also draws in players from areas of activity which may, at best, acknowledge a tenuous association with tourism and hospitality and, at worst, fail to see their responsibilities in this area at all--such areas can include national parks, leisure and recreational interests, the finance sector, the security services and parts of the retail sector.

One of the consequences of a fragmented public and private sector interest in tourism and hospitality is that there is rarely a clear, single authority with responsibility for the management and direction of education, training and development initiatives in support of the sector. In reality, there is frequently a range of organizations and agencies which have some involvement but also have loyalties and interests which lie out with the domain of tourism and hospitality.

Such organizations and providers may include:

- national, regional or local tourism development agencies, generally public but also in the private domain;
- national or provincial education providers;

- — public sector agencies or government authorities responsible for areas such as heritage, the environment, marine and other water resources, agriculture, national parks, etc.;
- — social partner organizations such as trade unions.
- — private education providers;
- — national employment, labour or manpower agencies and their respective government departments;
- — specialist training agencies, public and private;
- — the various industry sub-sectors and their representative associations;

Education providers may or may not be delivering appropriate curricula to meet industry's needs, is also an issue of policy concern and, in many respects, it is policy shifts that will be required to provide the lead, and assist the sector and the wider community to face up to predicted changes within tourism and hospitality in the future.

Amoah's (1997) study is one which seeks to establish the extent to which policy formulation in the area of tourism and hospitality evolves in tandem with, or in isolation from, that applicable within the education, training and development domain. While based on empirical work in Western Europe and similar developed-country contexts, the findings appear to be considerably more widely applicable. Amoah's study is based on a series of national case studies which were the outcome of local interviews and policy analysis.

Amoah postulates that effective linkages between policy formulation and implementation in the tourism and the education/labour market environments are an important building block towards meeting the human resource challenges which Spivack identifies.

She argues that this outcome is most effective where specific tourism education policies are articulated and put in place as a result of the convergence of the two supporting policy areas. Amoah has articulated this convergence process through presentation of a conceptual model which places tourism and education/training within a policy conceptual framework (Amoah and Baum, 1997), and identifies some of the key linkages which need to be in place for the effective delivery of tourism education, a delivery which can be fully responsive to the range of future needs identified earlier. In practice, Amoah's research suggests that few, if any, national or sub-national jurisdictions fully acknowledge the policy linkages which the framework proposes. Indeed, the reality, in many cases, is that the two key policy domains of tourism and education (where both are clearly identifiable) can operate in either virtual isolation or on the basis of dependency and adaptation where tourism and hospitality are required to respond to or accommodate, within policy and practices driven by education and training, priorities developed without specific sectoral reference.

It is arguable, for example, that the NVQ/GNVQ vocational education framework which was developed in the UK in the early 1990s was done so without specific sectoral consideration or recognition of policy priorities within tourism and hospitality. As a consequence, the structural and content focus does not fully meet tourism and hospitality industry needs. That said, it is difficult to fully verify this argument at a policy level because the UK, in common with many jurisdictions, has little more than embryonic components of a national tourism policy. Amoah's research points to approaches at a provincial level in parts of Canada and at a national level in the Republic of Ireland as representative of environments where policy convergence is most in evidence and most effectively implemented. In both situations, this policy convergence is achieved under the auspices of a national or provincial co-ordination agency. While commencing life as public sector bodies, a number of the Canadian models--for example, the Alberta Tourism Education Council (ATEC)--have been moved out of the public sector and now operate as private bodies. The Irish model, through CERT:

> ...is unique (in Europe) in that it provides by far the most comprehensive approach to co-ordinating the inputs of education and the tourism industry into a unified system and, through CERT, operates through total co-ordination and the identification of training and development needs at both macro and micro levels (Baum, 1995).

Summing Up

It is arguable that global tourism and hospitality have developed to their current status with limited policy focus and direction in a general sense and, more specifically, in relation to the human resource area, and have done so with reasonable success. However, increasing global competition and globalization of products and consumer expectations suggest that competitive edge, for organizations and destinations, will increasingly depend on the human factor, the ability to deliver quality products and services within all areas of tourism and hospitality.

In other words, the people dimension is likely to feature, with increased centrality, in corporate mission focus and destination objectives.

REFERENCES

Amoah, V., Baum, T. (1997), "Tourism education: policy versus practice", *International Journal of Contemporary Hospitality Management*, Vol. 9 No.1, pp. 5-12.

Baum, T. (1990), "Competencies for hotel management: industry expectations of education", *International Journal of Contemporary Hospitality Management*, Vol. 2 No.4, pp. 13-16.

Baum, T. (1993), "Human resources in tourism: an introduction", in Baum, T. (Eds), *Human Resource Issues in International Tourism*, Butterworth-Heinemann, Oxford, pp. 3-21.

Baum, T. (1995), *Managing Human Resources in the European Tourism and Hospitality Industry: A Strategic Approach*, Chapman & Hall, London.

Baum, T. (1996), "Unskilled work and the hospitality industry: myth or reality?", *International Journal of Hospitality Management*, Vol. 15 No.3, pp. 1-3.

Christensen, J. (1993), "The diversity dynamic: implications for organisations in 2005", *Hospitality Research Journal*, Vol. 17 No.1, pp. 69-86.

Cooper, C. (1993), "An analysis of the relationship between industry and education in travel and tourism", *Teros International*, Vol. 1 No.1.

Linney, C., Teare, R. (1991), "Addressing the human resource challenges of the 1990s", *International Journal of Contemporary Hospitality Management*, Vol. 3 No.2.

Mahesh, V.S. (1994), *Thresholds of Motivation*, McGraw-Hill, New York, NY.

National Liaison Group for Higher Education in Tourism (NLG) (1995), *Towards a Core Curriculum for Tourism: A Discussion Article*, NLG, London.

Riley, M. (1996), *Human Resource Management: A Guide to Personnel Practice in the Hospitality and Tourism Industry*, Butterworth-Heinemann, Oxford.

Ritchie, J.R.B. (1993), "Educating the tourism educators: guidelines for policy and programme development", *Teros International*, Vol. 1 No.1.

Spivack, S. (1997), "A consensus model approach for assessing gaps between education system output and human resource demands in the tourism and hospitality sector to aid in the attainment of quality service goals", University of Buckingham., unpublished DPhil thesis.

Walsh, M.E. (1993), "The Republic of Ireland", in Baum, T. (Eds), *Human Resource Issues in International Tourism*, Butterworth-Heinemann, Oxford, pp. 201-16.

Witt, S., Moutinho, L. (Eds) (1989), *Tourism Marketing and Management Handbook*, Prentice-Hall, Englewood Cliffs, NJ.

7

New Operations Management Curriculum: Change, Opportunity

In a country well governed, poverty is something to be ashamed of. In a country badly governed, wealth is something to be ashamed of.

—*Confucius*

All of education's stakeholders are currently in transition. Structural change within the hospitality industry has brought a need for new managerial skills, in particular the ability to integrate operational activities within a strategic organizational framework. Students continue to demand greater stimulus and challenge in workshops and classrooms; practical work, the core of vocational hospitality education, must thus be underpinned with management principle to an ever greater extent. The academic community is also in flux, edging towards new, service-related disciplines as Western economies shift inexorably away from traditional manufacturing industry. For hospitality education, the focal point of much of this change seems to be the operations management curriculum. This study examines environmental changes impacting on this important vocational area, and explores ways in which the operations management curriculum can shape itself to meet changing needs.

Structural Change

During the 1980s European hospitality (Hotel) firms have tended to become larger, better organized and more efficient in their quest to out-perform competitors by numerical and geographical expansion. Surveys conducted by Litteljohn and Slattery and by Olsen during 1990, predicted the continuation of both demand and expansion during the early 1990s. However, the potent cocktail of volatile and unpredicted events which emerged during the late 1980s, drastically forced the pace of change. A hostile business environment, characterized by demand instability and high interest rates, forced European companies to "delayer" or "downsize" their organizations, becoming "flatter and leaner" than at any point in their recent histories. Fewer senior managers are now working in specialist roles and the (somewhat reduced) employment opportunities are located mainly in operational areas. A new breed of managers is emerging, who need new skills and insight to cope with the complexities of changing corporate strategy. Olsen concludes: While the increasing competitiveness of the industry in Europe is well recognized and the downsizing of corporate headquarters is nearly accomplished, in most firms the managers in the field are not yet ready to accept the decentralization challenge. What are required are unique and innovative ways to try to educate, and in many cases socialize, these managers about the need for and value of thinking strategically. According to Nebel *et al.*, corporate downsizing continues in American luxury hotels, with the loss (as in Europe) of middle levels of management and those staff specialists not directly responsible for operational activities. These authors call for a curriculum of professional and technical skills, which will prepare graduates for the operational career paths which make up most of the demand. They stress that employees in the changing hospitality industry need a broader strategic view of operations. Further, Powers and Riegel consider that unit managers will be selected with increasing care, as they will be expected to adopt a wider managerial role.

The traditional view of operations managers as food and beverage or accommodation specialists with a comparatively narrow scope of responsibility is changing. As a result of restructuring, the modern manager may have to assume responsibility for other aspects of the business and must also have sufficient strategic insight to act effectively within organizational policy and strategy. In our view these developments demand a re-thinking of the operations management curriculum. It is necessary to review unit managers' key activities and establish the necessary content. We also feel that there is a need for an underlying theoretical paradigm which will allow the subject more scope to develop as an academic discipline. In addition, there are implications for co-ordinating and supporting appropriate teaching and learning activities.

Hotel Operations

Gamble *et al.* report on a study of hospitality managers' activities, conducted in six European countries. Their findings indicate the need for a more business-oriented hospitality manager who can deploy financial skills to analyse the business and can think strategically about customer needs. Traditional, autocratic management styles are steadily giving way to team-building and facilitation. The above authors attribute this to "total quality" aspirations, which require the harnessing of the creativity and energy of individuals at all levels of the organization. Gamble *et al.* summarize the tasks that hospitality managers perform in relation to four broad curriculum themes. Jones calls for educational programmes which blend technical, professional and personal development, supplying the basic tools needed for effective performance in the workplace. He sees the objective as nurturing individuals who have "a sense of commitment, vision and the ability not only to do things right but also with the wider understanding of doing the right thing". Closer partnership with industry is the logical way of achieving a better fit between the curriculum and the realities of operations management. However, this must be achieved without stifling the theoretical and abstract ideas which will be needed for innovation in the workplace as well as for students' personal growth.

Industrial involvement is not the only factor impacting on hospitality curricula. Calver, for example, lists formative pressures which include technological advance, internationalization and the dictates of government policy. The last few years have seen a rapid expansion in higher education and a dramatic increase in student numbers. In this busier, more turbulent environment, it is sometimes difficult to maintain a focus on the direction hospitality operations management is taking. Yet, a conceptual model of curriculum development which links managerial effectiveness to prevailing industry conditions, offers a relatively flexible way of keeping in touch. Jones uses the model show how the many aspects touching management effectiveness may be incorporated meaningfully into the curriculum. This model centres on a realistic work environment where students build a holistic understanding of managing operations effectively. The discussion so far has presented an industry-driven view that operations management should be positioned at the centre of the learning experience. A curriculum intended to serve industry must mirror the environmental changes of the last few years and must provide a balance of technical and professional skills to equip students with a detailed understanding of day-to-day operations. It must also offer a broader strategic outlook, dealing with every facet of unit and multi-unit business activity.

Operations Management

The changing nature of managerial work suggests a need to up-date and re-shape the operations curriculum, ensuring that it reflects industry needs and job prospects for students. In addition, the pressures of teaching more students and reductions in staff-student contact time have helped to ensure that student-centred learning is now firmly established. Under these circumstances, the logical first step is to develop teaching and learning courseware cheap enough to be within students' dwindling budget and sufficiently flexible for use in a variety of educational circumstances. The *Resource-Based Approach* series attempts to achieve these goals in a practical way. Published by Cassell plc, it reflects the issues raised in this article, in particular the need for an updated, student-centred operations curriculum. The pragmatic, problem-solving format provides an affordable, easy-to-use guide. Industrial relevance is assured by the use of business cases and situations to illustrate key principles in hospitality settings. Flexibility of use is a key consideration, the books being designed for courses at undergraduate level, for open/ distance learning and for short course programmes. To ensure continued relevance, the format of the book allows for regular updating and extension. The *IJCHM* Forum itself is seen as one vehicle for the process of consultation and subject development between all participant institutions. There are three hospitality operations management titles in the *Resource-Based Approach* series, providing a logical and progressive study. These are *Operational Techniques* (foundation level), *Operations Management* (intermediate level) and *Strategic Management* (advanced level), which together provide a progressively deepening understanding of operational practice.

Each of the titles follows a standardized format and draws from a core of recommended reading, including concise explanations, commentary and extension material. All of these titles aim at conceptual understanding of how to manage hospitality operations effectively.

However, the advanced level (strategic) study goes further than most current practice, by providing students with the broader strategic perspective of unit management demanded by industrialists. Another key objective is to integrate the curriculum at foundation and intermediate levels by focusing on operational themes shared between accommodation and food and beverage management. All of the books use systems theory as a basis for understanding the function and management of operations, organizations and the business environment. To some extent this provides the desired theoretical paradigm discussed earlier in this article.

Certainly it provides a foundation on which the academic discipline of hospitality management can build. It is intended that further development of this theoretical basis can be accomplished as the series develops and the consultation base is consolidated. The structure of the *Operational Techniques* volume, includes a review of "hard" and "soft" systems techniques, providing a broad methodological framework. This is developed by drawing parallels between food, beverage and accommodation operations so that hospitality operations are treated in an integrated, systematic way. Integration is maintained by including functional areas, such as personnel and marketing, wherever they occur naturally in the operational setting.

Thus, operational techniques are presented in a coherent way that makes them completely transferable. The second title in the series, *Operations Managemet*, builds on the integrated approach and systems orientation of the foundation level resource book. It is similarly divided into five parts, dealing with the scope of hospitality operations, the organizational context and the key issues of capacity, productivity and quality. In this way it broadens the study from the pragmatic to the more general issues of operations management.

Strategic Management, the third title, explores wider issues of the operational environment. All organizations must make decisions about the activities in which they wish to engage, the goals they seek to achieve and the overall direction they want to pursue. Activities must be planned and co-ordinated to make the best use of resources, meet customer needs, compete effectively, and permit a review of performance. Managers therefore need to define task-related boundaries and devise systems and procedures to carry out their decisions. Decision makers also need to think strategically about the wider implications of their actions for the organization as a whole.

Conclusion

Hotel operations management is once again the focal point for curriculum development. Structural changes occurring in the industry and elsewhere make it desirable to re-shape this specialist area to prepare students fully for employment opportunities. In addition there is a need to extend the subject to include a strategic dimension; to quote Olsen: "...unit managers are now being asked to compete effectively on the local level, where conditions are becoming extremely competitive, to scan the environment for threats and opportunities, and to build a strategic plan for their units based on this type of analysis. This leaves the unit manager with the need to become a much more independent decision-maker and one who is much more aware of the forces in the environment and how they affect the future of the unit".

Changes within education itself seem to require a more focused subject area, which enables students to build cognitively on a core of practical work.

REFERENCES

Calver, S. (1994), "Innovation in FE and HE tourism courses", *Transitions in European Tourism Education*, University of Exeter, No.July.

Fisk, R.P., Brown, S.W., Bitner, M.J. (1993), "Tracking the evolution of the services marketing literature", *Journal of Retailing* , Vol. 69 No.1, pp. 61-103.

Fowler, A. (1996), "How to manage your own CPD", *People Management*, No.October, pp. 54-6.

Gamble, P. R., Lockwood, A. , Messenger, S. (1994), "European management skills in the hospitality industry", HCIMA Conference Proceedings, Amsterdam, No.25-26 March.

Guest, D. (2000), "Human resource management at work", CIPD, available at: www.cipd.co.uk.

Higher Education Funding Council for England (2001), *Getting Ahead: Graduate Careers in Hospitality Management (HEFCE 01/30 May Report)*, Council for Hospitality Management Education/HEFCE, Bristol.

Impact Skills Network (2002), "An assessment of skills needs in tourism and cultural industries: Skills dialogues", July, available at www.impactskillbase.org.uk.

Jameson, S.M., Holden, R. (2000), "'Graduateness' who cares? Graduate identity in small hospitality firms", *Education and Training*, Vol. 42 No.4/5, pp. 264-71.

Johns, N., Edwards, J. (1994), *Operations Management: A Resource-Based Approach for the Hospitality Industry*, Cassell, London, pp. ii-iv.

Johns, N., Ingram, H., Lee-Ross, D. (1994), *Operational Techniques: A Resource-Based Approach for the Hospitality Industry*, Cassell , London, pp. ii-iv.

Johns, N., Wheeler, K.L. (1992), "Productivity angles on sous-vide", in Teare, R., Adams D., Messenger, S. (Eds), *Managing Projects in Hospitality Organizations*, Cassell, pp. 146-168.

Jones, P. A. (1992), "The effective hospitality manager", *Hospitality*, No.134, pp. 16-7 .

Kelley-Paterson, D., George, C. (2001), "Securing graduate commitment: an exploration of the comparative expectations of place students, graduate recruits and human resources managers within the hospitality, leisure and tourism industries", *Hospitality Management*, Vol. 20 pp. 311-23.

Kriegl, U. (2000), "International hospitality management. identifying important skills and effective training", *Cornell Hotel and Restaurant Administration Quarterly*, Vol. 41 No.2, pp. 64-71.

Learning and Teaching Support Network (2004), "Accepted students and applicants 1996-2003 in hospitality, leisure, sport and tourism", based on data provided by UCAS. Learning and Teaching Support Network, available at: www.hlst.ltsn.ac.uk/resources/ucas.pdf.

Litteljohn, D., Slattery, P. (1991), "Macro analysis techniques: an appraisal of Europe's main hotel markets", *International Journal of Contemporary Hospitality Management*, Vol. 3 No.4 , pp. 6-13.

National Statistics (2004), *Social Trends 34 - a Portrait of British Society*, National Statistics, London.

Nebel, E.C., Braunlich, C.G. , Zhang, Y. (1994), "Hotel food and beverage directors' career paths in American luxury hotels", *International Journal of Contemporary Hospitality Management*, Vol. 6 No.6, pp. 3-10.

O'Rourke, A. (2000), "Continuing professional development: too little ... too much ... too late", the Wisdom Centre, The Wisdom Virtual Conference in Clinical Governance, available at: www.wisdomnet.co.uk.

OECD (1998), *Human Capital Investment: An International Comparison*, Centre for Educational Research and Innovation, OECD, Paris.

Olsen, M.D. (1991), " Structural changes: the international hospitality industry and firm ", *International Journal of Contemporary Hospitality Management*, Vol. 3 No.4, pp. 21-24.

Porter, M.E. (1985), *Competitive Advantage: Creating and Sustaining Superior Performance*, Collier Macmillan, London.

Powers, T.F., Riegel, C.D. (1993), "A bright future for hospitality education: providing value in the 21st century", *Hospitality Research Journal*, Vol. 17 No.1, pp. 295-308.

Sadler-Smith, E., Allinson, W., Hayes, J. (2000), "Learning preferences and cognitive style some implications for continuing professional development", *Management Learning*, Vol. 31 No.2, pp. 239-56.

Schwartz, P. (1991), *The Art of the Long View*, Doubleday, New York, NY.

Scottish Executive (2003), *Life Through Learning; Learning Through Life: The Lifelong Learning Strategy for Scotland*, Scottish Executive, Edinburgh.

Shah, A., Pell, K., Brooke, P. (2004), "Beyond first destinations. Graduate employment survey", *Active Learning in Higher Education*, Vol. 5 No.1, pp. 9-26.

Shaw, M., Green, H. (1999), "Continuous professional development: emerging trends in the UK", *Quality Assurance in Education*, Vol. 7 No.3, pp. 169-77.

Teare, R., Ingram, H. (1993), *Strategic Management: A Resource-Based Approach for the Hospitality and Tourism Industries*, Cassell, London , pp. ii-iv

Van der Heijden, K. (1996), *Scenarios - The Art of Strategic Management*, John Wiley & Sons, Chichester.

VisitScotland/George Street Research Ltd (2002), *Stakeholder Opinion Research: Baseline Survey Report*, George Street Research Ltd, Edinburgh.

Wack, P. (1985), "Scenarios: shooting the rapids", *Harvard Business Review*, Vol. 63 No.6, pp. 139-50.

8

Performance Management

> The wise man does not expose himself needlessly to danger, since there are few things for which he cares sufficiently; but he is willing, in great crises, to give even his life--knowing that under certain conditions it is not worthwhile to live.
>
> —*Aristotle*

Process and Quality Improvement

Dodwell and Simmons (1994) posit that quality in hospitality services is concerned with "delighting the customer". It may be argued that this has always been the maxim of successful hospitality companies, but the need to create and maintain high quality standards could be said to be greater than ever. Day and Peters (1994) submit that a shared understanding of quality is a necessary antecedent to setting standards and that quality may be said to have static and dynamic components. Static quality is that which is normally expected by the customer such as a bed free of cockroaches, while dynamic quality represents "moments of truth" of human interaction. According to Coyle and Dale (1993), quality failures are often the result of gaps in perceptions between customers and providers.

They contend that more effort should be expended by providers in determining the needs and expectations of customers and that traditional methods such as questionnaires are inadequate for this purpose. Models of quality management for hospitality are proposed by Heymann (1992) and Atkinson (1994a). Heymann's holistic approach requires organizations to develop a positive, adaptive culture to ensure continuous improvement based on systematic planning and the judicious use of people.

This theme of programmed and sustained change is echoed by Atkinson's (1994a) "mix of six" approach to continuous improvement. The maintenance of quality over time requires commitment from every grade of employee and not just management.

Sparrow and Wood (1994) advance the proposition that experienced food servers have a far richer picture of customers than do training manuals and that their perceptual "maps" can assist in providing quality service. Further, such techniques produce enhanced feelings of trust and self-worth in employees as well as reducing absenteeism and waste. The task of setting of standards requires hospitality organizations to reflect carefully on the relationship between production and service processes to customer satisfaction. Kirk (1995) reviews the applicability of soft systems methodology to hospitality operations and concludes that it is necessary to take a holistic approach in which technical sub-systems are integrated with human activity sub-systems. Catering systems, for example, require technical objectives of safety, customer satisfaction and cost control as well as recognizing the importance of human relationships in implementing these plans. Hospitality systems too, can benefit from holistic approaches and Jones and Lockwood (1995) propose a hotel operations management model which integrates the analysis of process and outputs. Techniques for analysing processes in hospitality environments are offered in postgraduate studies by Orgonyi and Jienpetivate. He concluded that there are differences between manufacturing and service products, but SPC can be used in hospitality as a means of monitoring measured processes. Jienpetivate (1995) studied the service encounter through the methodology of critical incident technique (CIT) and concludes that the investment of effort into managing the service encounter can lead to an enhanced understanding between the server and the served. It is interesting to review the extent to which hospitality quality initiatives are reflected in the literature and the different approaches which are taken by firms. Breiter *et al*. (1995) remark that total quality management in hotels is becoming commonplace and recount the case in the USA of Bergstrom Hotels who have been practising quality principles since 1989.

Bergstrom's "quality commitment" has evolved into continuous improvement based on systematic decision-making, teamwork and human resource support systems. Also in the USA, Ritz-Carlton Hotel company have produced "Gold Standards" which include a credo, motto and 20 "Ritz-Carlton Basics" in the quality management programme. Their initiative has led them to be the first hotel group to win the Malcolm Baldrige National Quality Award (Partlow, 1993). In the UK, the Sutcliffe Group of contract caterers seeks to define quality as a means of sustaining growth, improving client retention and focusing employees on providing a quality service (Page, 1994). Callan (1992) reports the case of the Avant Hotel in Oldham, which was the first UK hotel recipient of the British Standard BS 5750. BS 5750 is a set of documented operational quality standards that is accepted by the British Standards Institution (BSI) and regularly monitored by them. Benefits of BS 5750 for the Avant Hotel include a keener focus on staff training, reduced staff turnover, waste reduction, and widespread publicity as the first registered for BS 5750. There is, however, little evidence that BSI standards of quality have been widely espoused by hospitality firms.

Business Performance and Performance Measurement

Business performance is related to success and the construct of "excellence" as proposed by Peters and Waterman in the 1980s. Caruana *et al*. (1995) comment that, although these so-called excellent firms in that study revealed themselves to be rather ordinary performers, the modelling technique called EXEL is able to be used in service firms with reliability and validity. Peacock (1995), like many other authors, emphasizes that there is no correct definition of good job performance and suggests that the conflicts between managerial perspectives of success should be recognized.

A more holistic approach is offered by Staw (1986) who contends that performance may be staged at the level of the individual, group or the organization. The performance implications of perceptual differences between these levels is referred to as "a strategic gap" by Edgar (1996) in his study of hotels in the short-break market. The results showed considerable variation between average hotel performance but that locational strategies might optimize performance. For example, in primary locations segmentation/packaging strategies work best while optimal performance is achieved with promotional strategies in hotels located in secondary and tertiary locations. In 1989, Witt and Witt (1989) remarked that productivity in the hotel sector is low and that hospitality managers are reluctant to use analytical tools to monitor performance.

Since then, technological advances have made information technology (IT) more widely accessible to business users. Liu's (1995) research concludes that the effective use of IT has the ability to increase overall revenue, improve customer services and to increase manpower productivity in hotel operations. The key factor is that there should be positive user attitudes to the potential advantages of the use of IT. Information technology can also be used to compare the performance of hotels and their managers.

Morey and Dittman (1995) have developed a computer model to benchmark general manager performance and to take into account environmental variables which contribute to profitability. Benchmarking is an important adjunct to continuous quality improvement in which the role of upper management is crucial. Yasim and Zimmerer's (1995) model of the benchmarking of hotel operations focuses on the need to match customer requirements with hotel service quality to achieve superior performance. Business performance may be viewed from the perspectives of a number of stakeholders and hospitality research has focused primarily on consumers and producers. Gu's (1994) study reviews US performance from the investor viewpoint in a ten-year comparative measurement of the risks and returns from hotel, casino and restaurant operations. He concludes that the casinos offers greater investment opportunities and uses two performance measures to compare the sectors. Brander-Brown and McDonnell (1995) review the use of Kaplan and Norton's "balanced score-card" to measure performance in the hospitality industry. The score-card offers an even-handed approach to performance management based on four perspectives: customer, financial, internal and innovation and learning. Although "bottom line" performance measurement is important, "softer" indicators may offer greater opportunities for organizational effectiveness in the longer term. A central strategy in hospitality performance management is to focus on customer satisfaction through quality improvement.

Teamworking

Teamworking is a force for co-ordination and communication and is of particular use to the hotel sector where inter-departmental conflict is a characteristic feature (Dann and Hornsey, 1986) and negative images of employees affect job performance (Palmer and Lundberg, 1995). Although hotels are traditionally grouped into functional departments, Nebel *et al*. (1994) propose a re-engineering approach in which hotels group tasks into coherent business processes such as customer communication, product development and problem resolution. Hotels may not wish to espouse such radical solutions, but the literature suggests that empowerment can offer benefits for hotels. Lashley

(1995) advances teamworking in hospitality as a means of empowerment and continuous improvement and cites examples such as the Accor Group (quality circles), Harvester Restaurants (autonomous work groups), the former Scott's Hotels (whatever-it-takes training), Hilton Hotels (team briefing). Brymer (1991) suggests that empowerment can affect guest satisfaction, employee satisfaction and bottom line profits.

In fact, a natural development to teamworking initiatives is the formation of self-managed teams to solve problems and drive continuous improvement (CI). Atkinson (1994b) argues that the foundation to CI is workplace improvement teams which probably started as quality circles and may have evolved into self-managed work teams. Their aim is continuously to seek improvements within their own remit and they are supported by corrective action teams. Actual hospitality examples of self-managed teams are scarce, but Newton (1992) reports the efforts of Harvester Restaurants who formed teams according to Belbin's typology and asked them to formulate unit strategies and personal objectives over a two-day brainstorming period.

Operational teams are led by an elected leader, self-managing and accountable for team recruitment and selection. Performance contracts are reviewed at meetings held bi-monthly and are supported by reward and recognition systems. To date, there is little evidence that teamworking has been as widely espoused in hospitality as in manufacturing. Ingram *et al*. (1997) contend that much of the literature on the subject is inconclusive and anecdotal and they propose a descriptive model of effective teamworking as a basis for future research. The comparative success of quality assurance schemes such as the government-led Investors in People scheme (Ball, 1993) suggests that hospitality firms are seeking new approaches to people which can address problems such as internal conflict and staff turnover.

Having reviewed some dimensions of business performance and performance measurement, process and quality improvement and teamworking, it seem clear there are links between the three themes. This part explores some of these interrelationships and illustrates them in a relationship.

An integrated process/people approach must specify balanced standards of performance and empower staff to perform more effectively by working together in teams. This will enable organizations to operate a quality assurance programme which is accompanied by improved customer satisfaction and performance improvement. Outside the hospitality industry there are many examples from around the world which indicate that teamworking has the power to improve the way that firms operate and their outputs. This section reviews literature evidence from other industries and the world of sport and considers the benefits of teamworking. Suggestions about appropriate structures and team development will be applied to the context of hospitality firms.

There is a considerable body of evidence which demonstrates that teamworking strategies are being applied in a range of industries with apparent success. Teare *et al.* (1997) have documented case study evidence which demonstrates the increasing role of teamworking in the new process paradigm approach to attaining higher levels of service and responsiveness. They cite examples of the role of continuous improvement and self-directed teams in identifying problems and applying solutions themselves. Brown (1996) reports evidence which concludes that a quarter of UK employers recognize teamworking in their pay systems and that another 17 per cent are actively planning its introduction.

The literature suggests that teamworking has the potential to provide such benefits as improved and sustained organizational outputs (Harris and Harris, 1996) and to act as an effective agent of change, especially with the trend towards horizontal structures (Stewart and Kleiner, 1996). Teams can refocus product design processes on the customer (Valdez and Kleiner, 1996) and help develop competitive advantage (Twomey and Kleiner, 1996). A major benefit of teamworking is greater co-ordination of departments (Nurmi, 1996) and the synergy that creates. The advantages for the teams and team members include greater job satisfaction and camaraderie (Elloy and McCombs, 1996) as well as self esteem and self-actualization (Stainforth, 1996). Shonk and Shonk (1988) submit that business teams can learn from the factors that make sports teams successful. These characteristics of unitary behaviour and "team spirit" in sports teams include, according to Syer (1986), morale, cohesion, confluence and synergy. Morale is an emotive term which refers to the contentment of the team, military unit or the organization as a whole. Cohesion is used by behaviourists who believe that an individual acts only according to the threat of a promise or reward and cohesive forces include commitment to success or task motivation, difficulty of withdrawing (due to inertia or fear of letting down the team) or social needs (Festinger *et al.*, 1950). It may be argued that cohesion is the result rather than the cause of improved performance. This is often demonstrated in football teams who, as a result of above average performance, derive what Syer describes as confluence or "peak experiences of intense concentration and awareness when it seems impossible to do wrong"

In order to succeed, teams need structures which enable them to develop and flourish. Elloy and McCombs (1996) describe a programme of greater employee participation in a US manufacturing plant based on the open systems concept. The process involved completely re-structuring the plant to form self-governing teams which were responsible for their own cost control, absenteeism, safety training, discipline and employee selection and in which leadership emerged naturally. Strachan (1996) reports on the formation of environmental action teams by such firms as Kodak, BT and Apple Computers and contends that traditional management structures may impose certain constraints on the way the team operates. He contends that "organic" cultures supported by participative styles of management best allow teamwork to flourish.

Practical advice about building teams is plentiful in the literature. McDonald and Keys (1996), for example, identify seven major errors in teambuilding programmes from real life episodes. They stress the mutual nature of teams, which they describe as "learning and sharing systems for organization". The point that is most often stressed is the need for upper management support, without which failure is likely. An example of an empowerment effort that "came undone" is recorded by Rothstein *et al.* (1995), who report the case of a sportswear manufacturer who attempted to establish self-managed work teams but, in the absence of whole-hearted management support, the scheme fell at the first hurdle. If the teamworking ethic is to permeate down an organization, it must first be fully espoused at the top and the commitment of middle management secured. This was the case at the First National Bank of Chicago in the mid 1980s, where there was a development from a staid culture to one which showed more risk-taking and innovation through team management (Harris and Harris, 1996). While it is important that top management set the scene and focus the goals, they must allow the teams the space to develop themselves because, as Fred Wilson (1996) suggests, "great teams build themselves". An important contributory factor to teams' success is a suitable leadership style which enables synergy to take place. Nurmi (1996) contends that synergistic teams can be "fertilized" by management, but after that, management has little to say in igniting the process. Another role of the leader is to manage the team processes effectively towards the goals and in a mature and supportive atmosphere. Esquivel and Kleiner (1996) stress the importance of conflict management in which the focus is on the issues and not individuals and in which teams develop "a sense of family". Team members must feel that they can contribute "safely" in an ambience of trust and confidence.

Summing Up

It is more difficult, however, to apply these lessons from other industries to the hospitality context. Part of the problem may be the traditional nature of hospitality management and its attendant functional departmental structure which can contribute to inertia, conflict and lacklustre performance. Another difficulty arises in matching a generic team strategy to hospitality units of diverse sizes, cultures and product offering, many of whom are struggling with the challenge of brand identity.

One hospitality firm who has consistently tried to reconcile the opposing tensions of standardization and empowerment is the Accor Group of France. From earlier experiments with quality circles, their Novotel chain of three-star hotels has developed a new approach to developing staff and ensuring standard brand quality. Susan Segal-Horn (1995) reports that flexible working patterns have broken down the staff demarcation normal within hotels and has enabled the creation of an "open space" approach to organizational learning. Firmly at the helm of this initiative is the unit general manager, whose role has been redefined much closer to the social role of a ship's captain.

Teamworking may not come easily, but its potential rewards are improved process and quality management as well as enhanced individual and organizational improvement. In conclusion, teamworking may be seen, not so much as a discrete force for change, but more as the social mechanism through which improvement may take place. In order for a teamworking programme to be successful management must have the vision to inspire and the courage to withdraw and let the process gain it own impetus.

REFERENCES

Atkinson, C. (1994b), "Continuous improvement the total teamwork way", *International Journal of Contemporary Hospitality Management*, Vol. 6 No.3, pp. i-ii.

Ball, S. (1993), "Investing in people", *Voice*, July/August, pp. 22-4.

Brander-Brown, J., McDonnell, B. (1995), "The balanced score-card: short term guest or long-term resident?", *International Journal of Contemporary Hospitality Management*, Vol. 7 pp. 7-11.

Breiter, D., Tyink, S.A., Corey-Tuckwell, S. (1995), "Bergstrom Hotels: a case study in quality", *International Journal of Contemporary Hospitality Management*, Vol. 7 No.6, pp. 14-18.

Brown, D. (1996), "Team rewards: lessons from the coal-face", *Team Performance Management*, Vol. 2 No.2, pp. 6-12.

Brymer, R.A. (1991), "Employee empowerment: a guest-driven leadership strategy", *Cornell Hotel and Restaurant Administration Quarterly*, Vol. 32 No.1, pp. 56-8.

Callan, R.J. (1992), "Quality control at Avant Hotels--the debut of BS 5750", *Service Industries Journal*, Vol. 12 No.1, pp. 17-33.

Caruana, A., Pitt, L.F., Morris, M.H. (1995), "Are there excellent service firms and do they perform well?", *Service Industries Journal*, Vol. 15 No.3, pp. 243-56.

Coyle, M.P., Dale, B.G. (1993), "Quality in the hospitality industry: a study", *International Journal of Hospitality Management*, Vol. 12 No.2, pp. 141-53.

Dann, D.T., Hornsey, T. (1986), "Towards a theory of interdepartmental conflict in hotels", *International Journal of Hospitality Management*, Vol. 5 No.1, pp. 23-8.

Day, A., Peters, J. (1994), "Rediscovering standards: static and dynamic quality", *International Journal of Contemporary Hospitality Management*, Vol. 6.

Dodwell, S., Simmons, P. (1994), "Trials and tribulations in the pursuit of quality improvement", *International Journal of Contemporary Hospitality Management*, Vol. 6 pp. 14-18.

Edgar, D.A. (1996), "The strategic gap: a multi-site, short break perspective", in Johns, N. (Eds), *Productivity Management in Hospitality and Tourism*, Cassell, London, pp. 38-54.

Elloy, D., McCombs, T (1996), "Application of open systems theory in a manufacturing plant", *Team Performance Management*, Vol. 2 No.3, pp. 15-22.

Esquivel, M.A., Kleiner, B.H. (1996), "The importance of conflict in work team effectiveness", *Team Performance Management*, Vol. 2 No.3, pp. 42-8.

Festinger, L., Schachter, S., Back, K. (1950), *Social Pressures in Informal Groups: A Study of a Housing Project*, Harper and Row, New York.

Gu, Z. (1994), "Hospitality return, risk and performance indexes: a ten-year examination", *Hospitality Research Journal*, Vol. 17 No.3, pp. 17-26.

Harris, P.R., Harris, K.G. (1996), "Managing effectively through teams", *Team Performance Management*, Vol. 2 No.3, pp. 23-6.

Heymann, K. (1992), "Quality management: a ten-point model", *Cornell Hotel and Restaurant Administration Quarterly*, Vol. 33 No.5, pp. 50-60.

Higgs, M. (1996), "Overcoming the problems of cultural differences to establish success for international management teams", *Team Performance Management*, Vol. 2 No.1, pp. 36-43.

Ingram, H., Teare, R., Scheuing, E., Armistead, C. (1997), "A systems model of effective teamworking", *The TQM Magazine*, Vol. 9 No.2, pp. 118-27.

Jienpetivate, M. (1995), "The management of service encounters", University of Surrey, Guildford., MSc dissertation.

Jones, P., Lockwood, A. (1995), "Hospitality operating systems", *International Journal of Contemporary Hospitality Management*, Vol. 7 No.5, pp. 17-20.

Kaplan, R.S, Norton, D.P., (1992), "The balanced scorecard--measures that drive performance", *Harvard Business Review*, Vol. 70 No.1, pp. 71-9.

Kirk, D. (1995), "Hard and soft systems: a common paradigm for operations", Vol. 7 No.5, pp. 13-16.

Lashley, C. (1995), "Towards an understanding of employee empowerment in hospitality services", *International Journal of Contemporary Hospitality Management*, Vol. 7 No.1, pp. 27-32.

Liu, M-C.B. (1995), "Information technology and management of hotel operations: an examination of the link between the effective use of IT, managerial effectiveness and improvement in business performance", University of Surrey, Guildford., MSc dissertation.

McDonald, J.M., Keys, J.B. (1996), "The seven deadly sins of teambuilding", *Team Performance Management*, Vol. 2 No.2, pp. 19-26.

Morey, R.C., Dittman (1995), "Evaluating a hotel GM's performance", *Cornell Hotel and Restaurant Administration Quarterly*, Vol. 36 No.5, pp. 30-2.

Nebel, III, E.C., Rutherford, D., Schaffer, J.D. (1994), "Reengineering the hotel organization", *Cornell Hotel and Restaurant Administration Quarterly*, Vol. 35 No.5, pp. 88-95.

Newton, S. (1992), "Customer obsession", *Managing Service Quality*, pp. 269-74.

Nurmi, R. (1996), "Teamwork and team leadership", *Team Performance Management*, Vol. 2 No.1, pp. 9-13.

Orgonyi, V. (1995), "An exploratory study into the applicability of statistical process control (SPC) in the hospitality industry", University of Surrey, Guildford., MSc dissertation.

Page, C. (1994), "Sutcliffe Catering's approach to continuous improvement", *International Journal of Contemporary Hospitality Management*, Vol. 6 No.1, pp. 19-24.

Palmer, I., Lundberg, C.C. (1995), "Metaphors of hospitality organizations", *Cornell Hotel and Restaurant Administration Quarterly*, Vol. 36 No.3, pp. 80-5.

Partlow, C.G. (1993), "How Ritz-Carlton applies 'TQM'", *Cornell Hotel and Restaurant Administration Quarterly*, Vol. 34 No.4, pp. 16-24.

Peacock, M. (1995), "A job well done: hospitality managers and success", *International Journal of Contemporary Hospitality Management*, Vol. 7 No.2, pp. 48-51.

Rothstein, L.R., Hackman, J.R., Pascual, E., Gelinas, M.V., James, R.G., Randolph, W.A. (1995), "The empowerment effort that came undone", *Harvard Business Review*, Vol. 1 pp. 20.

Segal-Horn, S. (1995), "Core competence and international strategy in service multinationals", in Teare, R., Armistead, C. (Eds), *Service Management: New Directions, New Perspectives*, Cassell, London.

Shonk, W., Shonk, J.H. (1988), "What business teams can learn from athletic teams", *Personnel*, Vol. 65 No.June, pp. 76..

Sparrow, J., Wood, G. (1994), "You're stopping me from giving quality service", *International Journal of Contemporary Hospitality Management*, Vol. 6 No.1, pp. 61-7.

Stainforth, D. (1996), "Teamworking, or individual working in a team?", *Team Performance Management*, Vol. 2 No.3, pp. 37-41.

Staw, B.M. (1986), "Organizational psychology and the pursuit of the happy/productive worker", *California Management Review*, Vol. 4 No.Summer, pp. 40-53.

Stewart, G.R., Kleiner, B.H. (1996), "The enabling power of teams and information technology", *Team Performance Management*, Vol. 2 No.2, pp. 13-18.

Strachan, P.A. (1996), "Achieving environmental excellence through effective teamwork", *Team Performance Management*, Vol. 2 pp. 25-9.

Syer, J. (1986), *Team Spirit: The Elusive Experience*, The Kingswood Press, London, pp. 13-14.

Teare, R, Ingram, H., Schueing, E., Armistead, C. (1997), "Organizational teamworking frameworks: evidence from UK and US-based firms", *Journal of Service Industry Management*, Vol. 8 No.3.

Valdez, R., Kleiner, B.H. (1996), "How to build teamwork in the defence industry", *Team Performance Management*, Vol. 2 No.2, pp. 41-8.

Wilson, F. (1996), "Great teams build themselves", *Team Performance Management*, Vol. 2 No.2, pp. 27-31.

Witt, C., Witt, S.F. (1989), "Why productivity in the hotel sector is low", *International Journal of Contemporary Hospitality Management*, Vol. 1 No.2, pp. 28-33.

9

Hotel Operations Management

Thank you for your wonder reception which I so richly deserve and so seldom get.

—George Jessel

The origins of operations management as a management subject lie in manufacturing where "production management" evolved to facilitate the production of tangible products. However, the growth and influence of service industries prompted a rethink of what constitutes "production", and as a result the more generic term "operations management" is gaining acceptance. As Heizer and Render point out: "Production management and operations management are activities which relate to the creation of goods and services through the transformation of inputs into outputs".

Hill's interpretation is more specific, by suggesting that: "Production management and operations management describe the same set of tasks. Both are concerned with managing those resources of an enterprise that are required to produce the goods or services to be sold to consumers or other organizations". Hence, in the broadest sense there is growing agreement that operations management is concerned with producing a product or a service. The concept of hospitality operations management has evolved from the fundamental activities associated with operating and managing the provision of rooms, food and beverages in a variety of hotel and catering establishments. However, before giving consideration to the implications of the study of hospitality operations management in higher education programmes it is relevant to reflect on the structure and content of the hospitality product.

A hotel example is used to illustrate this as, although various food-service and lodging concerns incorporate one or more of the major activities of rooms, food and beverage, hotels typically comprise all three.

The Hospitality Product

Clearly, the provision of rooms constitutes a near "pure service" product with a high service function, similar to a train journey, a college course or visit to the doctor. Essentially, the product is almost totally intangible, consisting simply of a memory of the experience. The provision of alcoholic beverages represents a service product, but contains within it a significant retail function. This function includes the purchasing, display and merchandising of goods in a similar way to those of department stores, shops and supermarkets. In addition, and in contrast to room letting, beverage operations contain an important stock management element which, among other things, aims to ensure demand is satisfied with a minimum of capital investment. Finally, the provision for food also constitutes a service product, but, in addition to containing a stock management element, also comprises a manufacturing-type production function. This involves the purchase and conversion of raw materials into finished products, i.e. dishes and meals, for distribution and service to the customer. Though on a smaller scale, this activity has similarities to that of a car manufacturer or a domestic appliance producer. The importance of reflecting on the separate kinds of functions involved in the provision of a hotel or hospitality product is that they can reveal parallels with other industries which specialize in similar functions, such as retailing and production. Once this is recognized it becomes possible to gain valuable insights into operating methods and associated systems which have been developed and refined over a considerable period of time.

For example, production firms place particular stress on total product costs and cost control systems, whereas retail firms emphasize material cost, gross margin and selling price control. By comparison, pure service firms largely ignore the control operating costs and focus on sophisticated pricing strategies and tactics. Whichever the case, there are lessons to be learned from these industries and the hospitality industry should not be slow to gain benefit from their experience. Where appropriate, certain methods and techniques can be transferred and adapted to suit the particular needs of the hospitality product. The above hotel illustration serves as a reminder of the deceptive complexity of the hotel product environment in which hospitality operations management is required to be implemented. However, the reality of the live situation is further complicated by the nature of the hotel product. For instance, although the food production function has definable similarities with the production function found in manufacturing firms, there are a number of major divergences. One of these relates to product range and volume.

While manufacturers are associated with the production of high volumes of a relatively limited range of products, hotels and other hospitality firms are normally characterized by their low volume and wide choice. For example, in many cases restaurants offer three or four varying product lists, in the form of menus, per day, e.g. breakfast, lunch, afternoon tea and dinner. With a relatively wide range of product choice within each menu, even the larger establishments experience a comparatively low volume of sales per menu item. Although in recent times the emergence of fast food and other speciality of restaurant types have ameliorated the situation, this basic characteristic, and others, still widely persist. Thus, the nature and complexity of the hospitality business presents a considerable challenge to the hospitality operations management curriculum.

Hospitality Operations Management

During past, operations management was broadly seen to fall within two distinct areas in hotels, namely house management including reception, housekeeping and reservations, and food and beverage management depicting restaurant, banqueting and bars. More recently there has been a growing recognition that the house and food and beverage management components are not discrete activities, but part of the whole hotel (lodging) or food-service product. While they may function as separate departments for organizational reasons, room, food and beverage activities form interdependent, rather than independent, components of a total service product. Elements such as product choice, quality of service and pricing policies should therefore be complementary. For example, guests' perceptions of a hotel product are likely to be adversely affected if reception provides swift and efficient registration, but bar service is slow and inadequate, or if the rooms tariff is competitive, but the restaurant menu is over-priced.

A Decision Framework

If the total hospitality product is to be administered effectively, operations managers need to acquire an understanding of the complete process involved in planning, implementation and control, including a knowledge of the design and development stages. As Schroeder argues: "Product design is seldom the sole responsibility of the operations function, but operations is greatly affected by new-product introduction and vice-versa. Operations is on the 'receiving-end' of new-product introduction. At the same time, new products are constrained by existing operations and technology.

Therefore, it is extremely important to understand the new-product design process and its interactions with operations". One notion of hospitality operations management is that it involves decision making in relation to the provision of rooms, food and beverage services. The decisions are fundamentally concerned with the transformation process, which takes inputs and converts them to outputs, together with the support functions required to complete the task.

Thus, in order to develop a curriculum which reflects the needs of industry, it is necessary to take account of both the decision making and the primary and supporting business functions involved in the process to form the basis of a conceptual framework. The kind of decisions involved in hospitality operations management are essentially operational (tactical) in nature, and these should determine the extent to which the other functional areas are required to underpin it. To take an extreme case, it could be argued that hospitality operations management encompasses all aspects of the primary and business function areas and that they should therefore be integrated in one single subject curriculum for the whole programme. Clearly, this is not academically sound or practically viable.

Disciplines such as marketing, human resource management and accounting, cannot simply be superimposed on operations management. This would give rise to an *ad hoc* and fragmented series of academic inputs, solely geared to the operational process associated with rooms, food and beverage activities. It would also disregard the development of the broader role of the business functions related to such activities as investment decisions, pricing strategies, and corporate planning. On the surface the functional application may be apparent in a particular situation, but the broader management implications of the theoretical underpinning will be lacking. Business and management disciplines have their own theoretical framework which should be developed logically and systematically in order for students to understand the principles, assumptions and limitations present. Thus, for example, if the kind of decisions made by hospitality operations managers are generally deemed to be tactical (operational) in nature, as opposed to strategic, this will provide a pragmatic basis on which to build a body of operations management knowledge into the curriculum. In this case there are a number of functional methods and techniques closely associated with tactical decisions which can be incorporated effectively in the curriculum. The examples illustrated below relate to the accounting function, but the principles and processes are similar for marketing, human resources, information systems and purchasing.

By identifying the major decision areas, involved in hospitality operations management it becomes possible to determine the appropriate "business function" knowledge integral to the decisions. In terms of accounting methods and techniques.

Stock management is an integral part of the transformation system involved in production of hospitality products and services. It is therefore essential that the hospitality operations management curriculum facilitates an understanding of the principles and practice that underlie stock management decisions. An intricate knowledge of stock recording methods and procedures is not relevant as this will normally be the domain of the accounting function. While the figure suggests the broad accounting content required to underpin stock management decision making, the detail will depend on the emphasis and orientation of the particular hospitality programme. By examining each major decision-making area and determining (drawing out) the methods and techniques, underlying factors and issues to be addressed, it is possible to establish the relevant curriculum content.

However, it is important not to be too rigid in distinguishing between tactical and strategic decisions as often it is necessary for students to appreciate the bigger picture in order to understand the context of the specific method or technique to be learned. The approach is similarly carried out for the other remaining functions referred (i.e. marketing, human resources and so on) to evolve the body of knowledge required from the hospitality operations management function.

Curriculum Delivery

The delivery of the hospitality operations management curriculum is also worthy of mention in terms of teaching and learning facilitation. To be effective, delivery should be carried out in a cohesive manner by operations management tutors rather than in a fragmented way with specialist lecturers in accounting, marketing, etc. The latter approach dissipates the operational management function and mitigates against its development.

Operations management is not subordinate to the traditionally accepted academic business disciplines and should not be treated so. Furthermore, if students are to learn and understand the interrelationships that constitute a "total hospitality product" in an operational context, then it becomes counter-productive to fragment the method of learning and teaching.

REFERENCES

Jameson, S.M., Holden, R. (2000), "'Graduateness' who cares? Graduate identity in small hospitality firms", *Education and Training*, Vol. 42 No.4/5, pp. 264-71.

Kelley-Paterson, D., George, C. (2001), "Securing graduate commitment: an exploration of the comparative expectations of place students, graduate recruits and human resources managers within the hospitality, leisure and tourism industries", *Hospitality Management*, Vol. 20 pp. 311-23.

Kriegl, U. (2000), "International hospitality management. identifying important skills and effective training", *Cornell Hotel and Restaurant Administration Quarterly*, Vol. 41 No.2, pp. 64-71.

Learning and Teaching Support Network (2004), "Accepted students and applicants 1996-2003 in hospitality, leisure, sport and tourism", based on data provided by UCAS. Learning and Teaching Support Network, available at: www.hlst.ltsn.ac.uk/resources/ucas.pdf.

National Statistics (2004), *Social Trends 34 - a Portrait of British Society*, National Statistics, London.

O'Rourke, A. (2000), "Continuing professional development: too little ... too much ... too late", the Wisdom Centre, The Wisdom Virtual Conference in Clinical Governance, available at: www.wisdomnet.co.uk.

OECD (1998), *Human Capital Investment: An International Comparison*, Centre for Educational Research and Innovation, OECD, Paris.

Porter, M.E. (1985), *Competitive Advantage: Creating and Sustaining Superior Performance*, Collier Macmillan, London.

Sadler-Smith, E., Allinson, W., Hayes, J. (2000), "Learning preferences and cognitive style some implications for continuing professional development", *Management Learning*, Vol. 31 No.2, pp. 239-56.

Schwartz, P. (1991), *The Art of the Long View*, Doubleday, New York, NY.

Scottish Executive (2003), *Life Through Learning; Learning Through Life: The Lifelong Learning Strategy for Scotland*, Scottish Executive, Edinburgh.

Shah, A., Pell, K., Brooke, P. (2004), "Beyond first destinations. Graduate employment survey", *Active Learning in Higher Education*, Vol. 5 No.1, pp. 9-26.

Shaw, M., Green, H. (1999), "Continuous professional development: emerging trends in the UK", *Quality Assurance in Education*, Vol. 7 No.3, pp. 169-77.

Van der Heijden, K. (1996), *Scenarios - The Art of Strategic Management*, John Wiley & Sons, Chichester.

VisitScotland/George Street Research Ltd (2002), *Stakeholder Opinion Research: Baseline Survey Report*, George Street Research Ltd, Edinburgh.

Wack, P. (1985), "Scenarios: shooting the rapids", *Harvard Business Review*, Vol. 63 No.6, pp. 139-50.

10

Food, Beverage and Accommodation

There is always a temptation to view the hotel industry as a number of discrete areas. For example, the classical approach is to consider catering as a separate issue to the function of hotel keeping. However, any true picture of the industrial situation demands that this gap be bridged by taking a holistic approach. Aspects and techniques which can be applied to the catering sector are frequently just as valid in the hotel sector and vice versa; only the examples are different.

Organizations can integrate closely with their members, or remain as incidental servants. They can be rigid, cold, and impersonal, or generate warm flexible relationships. Because of this diversity it is of little use providing business students and practitioners with something that purports to be a general solution to a generalized organizational problem. Undoubtedly ideal solutions to business problems do exist, but because of the diverse nature of organizations and the multiplicity of unit types, a given solution is often successful only in the specific situation for which it was designed. As a general rule, such solutions cannot be transported or replicated elsewhere.

This integrative approach may be taken still further. It is natural for vocational education, as exemplified by hospitality management studies, to emphasize the totality of processes common in organizations. This is just the way that operational managers cumulatively build up their bank of personal experience, a much valued commodity in a pragmatic industry, where managers must grasp the whole complexity of the workplace. Traditional business subject areas seem to tend naturally to a narrow academic focus, and as a result, integrative links between subjects taught in hospitality courses are sometimes lost. This may be avoided by reinforcing learning with practical examples demonstrating how topics complement one another and reflecting the operation of industry in practice.

The *Oxford Dictionary of Current English*, defines Hospitality as "the friendly and generous reception and entertainment of guests or strangers". It involves the satisfaction of primary human needs of food and lodging. Doswell and Gamble suggest that the total hotel product comprises not only the physical element (food, drink and accommodation), but also the emotional satisfactions of image and atmosphere. Such classifications are useful in advancing the understanding and theoretical analysis of the subject. However, the practice of hospitality management has much to learn from the global operational approach used in traditional operations management theory. This work has its foundations in manufacturing and during the 1970s was broadened to include services such as hospitals, office procedures and supermarkets. Vollman proposes a revised definition of operations management as "systems of men, materials, capital, equipment, information and money", while Hill more succinctly suggests that it consists of "... producing a product or providing a service"

Operations are in general regarded as possessing the broad characteristics of centrality and importance. They are also seen as system-led, time-constrained yet immediate entities. The principle of centrality is that operations are the central function and focus of most organizations and the means by which the consumer is provided with the product. Within the hospitality industry, this product and service delivery takes the form of a physical interaction between employee and customer. Human interaction is crucial to consumer satisfaction and its corollary, dissatisfaction, and therefore is of major concern to operations managers. The concept of importance reflects the fact that operations are an important core activity which have responsibilities for most of the organization's resources.

Most management time is spent in reviewing operational changes and allocating human and financial resources to those potential changes. Operations are regarded as system-led, because operations managers are concerned with satisfying customers by ensuring that the production and service system operates efficiently. They are time-constrained because consumer satisfaction depends on delivery of the product within time parameters. Fast-food, for example, is expected to be produced quickly and efficiently. Finally, operations are regarded as immediate because they represent a pervasive system of activities affecting every area of the organization. Without operations, no product would be produced or served and no profit would be made.

The immediate, all-pervasive and crucial nature of operations encourages the view that this activity should be studied as an integrated practice within hospitality management. Erection of barriers between the component activities of catering and accommodation is therefore spurious and unnecessary. However, the hospitality industry, being a service industry, must take account of the particular nature of the products and services offered, namely:

- they cannot usually be stored or kept for later use or consumption;
- they are often diverse and personalized in nature;
- they are perishable and cannot always be inventoried;
- most services have a high labour input.

— most services cannot be transported and must be provided or utilized on site; and
— demand can be difficult to determine and may fluctuate quite considerably, e.g. there may be a heavy demand at meal-times and none at other times of the day.

Business Cycles

The basic concepts which underpin operations in the hospitality industry are exemplified in the integrated systems approach to business organizations. Business systems may be viewed as cycles made up of inputs and outputs, an approach applicable to both the food and beverage, and accommodation sectors. The cyclical model can be applied at many levels and encompasses strategy and design, as well as operational and control activities. The starting point of the basic business cycle is the purchase of raw materials. These inputs are transformed into finished products and sold to generate wealth, which in turn is used to purchase more raw materials and restart the cycle. Labour costs can also be regarded as system inputs, as they are utilized at each turn of the operational cycle and are responsible for generating revenue. All hospitality operations thus fit this generalized business cycle, no matter what proportions of materials, service and labour are used.

Similarly, all hospitality operations are underpinned by a parallel financial cycle in which input costs are transformed into output revenue. As the stages of the material cycle run parallel with financial procedures, it is often convenient to use the cyclical model as a basis for control processes. Budgets often form the basis of such control through the comparative analysis of costs, labour, overheads or sales, which may be applied equally to both catering and accommodation departments. In the same way, catering and service systems may be incorporated into a universal cycle which takes account of the major activities as first suggested by Cracknell *et al.* in 1983.

This process, depicted graphically, recognizes that all hospitality operations are consumer-led and that the planning stage must reflect the nature of the market and target consumer. This course of action leads to the specification of products and the materials necessary to produce them. Goods are purchased, received, stored and issued in accordance with those specifications. In catering systems, this activity is an important one involving the physical movement of raw materials. However, it also applies to accommodation operations by, for instance, controlling the flow of laundry and cleaning materials. The production process transforms raw materials and labour into the finished product; a cooked meal or a serviced bedroom. At the service stage of the cycle, the product's attributes are displayed (through menus or tariffs) and delivered to the customer who has travelled to the hospitality unit to receive them. As suggested by Nightingale the service stage must be regularly monitored and reviewed to ensure that it conforms to the organization's standards and the customer's aspirations, thereby maintaining the consumer-led approach.

Most of the concepts and practices of operations management associated with manufacturing apply equally to the hospitality industry. Operations management can be defined as the study of concepts, procedures and technologies used by managers, administrators and employees in the operation of all organizations. In essence, it is concerned with the efficient conversion of resources into goods or services. The operation is a process of converting the inputs of equipment, material, money, people and time into outputs.

Measuring the time taken to carry out a particular task is an important aspect of operations management.

However, managers and supervisors in the hospitality industry often have only a vague idea of how long a particular task takes to complete and have seldom tried to establish whether this represents the optimum time. As a result, tasks are not always carried out in a cost-effective manner, either because insufficient time has been allocated, or more commonly, because too much time has been allowed and productivity is reduced.

The effective management of capacity is perhaps the most important responsibility of operations management. It is the principal planning responsibility and all other operations planning takes place within the framework set by capacity decisions. Capacity requirements in the hospitality industry can be identified from the perspectives of current, short-term and long-term capacity. The capacity of a hotel, for example, might be limited in the short-term by the number of rooms available. In the longer term, additional rooms could be built to increase the capacity. In the case of a restaurant, capacity is limited by the number of seats available. If capacity is to be adjusted or increased, alternative styles of food service or a different type of food or menu could be used to increase seat turnover. However, in doing this, the nature and style of the operation would be dramatically altered.

Forecasting is generally considered to be the starting point for any business planning activity and focuses on identifying and predicting likely demand. No single forecasting technique fulfils every operational requirement but if forecasts are to be of value, they must be as accurate as possible. They must provide the appropriate level of detail speedily, reflecting the up-to-date situation. The accuracy of forecasting techniques depends to a great extent on how far into the future it is required to predict. The further into the future, the more difficult it becomes and the greater the chance of error. The forecasting timeframe, in the hospitality industry, can generally be divided into four: the immediate, short-term, medium-term and long-term.

Immediate forecasting may be required to predict demand on a scale of hours or even minutes, for example, where responsiveness to the flow of customers demands constant rescheduling of production. Short-term forecasting has a time-scale of between one day and one month. It is used to predict periodic demand and to facilitate such activities as purchasing and staffing. Medium-term forecasting involves prediction of demand over the following three to six months. It is frequently used in areas such as the planning of maintenance projects and seasonal staffing levels. Long-term forecasting is normally for one year or more, and is used in areas such as the planning of new equipment purchases.

Capacity and the forecasting of demand are concerned with matching operational output to customers' needs. Scheduling completes this process by adding a time dimension to these functions and is concerned with the timing of actions that are either planned or may occur. It sets a timetable to any plans which have been drawn up in operations management so as to ensure that tasks are conducted in the correct order and at the right time. This enables items to be produced to meet a planned output or services to be provided on time. Activity scheduling, or activity planning, is used extensively in production management and provides the times at which activities should take place within an organization.

It is one means by which capacity can be managed whether the activities are the timing of a production process or the provision of a service. Several techniques are just as easily applied in the hospitality industry; for example:

— Just-in-time (JIT) takes its name from the idea of supplying raw materials with which to carry out production, and replenishing stocks as near as possible to the precise time they are required: extremely important in an industry which relies heavily on fresh and perishable products.

— Materials requirements planning (MRP), which is concerned with the scheduling and controlling of inputs and materials required for a production process. It involves decisions in areas such as: What is to be made? How many should be made? When they should be made? It could be used where large numbers of a single product are made, for example, in a cook-chill production centre.

— Reverse scheduling or backward scheduling uses the date or time when a product or service is required in order to determine the latest possible time at which the job could be started. Hence, if food is required to be served on a date at a particular time, then working backwards provides the time when production should commence, and back still further, when food should be purchased and received.

— Timetabling is the process of allocating particular activities a specific time for completion. The work of chambermaids, for example, may be timetabled to ensure that rooms are prepared in the most cost-effective way and made available in time for a guest's arrival. It also enables staff to be deployed in the most cost-effective way.

— Forward scheduling is the opposite of reverse and provides for jobs to be commenced in the order in which they come in. Hence, in an a la carte restaurant, the production of dishes will commence as the orders are received.

Conclusion

The diversity of organizations means that there is no such thing as a universal solution to business problems.

Many hospitality management courses currently make this situation still less practicable, by introducing spurious boundaries between operational areas (accommodation and food/beverage) or between the other business components of the curriculum. This article advocates greater integration of the curriculum, but suggests that the operational focus of many courses could be strengthened by applying operations management principles. Operations management has traditionally had its roots in manufacturing industry. However, using a practical and holistic approach, it can be applied just as effectively to the hospitality industry. This approach recognizes and emphasizes the fact that hospitality activities are inter-related.

REFERENCES

Cracknell, H.L., Kaufmann R.J., Nobis, G. (1983), *Practical Professional Catering* , Macmillan, Basingstoke, pp. 22.

Doswell, R., Gamble, P.R. (1979), *Marketing and Planning Hotels and Tourism Projects*, Hutchinson, London, pp. 19-20.

Harris, N. (1989), *Service Operations Management*, Cassell, London, pp. 3.

Hill, T. (1983), *Production / Operations Management*, Prentice-Hall, Englewood Cliffs, NJ.

Howard, B. (1992), *Operations Management*, Macmillan, Basingstoke, pp. 1.

Lee, S.M., Schniederjans, M.J. (1994), *Operations Management*, Houghton Mifflin Company, Boston, MA, pp. 3.

Nightingale, M. (1985), " The hospitality industry: defining quality for a quality assurance programme - a study in perceptions", *Service Industries Journal*, Vol. 5 No.1, pp. 9-22.

Slack, N. (1983), "Operations management and curriculum design", *Management Education and Development*, Vol. 14 No.1, pp. 19-32. Vollman, T.E. (1973), *Operations Management*, Addison-Wesley, Reading, MA.

Wild, R. (1984), *Production and Operations Management. Principles and Techniques*, 3rd, Holt, Rinehart and Winston, London, pp. 276.

11

Hotel Managers in Emerging Locations

As a universal phenomenon, Globalization has changed the business dynamics in the hospitality industry. Greenberg and Baron (1997) noted the increase in capital flows, competition, and economic interdependencies across countries. Choi *et al.* (2000) observed the evolving dynamics of international labor utilization, while Wilson *et al.* (2000) cited knowledge gaps in contract catering in the hospitality industry. In this landscape, it becomes important for hospitality managers to understand the implications of globalization and plan for the implementation of strategic approaches. For instance, Jones (1999) indicated the need to heighten attention to multi-location chain management through activities such as integration, location, configuration, organization, implementation, and adaptation.

Furhter, hospitality managers in emerging locations need to plan to respond to growing globalization. The World Tourism Organization (2004) forecasts that international travelers will reach 1.56 billion by 2020, with locations such as East Asia and the Pacific, South Asia, Middle East, and Africa posting over 5 per cent increase in arrivals each year.

The objective of the study was to explore the views of travel executives on the impact of globalization on contemporary business following concepts advanced by Thomas L. Friedman (2000) that:

- modalities for communication have expanded and changed;
- the approaches of contemporary business is far different compared to the period prior to the Cold War era;
- there are evolving investment approaches worldwide; and
- technology has paved the way for changes in the business environment.

The findings are presented, and discussed in the context of strategic implications for hospitality managers in emerging locations.

Travel executives as defined in this study refers to a professional performing a management function relating to travel and tourism. This definition includes individuals engaged in ventures such as travel agencies, travel research and consulting, travel technologies, hotels and resorts, hospitality management, travel media, airlines and aviation, car rental, tour operators, tourism boards, convention and exhibition bureaus, travel distribution systems, travel and tourism education, travel media, destination management, and destination investment companies. Survey forms were sent out to 1, 000 members of the Pacific Asia Travel Association (PATA).There were 118 valid surveys completed and returned.

Of the respondents, 35 per cent were in the travel services category, 34 per cent in tourism, 7 per cent in Airline, and 24 per cent in hospitality. The respondents came from 35 countries, namely: Austria, Australia, Bahrain, China, Canada, Cook Islands, Fiji, France, French Polynesia, Germany, Hong Kong, India, Indonesia, Japan, Korea, Macau, Malaysia, Mongolia, Nepal, New Guinea, New Zealand, Pakistan, Philippines, Saudi Arabia, Singapore, South Africa, Sri Lanka, Switzerland, Thailand, Tonga, Turkey, Turkmenistan, USA, UK, and Vietnam. Respondent profiles may be further qualified as follows: 73 per cent were male and 27 per cent were female; 50 per cent possessed a Bachelor's degree, 47 per cent with a Masters, and 3 per cent with a Doctorate; and, 88 per cent had at least 11 years of industry work experience.

Data are collected regarding the respondents' perceptions on the potential impact of globalization on business, communication, accounting and finance, technology, and individual psyche. Statements were offered through a corresponding five-point Likert scale. The quantitative and qualitative scales were 5 for Strongly agree (SA), 4 for Agree (A), 3 for Undecided (U), 2 for Disagree (D), and 1 for Strongly disagree (SD). Since the purpose of the study was to determine the central tendency of the responses to each statement, the weighted mean of each statement was calculated. In order to arrive at a definite interpretation of the respondents' central tendency, the author assigned the following hypothetical mean range to the scales in each item.

No doubt, globalization affects business management in at least five areas and point out relevant research pertaining to:

- evolution of business practices;
- changes in communication patterns;
- broadening of accounting and finance approaches;
- technological enhancements; and
- impact on individual and organizational psyche.

Business Practices

There exist certain business pressures brought about my greater market integration. Rosenzweig *et al.* (2000) indicated that for the past 50 years, declining tariffs and the emergence of regional trading blocs had an enormous impact on world trade and investment and encouraged companies to look at business in a global perspective. Haynes *et al.* (1999) noted the shortening of product life cycles in an information age, while Cateora and Graham (1999) emphasized the need to provide heightened attention to culture especially in the realm of international marketing and the segmentation of markets.

Communication Patterns

Breakthroughs in communication technologies have facilitated international communication. Kotler and Armstrong (1999) argued the need to utilize global communication adaptation strategies when communicating across borders, while Lussier (1996) alluded to the relevance of non-verbal communication in international business. Friedman (2000) observed the "democratization of information" in a global environment that allows individuals to reach out to others in a faster, deeper, and cheaper manner.

Accounting and Finance Approaches

The internet has made the search of financial information and international transactions easier. Malone and Laubacher (1998) referred to the emergence of "electronically connected freelancers" (e-lancers) that operate virtual organizations that facilitate the flow of financial transactions from anywhere in the world. Friedman (2000) highlighted that the whole world operates like Wall Street because global investing has become more convenient and accessible to many individuals.

Technological Enhancements

The global environment may require technological adaptation and adjustments. Bishop (1999) recommended undertaking international expansions assessments pertaining to telecommunication infrastructure, digital capabilities, and online resources. Buss (1982) articulated the challenge of management of information and technology across borders due to:

- divergence of equipment, software and procedures from one venue to another;
- changing costs of personnel, hardware, and data communication within and between different countries;
- increasing interdependence of firms' affiliates;
- fast-changing regulatory environments;
- unionizing of data processing department personnel; and
- the increasing rate of change of information technologies.

Individual and Organizational Psyche

In fact, environment has the ability to affect the mindsets of individuals. Fan and Mak (1998) observed that it is possible that international participants who lack social skills and aptitude may decide to withdraw from the process and prefer to stay within their comfort zones and interact with co-ethnic or like-minded members.

Gudykunst and Hammer alluded to the fact that individuals exposed to cross-cultural environments and are unfamiliar with varying cultural codes may experience a high level of stress in social encounters, and suffer from interpersonal anxiety and self-doubt. Theoretical literature suggests that business practices may change as a result of globalization. Insights of travel executives worldwide are gathered in order to identify viable strategic approaches.

Survey Results and Findings

Selected feedback of the travel executives on business issues relating to globalization.

The findings of the survey suggest the following:

- There exists heightened convenience in operational activities brought about by globalization.
- Modalities of business have been transformed in a global environment requiring strategic adjustments from field practitioners in the travel industry.
- Realignments in investment strategies are taking place.
- Business cycles have accelerated and require appropriate responses.
- Opportunities for inter-organization communication efficiencies can be achieved as global communication technologies are enhanced.
- Technological innovation along with corresponding organizational structure adjustments are perceived as avenues for building efficiencies.
- The heightened demands of globalization require that attention be placed on potential fears of adjustment that exist in organizations.
- There are perceived benefits in the creation of international financial alignments and standardization of practices worldwide.
- The global environment has the potential to shape individual and organizational mindsets and attitudes.
- Country infrastructure such as bandwidth is likely a location consideration.

Approximately one-quarter of the respondents in this study belong to the hospitality industry. The views and insights expressed on the globalization issues span the globe. While the respondent number limits generalizability of conclusions, the findings are potentially valuable in helping shape management approaches. Based on the survey findings, the author recommends five approaches for hospitality managers in emerging locations:

Prepare for globalization. The findings suggest that individual and organizational fears of the pressures of globalization exist in business organizations worldwide. Hospitality managers in emerging locations need to address these fears through organizational assessments, strategic planning, and the formulation of a global vision.

Enhance cross-border knowledge flows. The findings point to the convenience of cross-border communication flows in a global environment. Communication efficiencies can be further enhanced by hospitality managers through the improvement of international information flows, use of innovative learning and training approaches, and the broadening of marketing efforts.

Plan for financial practice modifications. In the survey, travel executives noted changes in financial investment strategies in a global environment, and saw the need for the standardization of accounting practices. Hospitality managers in emerging locations should be prepared to undertake adjustments in their financial operational systems and procedures for the sake of practice uniformity and commonality of standards.

Speed up business development efforts. The survey findings indicate greater conveniences in operational activities and the acceleration of business cycles. Regardless of location, hospitality managers are in a position to tap into the speed and trade conveniences brought about by globalization. Marketing and developmental efforts need to be intensified and adjusted in conjunction with new opportunities that arise.

Utilize technology strategically. Technology is viewed as a medium for efficiency enhancement and bandwidth has become an important business consideration. Hospitality managers in emerging locations should utilize technology in a strategic manner in their organizations. Forming innovative technological linkages with government and private enterprises in both local and international venues paves the way for technological enhancement and efficient organizational integration.

There is no exaggration that in a global environment, travel executives worldwide have built competitive advantages by strengthening efficiencies in business and communication practices, financial management, and technological usage. As hospitality managers in emerging locations face invigorated growth prospects, integrating these practices in their development agenda can become anchors for success in future.

REFERENCES

Buss, M. (1982), "Managing international information systems", *Harvard Business Review*, Vol. 60 No.5, pp. 153-62.

Cateora, P.R., Graham, J.L. (1999), *International Marketing*, The McGraw-Hill Companies, New York, NY.

Choi, J.G., Woods, R.H., Murrmann, S.K. (2000), "International labor markets and the migration of labor forces as an alternative solution for labor shortages in the hospitality industry", *International Journal of Contemporary Hospitality Management*, Vol. 12 No.1, pp. 61-7.

Fan, C., Mak, A. (1998), "Measuring social self-efficacy in a culturally diverse student population", *Social Behavior and Personality*, Vol. 26 pp. 131-44.

Friedman, T.L. (2000), *The Lexus and the Olive Tree*, Anchor Books, New York, NY.

Greenberg, J., Baron, R.A. (1997), *Behavior in Organizations: Understanding and Managing the Human Side of Work*, Prentice-Hall International, Upper Saddle River, NJ.

Gudykunst, W.B., Hammer, M.R.G. (1988), "Strangers and hosts: an uncertainty reduction based theory of intercultural adaptation", in Kim, Y.Y., Gudykunst, W.B. (Eds), *Cross-cultural Adaptation: Current Approaches*, Sage, Newbury Park, CA, pp. 105-39.

Haynes, A., Lackman, C., Guskey, A. (1999), "Comprehensive brand presentation: ensuring consistent brand image", *Journal of Product and Brand Management*, Vol. 8 No.4, pp. 286-300.

Jones, P. (1999), "Multi-unit management in the hospitality industry: a late twentieth century phenomenon", *International Journal of Contemporary Hospitality Management*, Vol. 11 No.4, pp. 155-64.

Kotler, P., Armstrong, G. (1999), *Principles of Marketing*, Prentice-Hall International, Upper Saddle River, NJ.

Lussier, R.N. (1996), *Human Relations in Organizations: A Skill-Building Approach*, The McGraw-Hill Companies, New York, NY.

Rosenzweig, P.M., Morrison, A.J., Inkpen, A., Beamish, P.W. (2000), *International Management: Text and Cases*, The McGraw-Hill Companies, Boston, MA.

Wilson, M.D.J., Murray, A.E., Black, A.M. (2000), "Contract catering: the skills required for the next millennium", *International Journal of Contemporary Hospitality Management*, Vol. 12 No.1, pp. 75-9.

12

Hospitality and Tourism Academic Research: Clusters and Gaps

The WHATT-CD Research Register has established a central resource of completed and ongoing research in the hospitality and tourism industries. From the researcher's viewpoint, it is useful to tap into a "one-stop" source of related studies and to have the opportunity to network with like-minded people. This article reviews the origins and content of the Research Register entries and comments on its relevance to the needs of hospitality and tourism researchers.

In total, there were 820 postgraduate research project entries (727 finished and 92 in progress) on the spring 1995 edition of the CD-ROM, with completion dates ranging from 1976 to 1999. The sources of the research entries and that all but 16 per cent were submitted from academic institutions.

The vast majority of entries (84 per cent) emanate from academic institutions and, in this category, 296 projects (43 per cent) are MPhil/PhD level and 175 MSc level projects undertaken by full or part-time research students or academic staff.

It is pleasing to note the wide geographical spread of sources, with entries from 209 institutions in the UK, Belgium, Austria, Spain, Sweden, USA, Canada, South Africa and Australia. Most of the institutions submitted small numbers of studies and only 16 contributed entries in double figures.

This article seeks to map the International Research Register entries by content-analysing subject terms. Users of WHATT-CD are able to access and filter the information they seek using the following categories:

- institution of researcher;
- research type, level and status (in progress or finished);
- names of researcher or adviser;
- glossary of subject terms.
- year begun or completed;

Each entry in the Register is classified according to its area of interest using four keywords, and to determine patterns keywords were clustered in intuitively-determined thematic categories as follows:

- general--overall subjects including management subject areas and techniques as well as external issues affecting organizations;
- hospitality--hotel or catering-related entries;
- tourism--entries associated with general tourism issues or destinations;
- "hot" issues--current areas of interest and concern.

Each of the four themes is examined and exemplified with reference to ongoing and completed projects. This is a large theme area comprising items of broad interest which transcend industry sectors or single disciplines and may be further divided into three sub-themes:

- general management, operations management, facilities management;
- services--legal, financial, marketing and research support;
- careers, education, training and human resource management.

A common feature here is the emphasis placed on planning and strategy. One example is Tracy Jones' 1991 MPhil project at Oxford Brookes University, UK, which recognizes that hotel managers need an effective information system to assist in decision making. She concludes that information needs should be more consciously determined using critical success factors and measures. Another important measure of organizational success is cash flow which is being studied by Eugene Gouws of the University of Pretoria in South Africa. His research aim is to identify the determinants of cash flow in a recreational setting as they relate to decision-making processes.

It is perhaps inevitable that the "general" area should be the largest thematic grouping in the Research Register and the one that demonstrates the widest scope. Each of the three sub-themes (operations, support services and people) reflect an interest in "managing effectively" and are fertile areas for academic research. They also recognize the importance of sociocultural and behavioural factors in managing organizations. This is manifest in a "softer" approach to systems and strategy characterized by flexibility and a greater awareness of the importance of people. The role of management is still seen as a pivotal one, but its focus is regarded by researchers as more facilitative than directive.

Hospitality

The hospitality category includes items relating to hotels, catering and other sectors such as leisure and gambling and one issue which cuts across all hospitality industry sectors is information technology (IT). The far-reaching implications of IT are exemplified by Marian Whitaker's PhD research project which suggests that there is nothing inevitable about the impact of new technology on employment. She observes that, when low thresholds of trust occur, employees' reactions to new technology are likely to be negative. Allen Freedman of Nova University, New York, considers the business ethics of hospitality managers and students in his DBA research. His findings suggest that while personal commitment scores were similar for male and female managers, female managers achieve higher overall scores in their commitment to the welfare of others, whereas their male counterparts tend to display greater commitment to profit maximization. The entries relating to "gastronomy" make interesting reading as this is an area where postgraduate research could be of benefit to industry and customer alike. There is much yet to be discovered about the sociocultural and sensory components of human taste and two PhD research projects from Bournemouth University, UK, and Cornell University, USA, respectively, tackle this topic in different ways. The first by Louise Blackwell investigates the role of the senses, particularly smell, in guiding food choice, selection and acceptability. Jennifer Crouch's research into public beer selection and consumption in the USA recognizes that social boundary-setting, as well as taste, are determinants of beer choice. Both projects suggest that sensory and environmental factors can be manipulated by managers to enhance sales or to attract selected customer segments.

Greater sophistication in food and drink marketing may be regarded as exploitative, but can also assist in the increasingly complex task of mapping changing consumer tastes. Most of the entries in this theme area relate to the leisure and hotel sectors while food and catering entries show a marketing or science focus and rarely relate to operational or service issues.

In general, the research entries reflect a widely-perceived need for a clearer understanding of the nature of hospitality and for increased levels of professionalism in the future. It is notable that many of the research projects seek to map emerging trends and study global strategies rather than address the problems of individual hospitality units.

Tourism

Tourism entries include items of general tourism interest and those which concern specific tourism destinations. General items span leisure, tranport and the future of the tourism industry. Both developed and developing nations seem to realize the benefits of tourism in earning foreign currency and stimulating local economies. Hard economic exigencies contrast with softer but equally valid concerns about the consequences for the natural environment. Desirable tourism is more often described as "sustainable"; an adjective which seems to incorporate both hard and soft ideals. Jane Rasbash's MSc research studies "green" tourism in Scotland and concludes (in common with many other tourism studies) that cohesive, strategic planning is a requirement for the future. The largest single area of research study is the European Community, but most tourism projects relate to destinations where tourism is, as yet, not fully developed such as Africa, South-east Asia and South America. One topic which transcends international boundaries is the classification and grading of hotels by public and private organizations. There are currently just four projects in this category which relate to Scotland, Europe and Africa respectively. Susan Kunkel's MA project at the California State University encapsulates the problems inherent in producing an accurate and digestible representation of a country or its accommodation. Tourist or accommodation guidebooks need to reconcile the divergent needs of the intended reader, the service provider and the competitive commercial environment. As tourism grows in economic importance, it is more often the focus of academic research.

Research in this area can assist in benchmarking good practice and detecting emerging trends in demand and tourism provision. The projects show that, although world tourism is growing, established tourism destinations are keen to maintain market share while newer destinations wish to develop their product. Destination development is seen as a long-term commitment in which environmental issues must play a part in the overall tourism strategy. Perhaps future research should seek to determine clearer links between micro and macro tourism issues; that is, to explain local tourism success with reference to tourism theory.

"Hot" issues are those which are regarded by society as increasingly important and which are the subject of lively debate in the wider community. The projects reviewed here have been grouped into five sub-themes. In the face of more intense marketplace rivalry, it is reassuring to note that nearly half the ongoing research relates to customers, service and quality. Despite the mega-growth predictions for tourism and hospitality, most firms realize that a market-oriented approach offers the best opportunity for survival and growth in the future. It seems that this perspective is shared by academic researchers, too. Most of the entries on "healthy eating" emanate from North America and they reflect concerns about the high level of fat and cholesterol intake in the North American diet. Ewan Gillon from Queen Margaret College in Edinburgh also addresses this issue and specifically the differences in the eating habits of men and women. His findings highlight relatively high levels of awareness of the link between food diet and health among women but also highlight the difficulties associated with managing dietary change.

Issues of current interest offer the academic researcher the opportunity to explore areas which need greater exposure and to provide an interpretation on their future importance to the industry. Such issues only remain "hot" if they have the potential to influence change in the medium to long term and to affect the way in which organizations respond to them. The judicious selection of research topic can be of benefit both to the career of the researcher and to the development of appropriate organizational approaches to emerging problems.

In the first annual review of hospitality and tourism trends (*International Journal of Contemporary Hospitality Management*, Vol.7 No. 7, 1995, pp. iv-vi), Julian Demetriadi comments on some perceived research "gaps". He suggests that some sectors have been ignored such as school meals, camping, forces catering, ferries and pubs. Despite the size and popularity of the uniquely British pub sector there are currently few research projects in this field. Alison Dingle's MSc research focuses on the British pub as a unique tourism opportunity with the potential to supply informal, value-for-money meals to an expanding dining out market. From the viewpoint of the drinks suppliers, a research project undertaken by the Brewers and Licensed Retailers Association predictably concludes that the reduction in beer duty is both socially and economically desirable.

Generally, it is the non-commercial domain that is most under-represented in the Register. Some examples are the hospital and institutional sectors which play so great a part in improving the quality of life of people and communities. Paradoxically, structural changes in these neglected sectors may make research even more important, but the choice of research project rests mostly in the hands of independent researchers. It seems inevitable that there will continue to be both gaps and overlaps in research focus, perhaps because of the different perceptions and priorities of practitioners and academics.

Practitioners might be expected to be concerned about seemingly irreconcilable issues that nevertheless affect operations and strategy. Such concerns include the problems of ensuring consistent quality despite staff turnover, shortages of key trained employees and pressures for efficiency improvements. Another key issue is the use of systems and information technology in decision making and operations. In addition, managers in the hospitality and tourism industries may be concerned with the identification of potential markets or products for the future. Other issues include the implications of privatization, the changing role of women in the industry and the continuous growth of short-break holidays. Overlaps exist in some of the tourism destination projects. Although the projects refer to different geographical destinations, the research findings are often similar in nature. The projects emphasize that tourism is an important potential source of revenue and foreign earnings for many emerging countries and it is understandable than postgraduate students would wish to relate their dissertations to familiar contexts.

The body of research as reflected by entries in the International Research Register seems to be shaped in two major ways. First the content of entries perhaps inevitably reflects the personal interests of the researcher rather than the needs of others such as those of industry or the wider academic community. In practice, subject choice is also affected by the availability and amount of information. Second, a comprehensive but voluntary Register relies on awareness and goodwill which will grow over time. Many vocational institutions of higher education have postgraduate students who need to research important issues in order to make original contributions to a field of study. Those who undertake postgraduate research, unless they are mature students, often have limited experience of the specific problems of the hospitality and tourism industries. While researchers need to take an objective view, they also need the co-operation of organizations to conduct and to shape primary research. These researchers have the necessary time, intellect and resources to make this possible, but need opportunities to conduct primary research in an industrial context.

In summary, bridges need to be built to span the perceived rift between industry and academia because there is much to be gained and little to be lost from greater interchange. Sectorial gaps may be inevitable, not least because of the long-term nature of postgraduate research. "Hot" issues may disappoint by cooling over time, and research can help in this regard. Primary research, informed analysis and interpretative comment can assist in mapping patterns in a mass of complex interrelated phenomena by differentiating the long-term trend from the short-term fad. If interpreted intelligently, research can also help to make sense of confusion and to predict likely events in the future.

Further, in the longer term, research methodologies may provide the key to learning in the future. The academic community is beginning to come to terms with qualitative methodologies as valid techniques with which to map the inherent richness of hospitality and tourism activities. More experimentation and interchange is needed to develop methodologies through which research may be made more accessible and credible to the world at large.

REFERENCES

Anderson, G.K. (1991), "The education and training of general managers in Scotland", *International Journal of Contemporary Hospitality Management*, Vol. 3 No.2, pp. 26-9 .

Atkinson, C. (1994), " Continuous improvement: the ingredients of change", *International Journal of Contemporary Hospitality Management*, Vol. 6 No.1/2, pp. 6-8 .

Balmer, S., Baum, T. (1993), "Applying Herzberg's hygiene factors to the changing accommodation environment", *International Journal of Contemporary Hospitality Management*, Vol. 5 No.2 , pp. 32-5.

Barron, P., Maxwell, G. (1993), "Hospitality management students' image of the hospitality industry", *International Journal of Contemporary Hospitality Management*, Vol. 5 No.5 , pp. v-viii.

Barrows, C.W., Hobson, J.S.P. (1993), "A model for teaching service management in hospitality", *International Journal of Contemporary Hospitality Management*, Vol. 5 No.3, pp. 32-6.

Brotherton, R., Coyle, M. "Managing instability in the hospitality operations environment: part three: variance", *International Journal of Contemporary Hospitality Management*, Vol. 3 No.1, pp. 26-31.

Brownell, J. (1994), " Creating strong listening environments: a key hospitality management task", *International Journal of Contemporary Hospitality Management*, Vol. 6 No.3, pp. 3-10.

Burgess, C. (1994), "The education and training needs of the hotel financial controller", *International Journal of Contemporary Hospitality Management*, Vol. 6 No.5, pp. 9-13.

Clifton, W.J., Johnson, K. (1994), "A structural analysis of the European hotel sector: a simple case of déjà-vu?", *International Journal of Contemporary Hospitality Management*, Vol. 6 No.4, pp. vii-viii.

Close, A., Teare, R. (1990), "Effective management development", *International Journal of Contemporary Hospitality Management*, Vol. 2 No.4, pp. i-ii.

Connell, J. " Branding hotel portfolios", *International Journal of Contemporary Hospitality Management*, Vol. 4 No.1 , pp. 26-32.

Costa, J., Teare, R. (1994), "Environmental scanning and the Portuguese hotel sector", *International Journal of Contemporary Hospitality Management*, Vol. 6 No.5, pp. iv-vii.

Counsell, S. (1991), " Fifty-seven-fifty and all that", *International Journal of Contemporary Hospitality Management*, Vol. 3 No.3, pp. iii-iv.

Crawford-Welch, S. (1991), "International marketing and competition in European markets", *International Journal of Contemporary Hospitality Management*, Vol. 3 No.4, pp. 47-54.

Crawford-Welch, S. (1991), "Marketing hospitality into the 21st century", *International Journal of Contemporary Hospitality Management*, Vol. 3 No.3, pp. 21-7.

Crawford-Welch, S., Tse, E. (1990), "Mergers, acquisitions and alliances in the European hospitality industry", *International Journal of Contemporary Hospitality Management*, Vol. 2 No.1, pp. 10-16.

Dodrill, K., Riley, M. (1992), "Hotel workers' orientations to work: the question of autonomy and scope", *International Journal of Contemporary Hospitality Management*, Vol. 4 No.1 , pp. 23-5.

Dodwell, S., Simmons, P. (1994), "Trials and tribulations in the pursuit of quality improvement", *International Journal of Contemporary Hospitality Management*, Vol. 6 No.1/2, pp. 14-18.

Doren, K., Blackman, D. (1993), "Communication systems and connectivity for the 'intelligent bedroom' of the future", *International Journal of Contemporary Hospitality Management*, Vol. 5 No.2, pp. 25-6.

Edgar, D.A., Littlejohn, D.L., Allardyce, M.L. (1994), "Strategic clusters and strategic space: the case of the short break market", *International Journal of Contemporary Hospitality Management*, Vol. 6 No.5, pp. 20-26 .

Gilmore, A., Carson, D. "Ferry travel: a case of comparative services", *International Journal of Contemporary Hospitality Management*, Vol. 4 No.4, pp. 16-20 .

Go, F. (1990), "Tourism and hospitality management education: new horizons", *International Journal of Contemporary Hospitality Management*, Vol. 2 No.2, pp. 43-8.

Goldsmith, A., Zahari, M.S.M (1994), "Hospitality education in Malaysia: filling the skill gap", *International Journal of Contemporary Hospitality Management*, Vol. 6 No.6, pp. 27-31.

Harris, P.J. (1992), " Hospitality profit planning in the practical environment: integrating cost-volume-profit analysis with spreadsheet management", *International Journal of Contemporary Hospitality Management*, Vol. 4 No.4, pp. 24-32 .

Hirst, M. "Creating a service-driven culture globally", *International Journal of Contemporary Hospitality Management*, Vol. 4 No.1, pp. i-iii.

Hobson, J.S.P. (1994), " Feng shui: its impacts on the Asian hospitality industry", *International Journal of Contemporary Hospitality Management*, Vol. 6 No.6, pp. 21-6 .

Hubrecht, J., Teare, R. "A strategy for partnership in total quality service ", *International Journal of Contemporary Hospitality Management*, Vol. 5 No.3, pp. i-v .

Ineson, E.M., Brown, S.H.P. (1992), "The use of biodata for hotel employee selection", *International Journal of Contemporary Hospitality Management*, Vol. 4 No.2, pp. 8-12.

Johns, N. (1992), "Quality management in the hospitality industry: part 2: applications, systems and techniques", *International Journal of Contemporary Hospitality Management*, Vol. 4 No.4 , pp. 3-7.

Johns, N. (1992), " Quality management in the hospitality industy: Part 1. Definition and specification", *International Journal of Contemporary Hospitality Management*, Vol. 4 No.3, pp. 14-20.

Johns, N. (1993), "Productivity management through design and operation: a case study", *International Journal of Contemporary Hospitality Management*, Vol. 5 No.2, pp. 20-24.

Johns, N. (1993), "Quality management in the hospitality industry: part 3: recent developments", *International Journal of Contemporary Hospitality Management*, Vol. 5 No.1, pp. 10-15.

Johns, N., Chesterton, J. (1994), "ICL Kidsgrove: engineering a quality culture", *International Journal of Contemporary Hospitality Management*, Vol. 6 No.1/2, pp. 25-9.

Johnson, C., Buehler, M. (1993), "Applying global concepts to individual hotels at Park Inn International", *International Journal of Contemporary Hospitality Management*, Vol. 5 No.5 , pp. i-ii.

Jones, P., Iannon, A. (1993), "Measuring guest satisfaction in UK-based international hotel chains: principles and practice", *International Journal of Contemporary Hospitality Management*, Vol. 5 No.5, pp. 27-31.

Jones, P.A. (1990), "A profile of management development and training", *International Journal of Contemporary Hospitality Management*, Vol. 2 No.2, pp. 7-12.

Kelliher, C., Blackman, D. (1991), "Human resource strategies for the 1990s", *International Journal of Contemporary Hospitality Management*, Vol. 3 No.2, pp. 4-9.

Kwansa, F.A. (1994), "Acquisitions, shareholder wealth and the lodging sector: 1980-1990", *International Journal of Contemporary Hospitality Management*, Vol. 6 No.6, pp. 16-20.

Larsen, S., Aske, L. (1992), "On-stage in the service theatre", *International Journal of Contemporary Hospitality Management*, Vol. 4 No.4, pp. 12-15.

Larsen, S., Bastiansen, T. (1992), "Service attitudes in hotel and restaurant staff and nurses", *International Journal of Contemporary Hospitality Management*, Vol. 4 No.2, pp. 27-31.

Larsen, S., Folgero, I.S. (1993), "Supportive and defensive communication", *International Journal of Contemporary Hospitality Management*, Vol. 5 No.3, pp. 22-5.

Larsen, S., Rapp, L. "Creating the service driven cruise line", *International Journal of Contemporary Hospitality Management*, Vol. 5 No. 1, pp. iv-vi .

Lee-Ross, D. (1993), "Two styles of hotel manager, two styles of worker", *International Journal of Contemporary Hospitality Management*, Vol. 5 No.4, pp. 20-4.

Linney, C.J., Teare, R. (1991), "Addressing the human resource challenges of the 1990s", *International Journal of Contemporary Hospitality Management*, Vol. 3 No.2, pp. iii-iv.

Littlejohn, D., Slattery, P. (1991), "Macro analysis techniques: an appraisal of Europe's main hotel markets", *International Journal of Contemporary Hospitality Management*, Vol. 3 No.4, pp. 6-13.

Littlejohn, D., Watson, S. (1990), "Management development approaches for the 1990s", *International Journal of Contemporary Hospitality Management*, Vol. 2 No.2, pp. 36-42.

Lockwood, A. (1994), "Using service incidents to identify quality improvement points", *International Journal of Contemporary Hospitality Management*, Vol. 6 No.1/2, pp. 75-80 .

Lockwood, A., Jones, P. (1990), "Applying value engineering to rooms management", *International Journal of Contemporary Hospitality Management*, Vol. 2 No.1, pp. 27-32.

Lowe, L.S., Kruger, A. (1991), "Motel advertising: practices and themes", *International Journal of Contemporary Hospitality Management*, Vol. 3 No.1, pp. 17-21.

Lucas, R., Laycock, J. (1991), "An interactive personnel function for managing budget hotels", *International Journal of Contemporary Hospitality Management*, Vol. 3 No.3, pp. 33-6.

Lucas, R.E. (1993), "Hospitality industry employment: emerging trends", *International Journal of Contemporary Hospitality Management*, Vol. 5 No.5, pp. 23-6.

Luckock, S. (1991), "Flexible working practices for women returners",

International Journal of Contemporary Hospitality Management, Vol. 3 No.3, pp. 4-9.

Luke, D., Ingold, A. (1990), "Planning for industry: a study in curriculum design ", *International Journal of Contemporary Hospitality Management*, Vol. 2 No.2, pp. 20-23.

Lundberg, C.C., Woods, R.H. (1990), "Modifying restaurant culture: managers as cultural leaders", *International Journal of Contemporary Hospitality Management*, Vol. 2 No.4 , pp. 4-12.

Lynch, P.A. (1994), "Demand for training by bed and breakfast operators", *International Journal of Contemporary Hospitality Management*, Vol. 6 No.4, pp. 25-31.

MacVicar, A., Brown, G. "Investors in People at the Moat House International, Glasgow", *International Journal of Contemporary Hospitality Management*, Vol. 6 No. 1/2, pp. 30-6.

Mazanec, J. (1993), "'Exporting' Eurostyles to the USA", *International Journal of Contemporary Hospitality Management*, Vol. 5 No.4, pp. 3-9.

Messenger, S.J., Lin, S.M. (1991), "International hotel advertising: the standardisation debate", *International Journal of Contemporary Hospitality Management*, Vol. 3 No.3 , pp. 28-32.

Meudell, K., Gadd, K. (1994), "Culture and climate in short life organizations: sunny spells or thunderstorms?", *International Journal of Contemporary Hospitality Management*, Vol. 6 No.5, pp. 27-32.

Mullins, L., Davies, I. (1991), "What makes for an effective hotel manager?", *International Journal of Contemporary Hospitality Management*, Vol. 3 No.1, pp. 22-5.

Mullins, L., Meudell, K. , Scott, H. (1993), "Developing culture in short-life organizations", *International Journal of Contemporary Hospitality Management*, Vol. 5 No.4 , pp. 15-19.

Sellah, H., Riley, M. (1994), "Measuring culinary learning processes: education and experience contrasted", *International Journal of Contemporary Hospitality Management*, Vol. 6 No.6 , pp. iii-v.

Senior, M., Morphew, R. (1990), "Examining structure in decision making in hotels", *International Journal of Contemporary Hospitality Management*, Vol. 2 No.3, pp. 3-9.

Waryszak, R.Z., Bauer, T.G. (1993), "Front-office staff selection techniques", *International Journal of Contemporary Hospitality Management*, Vol. 5 No.4, pp. 25-8.

Watson, S. (1991), "From a la carte to cafeteria-style management development", *International Journal of Contemporary Hospitality Management*, Vol. 3 No.4, pp. 42-6.

Weaver, P.A., Oh, H.C. (1993), "Do American business travellers have different hotel service requirements?", *International Journal of Contemporary Hospitality Management*, Vol. 5 No.3 , pp. 16-21.

Webster, M.M. (1994), "Strategic management in context at Swallow Hotels", *International Journal of Contemporary Hospitality Management*, Vol. 6 No.5, pp. 3-8.

West, A., Purvis, E. (1992), "Hotel design: the need to develop a strategic approach", *International Journal of Contemporary Hospitality Management*, Vol. 4 No.1, pp. 15-22.

West, A.J., Jameson, S.A. (1990), "Supervised work experience in graduate employment", *International Journal of Contemporary Hospitality Management*, Vol. 2 No.2, pp. 29-32.

Witt, C.A., Witt, S.F. (1989), "Why productivity in the hotel sector is low", *International Journal of Contemporary Hospitality Management*, Vol. 1 No.2, pp. 28-34.

13

The Future of Hotel and Catering Work

> 'Life is the art of drawing sufficient conclusions from insufficient premises'.
>
> —*Samuel Butler*

It is most apt to note that hotel and catering work is largely exploitative, degrading, poorly paid, unpleasant, insecure and taken as last resort or because it can be tolerated in the light of wider commitments and constraints. This is not to deny that there are many employed in a whole variety of work tasks who value their position and gain much satisfaction from their employment. Anyone who has even a moderate acquaintance with the industry is familiar with the many workers at all levels, 'the addicts', who work long hours in poor conditions for relatively little financial reward and for whom criticism of the industry is regarded as heretical. It remains to be demonstrated however as to whether these happy circumstances apply to anything more than a minority of the workforce.

International Scenario

The problems and experiences of the UK hospitality industry workforce are not unique, but are repeated on an international scale. In the mid-1960s and 1970s the International Labour Office (ILO) published a number of reports based on the proceedings of symposia held under the auspices of the International Labour Organisation (International Labour Organisation, 1965, 1974, 1980). A close reading of these rapidly reveals that little can be added to the judgement of Mars, Bryant and Mitchell:

> The I.L.O. reports describe the structural properties of the industry in a number of different countries. Although there are some very obvious cultural variations, particularly in terms of attitudes to the service role the industry performs, many of the social and economic problems of the industry tend to have general applicability.
>
> (Mars, Bryant and Mitchell, 1979: 153)

Mars and his colleagues have of course, identified that key difference between the UK and other countries which is supposed to mark the fact that other hotel and catering industries are in some way better than our own and their workers better off in some absolute terms. This is the attitude to service which can and does differ radically in *some* countries from the British aloofness and disdain for personal service industries. However, appearances have little to do with reality, particularly in the hotel and catering industry.

Ackerman's observations are confirmed in a study by Alpert (1986) of the American restaurant industry. His statistics are no less illuminating: 64 per cent of all restaurant workers are women; most workers are young, with half under the age of 25 and 32 per cent less than 19; most work less than twenty hours per week; most are relatively badly paid, restaurant workers' wages being only 52 per cent of employees in manufacturing. Alpert also claims in support of the British evidence that tipping is extensive and serves to subsidise the cost to the operator of service delivery (though only 37 per cent of restaurant workers are actually in service positions and therefore likely to receive tips); that deskilling in the industry is extensive as a result of increasing use of technology; and the level of unionisation is low at around 10 per cent. Hiemstra (1990) in a study of the personnel practices of a sample of American hotels and motels in response to an apparent labour shortage reports labour turnover rates of 89 per cent for hourly paid staff and 44 per cent for salaried staff per annum. When asked what personnel policies were being pursued in the light of the putative labour shortage, in a list of nine 'paying relatively high wages' came bottom with, just above, 'providing job security'. The most common hiring practice reported by Hiemstra's respondents was local recruitment through newspaper advertisements or personnel recommendation, thus emphasising the no less local nature of labour markets in the American hospitality industry.

The evidence of Ackerman, Alpert and Hiemstra confirms the findings of Henderson's 1965 study of the American lodging industry and, when taken with the other North American literature discussed elsewhere in the text, suggests that there are few fundamental differences in the nature and experience of work on either side of the Atlantic. This appears to extend to other countries. The picture of hotel and catering work in Australia differs hardly at all. Worland and Wilson (1988) examined hotel and catering labour in the state of Victoria and report above average levels of part-time work and female participation in the labour force of the hospitality industry, aspects of employment they suggest minor national trends. Casualisation, linked to trends in multiple-job holding, is also common. Tomoda (1983) in a study of working conditions in Japanese hotels similarly found many of the common industry characteristics described earlier. Wages were generally low, women and part-timers were particularly affected in this respect and, of course, many part-time workers were women. Explicit discrimination appears to have been a feature of Japanese employment at that time. Hardly any wage gap existed at all between men and women upon graduation from high school but pay gaps increased markedly between the second and fifth years of employment in the hotel and catering industry largely,

Tomoda suggests, as a result of some women receiving smaller increments than their male counterparts. Men also enjoyed greater chances of promotion within the industry.

A report in the industry magazine *Asia Travel Trade* (May, 1989) focused on six countries with labour shortages and pointed up all too familiar problems and practices. In Hong Kong, employers were seeking to overcome the labour shortage in terms of offering more perks, poaching staff from one another's hotels and in some cases paying large loyalty bonuses--four months salary at Chinese New Year is the example cited. Staff poaching was also common in the much smaller Malaysian hotel industry where, however, the reports' authors note concern about the lack of staff training. The Philippines appeared to be the least problem-ridden of the countries examined and it is interesting to note that there is an established system of hotel management education in the Philippines! Labour shortages and high labour turnover were both common problems in the Singapore and Taiwanese hotel industry, compounded by reportedly poor conditions of work and a view of the industry as offering low status jobs. In Thailand, the authors of the report noted more fundamental problems in terms of an acute skills shortage (including language skills) but found recruitment to be buoyant as pay and conditions of work in the hotel industry tended to be better than average for the country as a whole. This view is borne out in a study by Samalapa (1990) who suggests that Thais have a considered and positive approach to hospitality not necessarily characteristic of many other Asian societies. Personal and community bonds deriving from close religious observance render personal service a relatively valuable social commodity that is not regarded as degrading. At the same time, the That hotel industry is characterised by a substantial number of indigenous hotel companies and internationalisation is as yet in its infancy in terms of the presence of significant numbers of multi-national firms. The indigenous firms thus set employment standards in the industry and these tend to be predicated on the predominant social values of Thai society which are paternalistic but, at some levels at least, less inclined to economic exploitation.

In many developing countries, those of the so-called 'Third World', the indigenous hospitality industry is often limited in scope to the needs of the resident population. The growth of the multi-national hotel industry is slowly changing the face of hospitality in many of these countries, at least in large cities and tourism destinations. Hotel companies operating in less developed countries may pursue a range of strategies in running their hotels: franchising the operation, utilising management contracts, and direct management by their own staff amongst them. Similarly, hotel construction can be achieved in a variety of ways: solely financed by the company, financed jointly by the company and the government of the country concerned and so on. Ultimately, however, the resulting product tends to be very much in the cultural traditions of Western hotels, unsurprising given that a substantial proportion of the tourist trade is drawn from the West. The spread of the international hotel industry to less developed countries may be seen as a form of cultural imperialism and though knowledge concerning the effects of development on employment is virtually non-existent, the effects of tourism on these and other non-industrialised countries have attracted the attention of some researchers.

Belisle (1983) in a study of tourism and food production in the Caribbean notes how the requirements of the former distorts local food production. Many Caribbean islands import the majority of their foodstuffs. There are a number of reasons for this. Tourists prefer the type and taste of food they customarily consume at home, imported food is sometimes cheaper than local food and of a superior quality, and local farmers are unable to either change the type of food they produce or supply sufficient quantities of what they do grow. Importing food leads to loss of foreign exchange but, more significantly, there is a loss of opportunity to expand and diversify the indigenous food production and processing industries with concomitant loss of potential employment and income. This scenario is a familiar one to tourism analysts. In terms of employment local economies can be distorted by an over-emphasis on tourism and hotels as revenue generators. Employment patterns in support of tourism industries may develop in such a manner as to irrevocably alter and distort the economic and social fabric of whole communities and regions.

This process is not confined to less developed countries or established overseas resort destinations. In Britain, the recent growth of the 'heritage industry' and internal tourism, encouraged by government and others as a potential employment solution to long-term decline in traditional manufacturing and 'smokestack industries', has led many commentators to express concern at the growing dependence on so narrow an economic base. Arguments about the British hostility to service industries apart, the implications for employment seem clear not only do the service industries appear incapable of absorbing sufficient numbers of workers from declining industries but service jobs are often part-time and of dubious 'quality' (Gabriel, 1988). But this does not have to be the case. The potential for wholesale distortion of economy and employment as a result of growth in service industries in general and tourism in particular is a potential that can be ameliorated by preventing unfettered development and taking action to provide an economic framework that accords service industries a central rather than peripheral role in economic policy. There is no intrinsic reason why service employment should be poorly paid: poor pay and conditions are a matter of employers' policies and these are mediated by wider social and political values and ideologies. Discussion of attitudes to service and service industries have recurred throughout this book (and are returned to several times below). Without seeming to trivialise what are obviously complex economic issues, it is nevertheless important to recognise that exploitation in employment is not a characteristic of particular types of industry but of the social and economic system in which industries operate--and all systems are susceptible, with varying prospects of success, to some form of management.

Employment Trends, Professionalisation and Education

Given the limited availability of detailed evidence, there is little merit to any extensive country-by-country account of the conditions of hotel and catering labour. What is clear is that despite cultural variations general trends can be perceived and these bear out much of what has been said about the degradation of work in the industry and the exploitation of employees in the UK context. Changes in the nature of hotel and catering employment in modem times have not, in the main, been for the better. The historical fact of low pay, low status and highly stigmatised jobs has been compounded by employer strategies to weaken further the power of employees by moving towards increased numerical flexibility in the use of labour, the increased employment of workers limited in bargaining power, most notably women; the creation of a multi-layered workforce incorporating a strata of low skill, deskilled and degraded jobs many of which are heavily sex-typed; and heightened divisions within the workforce engendered by the utilisation of greater numbers of peripheral casual and part-time workers at the expense of full-time core staff.

The frequent efforts of employers to convince the outside world that the nature of hotel and catering work has unproved or is improving look ever more shallow with each new piece of research confirming the true state of employment in the industry. So too do claims concerning the increased professionalisation of, in particular, hotel and catering managements. Views like these have always formed part of the rhetoric of hospitality industry employers, educators, representative organisations and professional associations. They now seem to be gaining wider circulation.

For example, Crompton and Sanderson note that 'Within the hotel trade in particular it was constantly stressed that progress through management without an HCIMA [Hotel, Catering and Institutional Management Association, the UK's professional and educational association] qualification would be extremely difficult' (Crompton and Sanderson, 1990: 156). This is a pleasant fantasy that mistakes both the extent of unqualified managers in the industry (particularly in those areas where management functions have been devolved to largely unqualified 'supervisors' for the purpose of containing labour costs and increasing the value to the employer of certain categories of labour) and the nature of hotel and catering management education as a form of pre-entry socialisation to an occupation which itself is extremely degraded in terms of job content and remuneration except at the most senior levels. Certainly, the hotel and catering industry has always been surrounded by the paraphernalia of education and certification (Lennon, 1990). To dignify this as evidence of professionalisation is, at its kindest, misguided for it makes certain unspecified assumptions about the content and quality of such education. Despite many pockets of excellence, detailed study of aspects of British hotel and catering management education raises serious questions about the quality and standards of provision (Department of Education and Science, 1987, 1988; Wood, 1988; Lennon, 1989, 1990).

More important is the extent to which hotel and catering management education, at least in Britain, buttresses existing systems of inequality and exploitation in the industry by virtue of its very existence as a form of training separate and distinct from general business and management studies. As Mars, Bryant and Mitchell (1979) imply, hospitality management education is something of an industry in its own right, promulgating reactionary platitudes as potential managerial solutions to the 'problems' faced by the hotel and catering sector. Education, the authors suggests, 'makes any problem appear soluble at an acceptable cost . .[and]. . .has allowed difficult decisions to be avoided by discouraging the kind of searching analyses that may reveal unpalatable realities' (Mars, Bryant and Mitchell, 1979: 129). Though they do not say it in so many words. Mars and his colleagues appear to be suggesting, rightly, that management is, in the words of the aphorism, pan of the problem rather than part of the solution.

One thing is certain and that is that if the success of hotel and catering management education was judged solely in terms of the contribution of trained managers to the quality of working life in the industry then it would be difficult indeed to Find something even remotely charitable to say in defence of both past and present performance. From the evidence reviewed earlier (and some limited reading between the lines) it seems that the situation in the education systems of other countries is not radically different. In Britain, there is a certain resistance in the hotel and catering industry to the blandishments of educational institutions and great emphasis is placed on practical skills and experience. Ironically however, there is a lurking suspicion that one issue on which educationalists and industrialists would be agreed upon would be the need for specialist separate hospitality management education if there must be education at all. There are few industries in the United Kingdom or elsewhere whose potential source of managerial labour is trained quite so extensively at the taxpayers' expense prior to them taking up their first job. The response of employers to this considerable subsidy is to pay their management staff salaries which for the most part are substantially below those of managers in other industries, constituting further cost savings in the acquisition of skilled administrators.

At the time of writing there are over twenty degree courses in hotel and catering studies available in UK higher education institutions compared to just two courses in 1965. In addition there are innumerable Higher National Diploma (sub-degree) courses and programmes leading to certification in a variety of operative skills. The long-term post-war investment of government, not only in education but in training (via such organisations as the Hotel and Catering Industry Training Board), has had ample time to show concrete returns not only in terms of product quality but in the quality of working life in the hospitality industry that might be engendered by 'professional' approaches to administration. No such returns are in evidence. The hotel and catering industry has succeeded in talking about training and the need for training whilst pursuing, at many levels, development and employment policies designed to eliminate the need for motivated and accomplished employees.

Management and management education is of course a soft target for the desk-bound critic and there are many, including academic commentators, who point with varying degrees of explicitness to the role of the workforce in perpetuating poor terms and conditions of employment. These arguments operate at a variety of levels. Hotel and catering workers are, supposedly by their own admission, 'different from other people' (Shamir, 1981). They 'enjoy' mobility and transient social relationships. As Crompton and Sanderson (1990) put it on a number of occasions, the industry is a 'turbulent' one. Turbulence is not a basis for sound industrial relations or collective action. The more these kinds of argument are analysed the more it becomes obvious that victim-blaming is still alive and well. The problems faced by many employees are not seen as the the result of socio-economic inequalities and appalling management: workers themselves must bear at least some of the responsibility for their situation.

That hotel and catering workers tolerate their lot because, despite the privations of their employment, they derive some psychological gratification from being exploited or rather enjoy the instrumentalism forced upon them by a highly competitive work environment, is a view that is as fatuous as it is dangerous.

From Orwell's autobiographical excursus through Whyte's study to much contemporary research, the idea that some or all hotel and catering workers obtain masochistic pleasure from performing degraded and unpleasant work tasks for minimal reward has provided an explanatory bolt-hole of extraordinary convenience. Sometimes, this aspect of hotel and catering work has reflected analysts' genuine puzzlement at the conditions under which industry employees are prepared to labour.

On other occasions, researchers' dazzlement at the seedy and informal side of hotel and catering operations can be identified as the source of arguments predicated on victim-blaming. Too frequently, however, holding workers responsible for their own situation derives from an unwillingness to recognise the importance of labour market factors and more general trends in work that provide the wider context for conditions of employment in the hospitality and other industries.

Such an unwillingness has been, until relatively recently, at the heart of the orthodox view of research into hotel and catering labour. As suggested in Chapter 1, increasing research interest in hotel and catering employment has begun to widen perspectives and lead to a questioning of these orthodoxies. Despite this, there is an all too ready willingness when avoiding 'victim-blaming' explanations to accept that there is little that hotel and catering workers can or want to do to improve their situation. The sense of hopelessness experienced by many employees is in other words matched by a similar sense of hopelessness amongst researchers. The point is, of course, that the extent of workers' resistance is limited as a result of the general lack of importance attached to employment welfare and particularly that of workers in service industries. General social disdain for service employment is complemented in common-sense perceptions by a curious attitudinal paradox that on the one hand sees service work as 'not quite the thing' and on the other as offering opportunities for 'helping' others and thus performing valuable tasks.

Most of the general public only ever appreciate hotels and catering in terms of the work of waiting staff and other front of house employees and this can lead to the 'lion and hyena' situation whereby the vulture, having observed the lion rip the hyena to shreds, alighted next to the unfortunate victim and, upon being asked with a dying groan why he had not come to the hyena's aid replied 'You were laughing so much I thought you were enjoying yourself. The general social perceptions of hotel and catering and other service work, with all the contradictions they entail, have far more concrete implications. Apart from minor concessions to wages protection, government takes little interest in the lot of service workers and other low-paid employees (a point elaborated upon briefly in the next section). Trades unions have demonstrated what by any standard is only marginal interest in the hotel and catering industry and more significantly have failed to back both their rhetoric and frequently stated desire to maintain membership levels in the provision of resources necessary for organising the industry.

It is interesting to reflect upon the plight of hotel and catering workers in terms of the root character and purpose of their labour--the provision of food, drink and shelter, and to consider just how widely the majority of people take these things for granted. Hotel and catering workers have always been taken for granted and their situation, far from being a product of their own inertia, constitutes more the outcome of wider social attitudes to service and hospitality that are ruthlessly exploited by those who provide it. What then is the future of hotel and catering work? One view based on current trends might be that the UK is developing along similar lines to the situation that seemingly exists at present in America if writers such as Alpert (1986) are to be believed. The industry is becoming a sector in which people work for a brief time, it is a staging point on the career path that leads to somewhere better. This scenario is supported in the American context by the observation that the hotel and catering industry offers a ready and plentiful supply of part-time jobs particularly valuable to young people in education who require sources of finance to support their studies (Alpert, 1986).

Crompton and Sanderson undoubtedly paint the prospect of an industry that has little qualms about employing the cheapest labour. The substitutability of labour (or should it be disposability?) is a matter of little concern to employers where part-time and casual employees enjoy few legal rights of protection and can be excluded by law or company policy from certain remunerative benefits such as holiday pay and work-related bonuses. Certainly, in the case of young workers under the age of 21, where the encouragement to low pay is enshrined in statute law, Crompton and Sanderson's arguments acquire special salience. It would be dangerous, however, to fall into the trap of regarding such a scenario as either wholly real or unavoidable. The hotel and catering industry is not heterogeneous and it is clear that local labour markets are an important factor in determining both the supply and price of labour as well as hotel management's attitudes to staffing.

As the earlier study by Lockwood and Guerrier (1989) demonstrated, there are certain areas in which hoteliers build up a core of more or less permanent staff. Just as it is clear that in some areas practices such as these are alien to hotel managements then there are locales and sectors in which labour stability is an important factor in employer strategy. Nor does this apply only to full-time staff. There are many instances of even casual, seasonal and part-time staff working for only one firm or unit as the need demands (cf. Lowe, 1988). Youth labour is likely to remain an important element of the supply for hotel and catering labour in many countries and it seems that in some cases at least, 'the young' will predominate in the workforce overall.

Some employers, notably McDonald's in the USA (with whom 7 per cent of the working population gain their first job -Transnationals Information Centre, 1987), have made a point of employing older workers, including the early retired, but this trend does not seem to have gathered momentum elsewhere. Clearly the shifting composition of the hotel and catering workforce will remain an interesting focus for research, though it is important to remember that the action (or indifference) of employers and prevailing influences in the labour market are not the only variables of importance in considering the changing nature of hospitality work.

This is particularly true in industries such as hotel and catering traditionally 'protected' by legislative structures centred on pay regulation. Here governments can make a difference. During the 1980s in Great Britain a central plank of employment policy has been, as indicated earlier in the text, to lower the cost to employers of youth labour through a variety of devices including exclusion of under-21s from the scope of Wages Councils in protected industries. There is nothing necessarily inevitable or concrete about such policies however and a government of different political colour may well reverse these legislative measures or at least make important adjustments to them. In one form or another, the Trades Union Congress (TUC) is committed to pressurising government for the introduction of a statutory minimum wage (SMW). Under a government of the Labour Party such a development is not unlikely, though nor is it necessarily practicable.

The United Kingdom's membership of the European Community is also a likely important influence on industry and employment in general and low-pay industries like hotels and catering in particular. The attempts by the European Community to introduce a 'Social Charter' regularising *inter alia,* employment rights in member states was resisted by the British Government to the extent that Britain was the only country not to sign the Charter in December 1989. European-wide influences on both employment legislation and employment itself seem likely to increase in importance, especially with the advent of the Single European Market in 1992.

Certainly, the failure of the hotel and catering industry in Britain and elsewhere to 'put its own house in order' (a charitable description) means that it is only action by governments that will make any real change to the nature of hospitality sector employment. Even here, however, past experience shows that the scope for government is limited if policy is merely directed towards employee protection. Wages Council protection is of little use if it is not policed rigorously.

For this reason, even returning under-21s to Wages Councils protection would probably make little difference without substantial improvements to monitoring the system. The kind of governmental intervention that would be required to ensure that hotel, catering and all other employers provided decent terms and conditions would require a radicalism not seen in British politics for many years, if at all. Even then, it is not certain that many industry employees, given their diverse motivations, would either welcome or benefit from such changes. Employers and proprietors could no doubt be relied upon to respond with their usual hostility. It is a measure of the extent to which service industries in Britain are viewed as unworthy of serious attention that tourism, hotels and catering--one of the nation's biggest money-earners--are not represented significantly in the higher reaches of government, either in policy or administrative terms.

The United Kingdom has no Ministry of Tourism, it has no coherent set of policies on tourism development and the internal administration of tourism is handled by a range of bodies that are not co-ordinated in any significant way. There is little or no unifying focus for tourism-related industries nor any widespread sense of their value and limitations to economy and society more generally. This *laissez-faire* approach seems likely to continue for the foreseeable future, with all that entails in terms of the continuing misery of employment for those who service the leisure and business needs of others.

Predicting the future is a sometimes interesting but rarely meaningful exercise. Chivers (1973) suggested that the deskilling of cooks and chefs would lead to a greater unionisation of that occupation. A similar portent was divined by Mars and Mitchell (1976) in respect of the growing involvement of breweries in the ownership of hotel and catering organisations. Breweries, they argued, had sophisticated management and personnel administration techniques and were unlikely to tolerate the workplace practices common in the hotel and catering industry. These were optimistic prognoses and they have (so far) been proved quite wrong.

Indeed, any understanding of both the history of the hospitality industry and the laws of probability suggest that optimism about the future of hotel and catering work is bound to be misplaced. Each new study of employment in the industry tends to 'rediscover' the wretched situation of many hotel and catering workers. The provision of hotel and catering services at anything other than the most basic level has always entailed an element of the feudal, of the poor servicing the rich. Conflict in the workplace is not a new phenomenon in hotels and catering but one, as Gabriel (1988) suggests, with its roots very firmly planted in the soil of capitalist exploitation. In these respects, hotels and catering differ little from other industries and it is the similarities that the industry has with others that deserve to be stressed, not the putative differences on which many employers, educationalists and academic researchers repeatedly dwell.

To take refuge in platitudinous generalisations is, of course, to abandon the responsibility for accepting that improvements are possible within any social and industrial system. Mars, Bryant and Mitchell (1979) argue for reducing the importance of individual contract-making and breaking down the informal rewards system by encouraging multi-skilling and the employment of workers with little or no experience of hotel and catering employment and therefore limited expectations of industry traditions and conventions in respect of additions to basic pay.

To a certain extent, many large hotel and catering organisations have pursued just these policies. However, there is every suggestion that, insofar as they ever existed at all extensively, individual contract-making persists as do informal reward elements in remuneration. Mars, Bryant and Mitchell's goals are directed towards an essential undermining of the culture of hotels. Thus in arguing for multi-skilling, they accept that one price for this will be some deskilling. They are not so clear about the necessary corollaries to elimination of individual contract-making and informal rewards, i.e. higher basic wages.

Their still eminently realisable objectives could be achieved by management action but this would require the uniformity of purpose and level of foresight necessary to the sparking of a conversion of the kind unseen since that of Saint Paul. More importantly, without the concomitant provision of decent basic pay and conditions, many workers would be disadvantaged. Partnership between industry and government, with action by the latter to introduce an element of compulsion into the process of reform would be one alternative.

Indeed, whilst laudable, it is difficult to see how the sorts of objective Mars, Bryant and Mitchell have in mind could be realised without government intervening to either initiate or contain reforming action.

This is clearly the view of campaigning groups. In Britain, the Low Pay Unit network of regional pressure groups has for some considerable time performed singly what should be a role shared with trade unions, that of campaigning to protect low-paid workers in hotels, catering and other industries. Potter (1988) concentrates on the extent to which employment conditions in hotels and catering might be improved as a result of developing highly co-ordinated local strategies of monitoring, control and action involving the tourism departments of local authorities, trades unions and other interested parties.

There is a rather sad air in Potter's work reflected in her exclusion of employers from a potential list of 'action points'. Considering employers' track record on innovation and change it is probably realistic to assume that it is only legal and quasi-legal controls and external pressures that are likely to produce significant improvements. However, given the local nature of hotel and catering product and labour markets, it would be unwise to assume either that hotel and catering employers can be negated in any strategy for change or that *all* employers would themselves be opposed to involvement in a scheme that could be designed to bring manifest benefits.

Certainly, one benefit of local strategies to combat conditions of work in hotels and catering is that they can lake account of local circumstances and need not rely on the idealistic hope of initiatives by central government The main stumbling block is of course the willingness of local authorities to participate in such schemes which, it is safe to hazard, would be ideologically unacceptable to some forms of political control.

Discussion of the kinds of policies that are needed to effect meaningful change to the terms and conditions of hotel and catering workers inevitably returns attention to the scope for making generalisations about what is an industry of considerable diversity. And yet generalisation is possible. The evidence reviewed in this book is suggestive of a deep-rooted and widespread malaise in the hotel and catering industry. It is a malaise also to be found in many other low-paid industries.

The issues are somewhat blurred in the academic literature by the persistence of arguments concerning the willingness of hotel and catering workers to accept their lot 'with a nod and a smile'. These arguments must contain an element of truth but they should not be regarded as typical. For the most part, their expression is itself the result of researchers examining relatively untypical examples of hotel and catering operations. Perhaps the biggest obstacle to change in hotels and catering however is the widespread prejudice that goes hand-in-hand with concepts of service. To reiterate the point, service is simply not regarded as important in contexts where it is associated with things like food, drink and accommodation, things that most people take for granted.

By association, those who work to meet these needs in the public sphere of hospitality receive little acknowledgement of their efforts and only limited acknowledgement of their service. It is a wretched situation made more wretched by the knowledge that change is possible but unlikely.

14

Staff Management in Hotel Industry

Staff management in Hotel industry is of prime importance. Staffing pattern from bottom to top needs a careful investigation, planning and implementation. A difficulty that has to be confronted from the start is that studies of some occupations lend themselves more easily to demonstrating certain points rather than others. Hotel and catering managers may have the best deal of all employees in the industry but it is not that much easier in practice. This largely reflects the piecemeal development of research in the field and the particular preoccupations of the researchers involved. Studies of management work in hotels and catering have grown considerably in recent years. By focusing on hotel managers, it is possible to gain some insight into how conditions of work in the hotel and catering industry are perpetuated. Discussion of hotel management work demonstrates the extent to which managers themselves might be perceived as victims of the same conditions of work that make hotel and catering employment so unpleasant for operative staff.

1. Reception Staff

The work of the receptionist is also undertaken more often than not in full-public view, in the 'front office', and receptionists are usually the first people hotel guests encounter, particularly in those hotels where hall porters are not employed. They thus occupy a 'gatekeeper' role, frequently bearing the responsibility for guests' first impressions of the hotel. In fact, the responsibilities that receptionists bear for the image of the hotel arguably extend beyond first impressions. The varied nature of these responsibilities is rarely reflected in adequate remuneration and reception work, no less than other hotel and catering occupations, suffers extensively from labour turnover.

The ETAC, 1983 studied 40 receptionists of which twenty-three admitted to *regularly* being involved in book-keeping, letter writing, inventory taking, typing, record keeping, answering queries, filing, taking reservations, dealing with mail and lost property, dealing with room changes, taking payment of customers' bills, banking monies, holding responsibility for room keys and producing reports and statistics. Further to these diverse dudes, the position of the reception at the 'crossroads' of the hotel ensures that the potential for pressure emanating from the demands of the client are considerable: the visibility of the reception desk ensures that it is the first port of call for any disgruntled guest Shamir, 1975, found that receptionists frequently act as conduits for communicating requests and complaints to other departments of the hotel.

In addition to a gatekeeper role therefore, the receptionist is expected to be a mediator. It is these roles, Shamir argues, that can lead the relatively high status of receptionist to suffer in terms of role stress and incongruity. He found that receptionists were perceived by senior kitchen and restaurant staff as low in status and by lower kitchen and restaurant staff as arrogant and self-important.

The 'in-between' role of the receptionist both in terms of physical location within the hotel and their position in the hotel's communications system creates the potential for a particularly unrewarding job characterized by conflict, both actual and in terms of role image amongst colleagues in other departments. As with chambermaids, little information is available on the extent to which receptionists benefit from informal rewards and fringe benefits. First general point of note is the extent to which illicit activities are constrained by receptionists' lack of mobility to access the latter and their high trust relationship with management. Their responsibility for monies often entails close supervision and monitoring thus making fiddles difficult. Where information technology has been introduced the scope for fiddling is further reduced.

2. Waiters

The waiter is the very important part of the hotel and catering industry. Waiting-on-table is the most crucial and widely studied hotel and catering industry occupation which provides the basis for much of what is regarded as the conventional wisdom in the theoretical analysis of hospitality labour. With so much research effort it might be thought that studies of waiting-on-table offer, cumulatively, a plethora of analytic detail about the occupation. They do not. Two main methodological handicaps limit the collective value of studies of *waiting on table*. These are, firstly, the types of establishment studied. Thus there is a problem of representativeness. Secondly, the majority of data has been collected using ethnographic techniques, leading to a preoccupation with studies of the relationship between waiters and waitresses and the informal rewards system and, in particular, that competitiveness in wailing work that centres on the tipping practice. The waiting staff can to some degree control the amount of their remuneration by engaging in activities that increase monies from tipping and by becoming involved in fiddling and knocking-off. Thus, Butler and Snizek (1976) found that waitresses can exert control over their clients by employing various 'guidance' techniques. The most important of these is *product promotional activity* which entails attempts to maximise the sale of food and drink. The rationale underlying this strategy is that by increasing the size of the customer's bill, the size of any tip will be increased since *tip size*, by convention, normally bears a proportional relationship to the bill's total. The other two methods of influencing the reward structure are regarded as less likely to succeed but are nevertheless of importance. *Increased ritualization* involves putting excess emphasis on service acts. *Friendly rapport techniques* entail, in essence, fawning to the customer and striving to reduce the social distance between server and served. Neither activity necessarily serves to increase the chances or size of reward since both are intrusive and are thus high-risk strategies that may result in waitresses being 'stiffed'--receiving little or no tip--a source of criticism by other staff who view being stiffed as evidence of incompetence and inability to control the work condition

To improve the size of tip, the activities in which waiting staff engage is not determined in a wholly arbitrary fashion. Most food service staff develop customer classification schemes which determine the types of customer to whom product promotional activity, friendly rapport and increased ritualization may be directed with some expectation of success.

Bowey (1976) noted that waitresses regarded the most promising customers as those adults in lunch parties of two or more; individuals alone were not regarded as having quite the same potential for tips and involved staff in more work. Parties with children were regarded as being of only limited potential for ups since parents rarely left a pro rata tip on their children's behalf and children also often involved considerable extra work. The use of classificatory schemes by waiting staff was also observed by Mars and Nicod (1984) who found that different types of classification can be operated at any or the same time. Some schemes attributed quite specific labels to individuals. Further, a series of generally applicable industry-wide beliefs about upping. These are:

— people on package tours are poor uppers;
— older persons are better tippers than the young ;
— men are considered better uppers than female (because they are more experienced diners);
— male accompanied by female rather than men are better tippers (because they seek to impress);
— large parties are poor tippers (because as the cost of the meal rises there is a tailing-off in the amount tipped).
— customers with children are poor tippers (because they have less money and do not regard the serving of children as involving extra effort), and
— the socially insecure are poor tippers (because they are usually inexperienced in dining and therefore are not *au fait* with the correct amount to tip);

An effort to supply a systematic account of how waiters work in this respect, use the concepts of boundary-open and boundary-closed transactions. Boundary-open transactions exist between server and served where the served prefer to foster intimacy with the server, treating them as friendly or even quasi members of the family. Boundary-closed transactions reflect a desire by customers to reduce intrusion by waiting staff and a fostering of intimacy between host(s) and guest(s) on the part of the host. Such transactions are typical of business diners. Emphasis is placed on maintaining the ritualized formality of the waiting game, evidenced most in the exaggeration attached to service ritual. According to Mars and Nicod, both types of boundary transactions are governed by common rules which do not vary. These include: always serve a guest before a host, a woman before a man (unless she is the host), and an older person before a younger person; always address a customer by his or her surname or as 'sir' or 'madam'; and always serve from the right and clear detritus from the left.

However, the problems faced by waiting staff are complicated by the fact that, in any single transaction, clients may vary between being open and being closed. Similarly, guests who use a facility regularly may do so in different role guises--as businessman or as a man entertaining his wife. Interactional difficulties can arise particularly in respect of searching for host/guest clues when diners are of the same gender. Mars and Nicod found that this occurred in the case of homosexual males dining together, citing one instance when a guest believed to be a transvestite caused substantial classificatory difficulty. In general, however, the nature of social transactions can be determined by reference to the following patterns of primary cues (*i.e.* gender, age, race, class and state of health):

— *place of origin:* those of the same place of origin will enjoy boundary open transactions and vice versa;
— *age:* waiters and diners of roughly the same age will tend to experience boundary open transactions and vice versa; and
— *sex:* when waiters and diners are of a different sex transactions will be boundary open and vice versa: there is an assumption by male clients that female waiting staff should be more boundary open.

The 'screening' process is crucial to the assessment of the kind of service relationship into which waiting staff are likely to enter and therefore the types of activity in which they will have to engage in order to maximise the likelihood and size of gratuities. The level of service received by customers is thus determined as the outcome of a complex of interactional processes centring on the server's assessment of the likely temperament and disposition of clients. In fact the preoccupation in Mars and Nicod's study, evident in similar reports, with the actual mechanics of occupational sub-cultures tends to obscure not only how difficult it is to obtain tips, but the extent to which the occupational experience of *waiting on table* is far from uniform. Nowhere is this clearer than with the case of female waiting staff.

Many female waitresses may find themselves confined to labour markets associated with the lower end of the product hierarchy and thus unable to progress to establishments associated with better conditions of work, better opportunities to exercise discretionary skills and the opportunity for greater informal rewards. More importantly there are fundamental differences in the terms, conditions and experiences of employment enjoyed by female staff more responsibility.

One example centres on the generalized exploitation of female's sexuality at work which in the hotel and catering context can achieve extra salience. In the opinion of Dronfield and Soto: "Trusthouse Forte tried to train female to be all-round hostesses, combining the images of the sexy receptionist with the caring housekeeper. The plan would allow Trusthouse Forte to cut down on the waiting around rime inherent in many hotel jobs. The female would supposedly serve breakfast, check the clients in and out, go upstairs to make the beds, and be ready to serve lunch. After a while the female refused to do the worst jobs and the scheme broke down."

Hotel and catering employers often seek persons who exhibit a reasonable degree of physical attractiveness for jobs with high levels of public contact. Male employers tend to be perhaps more self-conscious in the extent to which they attempt to capitalise upon female sexuality. In the studies by Roebuck and Frese (1976) and Mann & Spradley (1975) of, respectively, an American after-hours club and cocktail bar, sexuality was an integral part of the role of the female waitresses, stopping short of responding to sexual advances from clients--though for reasons, primarily, of avoiding the attraction of management displeasure. Frese & Roebuck (1976) found that barmaids and cocktail waitresses were explicitly selected on the basis of their physical appearance--along with *class*, personal habits and other attributes of social and technical skill. Most of the female workers in this establishment were, Byrne claims, middle aged, long serving staff popular with regular customers and competent at their jobs who did not, however, fit 'with the dolly bird fantasies of the Berni Inns Management'. The exploitation of sexuality at the level of the employment decision is often compounded by sexual harassment. A report on the European hotel industry found that some 23% of hotel staff knew of instances of sexual harassment.

One more aspect of the generalized differential experience of female at work is the extent to which female are more rigorously controlled by men. This control can be formal in the sense that men tend to hold positions of authority, or more informal in the sense that within nominally collaborative work teams with relatively little visible role differentiation female are still subordinated to male control. Again in the hotel and catering context, a good example of this is provided by Mann & Spradley in their ethnographic study of the cocktail waitress. They examine the patriarchal relationships in *Brady's Bar* engendered by the male proprietor and show how these lead to role conflict

The two male bartenders, custodians of Mr Brady's trust, were also managers to whose authority the female cocktail waitresses had to submit. As bartenders, however, there was scope for disagreement, for the questioning of authority and opinion. To the outside gaze, the relationships between waitresses and bartenders were nominally cooperative. Indeed, for the male bartenders, resort to the use of managerial authority in controlling waitresses was seemingly rare.

However, the informal control exercised over female workers was considerable. The bartenders had control over the speed at which the waitresses' orders were filled and in what priority, control that could cause friction at busy times as several waitresses vied for orders. Any mistakes made in ruling orders or in respect of other aspects of service had to be shouldered by the waitresses, even if they were due to errors on the part of the bartenders. This 'keeping the peace' was essential to harmonious relationships. Bartenders' control extended to what female waitresses were allowed to drink at the end of the service period and male notions of acceptable entitlement could not be broached without retribution. Waitresses allowed the 'privilege' of assisting the bartender at the bar during busy limes had to thank him for the opportunity to participate in the male sphere of operations.

Whilst this may all seem a little bizarre, it begs the question as to whether male waiting staff would receive the same treatment. As Mann & Spradley, 1975, point out, the waitresses in their study relied on men not only for technical support to do their work but depended on male approval for their sense of well-being to the extent that pleasing male bartenders became more important than pleasing customers. There are echoes here of Whyte's study. He reports the ways in which female workers frequently coped with the stress placed upon them by (usually) male counter workers or similar by crying. There is of course evidence to suggest that waiting staff in general are often looked upon by chefs and others as something approaching a lesser species. As noted in the previous chapter. Snow found that references to the homosexuality of male waiters acted as a device to further justify contempt on the part of chefs. However, the creation of such handicaps is an essentially arbitrary affair. Female workers must ever carry the dual handicap of discrimination against them, based on their occupational location in the hospitality industry hierarchy and their gender. The effects of this on producing an experience of work different to that of men should not be either ignored or underestimated.

3. Kitchen Workers

The kitchen in which she worked provided 700 meals daily for all staff and patients and the maids had a dirty job that entailed not only food preparation but the cleaning of floors, surfaces and equipment. In a manner reminiscent of Saunders' claims concerning the role of the menu in determining social relations in the kitchen (Saunders, 1981b), Paterson argues that the structure of maids' working day was fleshed out by the weekly menu cycle. For example, when food had been processed for one day, it was often the case that ingredients were prepared for the following day's menu, the menu dishes indicating the necessary 'food work' that had to be undertaken.

Maids' work experience was characterized by a sense of overwhelming drudgery. Dealing with food in bulk led to a fragmentation of perceptions of food production, a disassociation of experience gained in the domestic provision of food made manifest in that the maids brought their own food to eat Because of role-strain engendered by the conflict between their positions as food producer in the home and hospital bulk food producer, they had difficulty in adjusting to the dissemination of small portions when instinct led them to feel that larger amounts were 'normal'. The experience of 'food as work' also led maids to develop different criteria of 'good' and 'bad' food, based not on taste but on the relevance of preparation for work control and experience. 'Doing lettuce' (*i.e.* washing and preparing) was therefore regarded as an arduous task, generally eliciting sympathy from colleagues.

Good foods were those requiring little or no preparation by the maids or which meant that few items of equipment had subsequently to be cleaned. Paterson's study reveals continuities in the themes highlighted previously. Kitchen maids were at the bottom of the departmental hierarchy and felt this subordinate position acutely, a feeling heightened by arbitrary and erratic supervision. It was difficult for them to take pride in their work since nobody praised them and most other higher grade kitchen workers treated them as skivvies. Also, because maids were unable easily to reconcile the perceived low standards attendant on the preparation of hospital food with their own personal domestic standards, a good deal of frustration was experienced. As a result of these experiences, a number of coping strategies were evolved, including distancing, marked by protestations that skivvying was 'not really them' and activities such as joking cheekily with amenable cooks-pretending to refuse to undertake instructions and suchlike. In addition to these distancing tactics, kitchen maids abused the control system almost as a form of compenzation for being employed there. Food was taken and eaten and when food was not available this led to annoyance and frustration. The appropriation of knock-offs was not simply related to expectations of total rewards but was also a manifestation of resistance, of fighting back against menial, degraded and monotonous jobs.

Now kitchen porters. kitchen portering serves as a reservoir to take up those into work who have suffered as a result of changes in local industrial employment or some personal reason for which they had to leave other work. The majority of kitchen porters in Saunders' sample were men with few if any school-leaving qualifications. Only 21% were married and 64% had no children. Over half Saunders' respondents said that they became kitchen porters because it was the only job they could get. Their work was predictably degrading, though there are some hints that a minority of workers made something of it. Interestingly, the work of the kitchen porter is often monotonous and dull and little effort is made to invest in technological aids. Saunders found no evidence of the existence of mechanical or technological aids to minimise the drudgery of the job and the picture he paints would appear to confirm a lack of advance in the treatment of kitchen porters since Orwell's (1933) account of his own experiences in *Down and Out in Paris and London.* Of course technological investment is expensive and kitchen porter labour cheap and disposable.

What arises mostly clearly from the works of writers like Paterson (1981) and Saunders (1981a), however, is the lack of dignity allowed to workers in these low grade posts. These authors direct attention to the routine, everyday aspects of hotel and catering work, processes that have become increasingly common with new forms of food work, notably those that characterise capital intensive chain restaurants. These systems of catering exists alongside the more traditional forms of food provision but there is little evidence to suggest that they provide employment which is any less engaging.

4. Chefs & Cooks

Several studies contain incidental comment but seemingly only Chiver's now dated research is devoted entirely to the occupation of chef. As an occupational group, chefs and cooks are interesting for two principal reasons. First, they have been identified as the victims of hotel and catering managements' attempts to deskill and degrade work in the search for reduced costs. The second reason for interest in this occupation, and the one that provides the focus for the following discussion, relates to the position of chefs and cooks in hotel and catering organizations vis-á-vis other workers, particularly in respect of claims made for the cohesiveness and solidarity of chefs and cooks as an occupational group. This view derives from the report by the Commission on Industrial Relations (CIR) (1971). It will be recalled that the Commission found the hotel industry to be highly status conscious, hierarchical in organization and conducive to the encouragement of entrepreneurial, individualistic and competitive attitudes amongst workers. Combined with the personal service nature of employment and the isolation in which many workers undertook their tasks, these factors led to an unstable workforce and stressful working conditions, but also the development of strong identification with management and the aspirations of management, particularly in respect of the desire for promotion less realistically proprietorship of a hotel or catering unit.

Whilst chefs no less than other workers exhibited the latter tendency, the CIR argued that they also demonstrated greater cohesiveness and solidarity than other occupational groups. The CIR hypothesized that the greater cohesiveness and solidarity of chefs was attributable to three factors: the collaborative 'teamwork' involved in hotel and restaurant cookery; the craft orientation of chefs and cooks; and chefs' removal from the competitive forum of service that denies them access to tips and other informal rewards.

On the last of these there is little information. In theory, chefs have opportunities to run a variety of fiddles and knockoffs in the kitchen, opportunities reinforced by the fact that the geographical isolation of the kitchen and high-trust relationships with management often mean that the latter rarely intrude into the work of the chef. The other two characteristics of chefs identified by the *CIR* (1971) have found resonance in later studies. The crux of the CIR's argument in respect of the collaborative nature of chefs' work is that whereas many hotel and catering employees undertake their tasks on an individual and peripatetic basis, chefs' work takes place in a single location and by definition requires a collective, interdependent approach to labour.

Further, because in many hotel and restaurant

organizations the kitchen brigade is controlled by a Head Chef rather than a conventional manager, loyalty is induced not only to the craft but to the occupational group as a whole. That teamwork is an important element of chefs' lives was also suggested by the ETAC (1983) report which found that 85% of those asked said that being a good member of a team was very necessary or essential to their job. The kitchen is arguably the only true 'product' creating department in the hotel: the kitchen's output is tangible and real and the kitchen's products like meals & dishes can be complex to assemble. The basis of food production in traditional kitchens is the *partie* system, the origination of which is normally attributed to the French chef, Escoffier, and involves a division of labour along commodity and dish type lines, though to what extent Escoffier refined rather than devised the working practices associated with the system is unclear.

Saunders (1981a) postulates a generic hierarchy for the *Brigade de Cuisine* running from Chef de Cuisine (Head Chef) through the Sous Chef (Deputy Chef) to the *partie*--the sauce chef, larder chef, pastry chef, fish chef, roast chef, soup chef and vegetable chef. However, a variety of practical interpretations have been put on kitchen organization and variations in such organization are clearly a function of the type of restaurant and the market in which it operates. These differences reflect the essential malleability of the system. It is evident that in many hotels and restaurants, including many smaller operations, the *partie* system persists, however weakly, in one form or another. *The partie* system involves considerable specialization whilst fostering interdependency.

Though the majority of workers may be involved in producing individual tangible dishes like a fish dish, a soup, work in a hotel or restaurant kitchen is organized according to the tacit assumption that the proper meal comprises two or more courses. The specialized tasks of individual chefs and cooks are thus brought together in a whole and the whole is to a very large extent the result of social negotiations over the menu. This point is made by *Saunders* (1981b) who argues that the work experience of chefs is governed by two mutually influencing factors being:

— the position of the individual worker within the occupational hierarchy of chefs; and
— the cycle of meal provision.

Both of these are ultimately related to the status of foodstuffs, the status of particular meals and the relationship of the unit to the wider market in terms of staff skill and the technology employed. Five determinants of status amongst the kitchen brigade: The first four are: high skill over low skill; high pay over lower pay; long service over short service; and product finishing over product preparation at the earlier stage. The fifth determinant is probably unique to the activity of food preparation--"the working supervisor of the fish station ranked towards the top of the kitchen in all of these factors [the first four status determinants above], and yet her status in the kitchen was low. Evidently there is another factor powerful enough to overrule all these considerations--*the prestige value of the materials used*."

Now to commercial cookery. Certain meals enjoy higher status than others. Also, the position of each of the *chefs de partie* in Saunders' hierarchy mirrors relatively closely the hierarchy of foodstuffs proposed by *Twigg* (1983), with red meat being most valued followed by white meat, fish, dairy products and vegetables and fruit. Certain other resonances with the claims made by sociologists of food and eating are also evident. Thus the sauce chef is senior because sauces bind dishes together, spoil easily and, in the traditional repertoire of French *haute cuisine* are characteristic features of virtually all dishes. The larder chef is similarly important because s/he is responsible for perishables—for fresh food which is attributed considerable importance in traditional hotel cuisine.

The positions of soup and vegetable chef are also consonant with the general (low) value attached to these foodstuffs. The predication of kitchen organization on culinary skills directed towards particular commodities and parts of the meal is important not only in defining individuals' place within an organization or the occupation more widely, but in charting career development.

Progress in the traditional chefs' hierarchy is, in simplified terms, usually from apprentice to a *partie* position and ultimately to the positions of sous chef and chef de cuisine, in other words a progress from dealing with the specific to dealing with the general and usually involving some mastery of a large number of *partie* positions. The relatively well developed career structure for chefs means that, when taken with the mode of work organization, it is easier for individuals to see their role with clarity which, whilst not guaranteeing cooperative and interdependent working arrangements, is likely to foster individual skill and responsibility that allows for controlled creativity within a bureaucratic work structure. Further evidence to support the hypothesis that chefs' work is characterized by a high degree of cooperation comes from Chivers' (1971) study of chefs' perceptions of conflict.

Chivers notes that the pressure under which the kitchen is placed, particularly by waiting staff, can lead to losses of temper although he suggests that such outbreaks are rarely malicious, rather they add to the camaraderie of the kitchen since friendship and harmony must survive transient divisions in order for the kitchen to function adequately. Chivers also suggests that temper loss may be a useful strategy for asserting the temporary independence of an individual or the kitchen as a whole. What Chivers does not mention is that the cultural stereotype of the temperamental chef may actually lead to a situation where such behaviour is expected and where the expectation itself glosses real divisions and serves as an institutionalized form of defusing conflict between individuals. Some support for this view comes from Saunders' observation that in traditional kitchens the formal pattern of authority matches closely the informal pattern. Head chefs often occupy like a god status, and age and experience rank more highly than informal leadership not backed by these criteria. The clear implication is that there exists less scope for 'dissent' because a professional and highly formalized ethic of behaviour prevails. That chefs are team oriented in their approach to work is held to be closely related to their craft orientation and a sense of status superiority. Confirms this view, suggesting that occupational solidarity is reinforced by dedication to task and a genuine interest in the work and opportunities offered by the use of manual skills (Chivers, 1973) .

However, being able to exercise manual skills is not everything. The context in which such skills are exercised is important. *Chivers* (1973) argues that chefs and cooks, like other hotel workers, are located in a wide range of hotel and catering units and this geographical spread militates against collectivism. This spatial constraint to collectivism is compounded by chefs' own perceptions of the range of establishments and their relationship to them. Chivers focused mainly on chefs and cooks in upmarket establishments and found that these workers viewed themselves as distinct from those employed in lower market establishments--the former were chefs whereas the latter were merely cooks. What is unclear is the extent to which this is rationalized by chefs/cooks working in less prestigious establishments. The bottom line appears to be that chefs are fairly realistic about their job prospects and are encouraged in this by two simple truths: that there will always be a need for their skills & there exists very clearly demarcated career structures for chefs and cooks in the hotel and catering industry. In support of this are Chiver's findings concerning the career aspirations of chefs and cooks.

Many respondents to his study cited the ownership of a restaurant as a business goal. However, the extent to which managerial and employer positions were realisable aspirations was very clearly reflected in a second choice career goal career cooking--which Chivers interprets as reflecting more realistic assessments on the part of his respondents. A strong craft orientation and status superiority is thus seemingly maintained by chefs precisely because career structures embody relatively precise alternatives in terms of the opportunities to develop and exercise skills and increase status and rewards. A waiter in a small privately owned restaurant working split shifts may, in theory, improve his career prospects by moving to a high-class hotel.

However, the waiter is always going to be involved in the same type of work. Being a waiter in one type of operation is not vastly different from being a waiter in any other. For the chef, however, the options are much more clearly defined. A chef, particularly one fairly senior in the kitchen hierarchy, is always going to be an employee whose occupation automatically confers some status irrespective of the organization. Further, within the hotel and catering industry there exists sufficient sectoral differentiation to present chefs with several quite distinct career options, that, whilst always involving cookery as the central task, vary in quite precise ways in terms of benefits relating to conditions of work and remuneration.

Thus, Chivers found high mobility amongst the chefs he studied with a net loss of employees from the hotel and restaurant sector. A third or more respondents in hospitals had experience in the commercial sector whereas only 7%

of those in the latter had worked in hospital cooking, suggesting, Chivers argues, a move towards jobs where working conditions were better. It is not simply a choice between institutional and commercial catering, however. Because their skills are less confined to local labour markets, chefs can job hunt in a national market. However, fewer senior positions exist for chefs in the commercial sector, particularly in those high-quality establishments the aspiration towards employment in which is very much a part of the occupational culture. This faces many chefs with career choices that are to a very large extent determined by the state of the market for their skills.

For access to incrementally superior or better paid posts of responsibility in the commercial sector chefs might have to accept charge of a small unit, the tradeoff of which is less opportunity to exercise their skills and diminished opportunities to reach the top of their trade unless the unit in question is very famous. In the commercial sector, career choice is very much in terms of hoping for a senior position in a high-class establishment, remaining a member of a team in such a unit or a less prestigious establishment, or taking up a senior position in a smaller unit. Chefs could, like other hotel and catering workers, flit from establishment to establishment, but in terms of career development this can be pretty pointless since clearly defined options in the market place exist with genuinely calculable consequences for work experience.

Bowey states in this connection that: 'Careers' for chefs are slightly different from those of waiters and waitresses since their earnings are less dependent upon the volume of trade and the generosity of customers in the restaurant. They are taken on as 'commis chefs' and trained as chefs, being promoted to posts carrying higher responsibility as their skills and experience increase. They also move from restaurant to restaurant seeking to move each time to a higher status restaurant where the food preparation is more intricate and therefore the skills learned more valuable.

The differentials between the different grades of chef become increasingly more substantial as the skill level of the chef increases. A restaurant builds its reputation on the quality of its food and this depends largely on the abilities of the head chef. The head chef is typically a much honoured, respected and well paid employee in a restaurant. Like the waitresses, however, a chef who is, say, three grades below the head chef in a high status restaurant may earn more money by accepting a head chefs job in a lower status perhaps smaller restaurant. If he does this he is likely to find himself without the opportunities for practising and developing many of his skills, and his chances of reaching the top of his profession are lessened.

Now chefs and cooks' career options which are firmly cemented in a context of highly formalized systems of training. The Education and Training Advisory Council (ETAC), 1983 in its study result that of 70 chefs or cooks, some 41 had formal educational qualifications in cookery. Amongst head chefs, 34 out of 41 had such qualifications. Chefs can obtain standard qualifications which are *trade* qualifications--that is, they are universally recognized as appropriate to a career as chefs or cooks. This system of certification based on what is essentially a national curriculum ensures not only the transmission of basic craft knowledge but also of tacit skills and values, the *culture* of the occupation. Measurement of individual worth therefore extends beyond the actual practice of cookery to a more generalized appreciation of the level of qualification: formal certification links chefs and cooks together in an educational framework that validates their occupation over and above relatively subjective criteria such as craft competency, employment record and so forth. This process of certification is reinforced by the involvement of chefs in their occupation beyond the workplace. In addition to formal certification, there are many associations for chefs to join and the whole occupation is held constantly in the spotlight through the activities of such associations, through the achievements of individual chefs and through the bourgeois concern with food reflected in food guides and specialist magazines.

At a less formal level, Chivers (1971) argues that the nature of hotel and catering work encourages patterns of friendship within the trade and this is reinforced by involvement The occupation is centrally concerned with the craft and craft provides the focus for self-improvement and advancement via the development of social networks--a feature, to some extent, of other industry occupations also. The attitudes and culture of the occupation are highly generalised: involvement in the craft, national support systems and professional reference points all combine to reinforce a relatively uniform and highly systematic approach to work--perhaps most obviously experienced by the outsider in terms of the perception of chefs as arrogant, superior and self serving.

5. Accommodation Workers

The term 'accommodation workers' is used to describe a diverse group of employees including receptionists, hall porters, housekeepers and room-cleaners of all hotel and catering employees, those engaged in accommodation services work have received least research attention. The limited literature on the third and non-existence of any significant commentary on the last means that discussion here is slanted towards the first two, the largest categories of accommodation workers in the industry. In the Hotel and Catering Industry Training Board (HCITB, 1985) classification of occupations, chambermaids are subsumed in the category 'domestic staff and number some 81, 000 in the commercial sector. Some 97% of workers in this category are female. Chambermaids, like all accommodation workers, are more or less exclusively concerned with the hotels sector. Shamir (1975: 178-183) in his study of London hotels adopts a typical attitude to room cleaning work. Chambermaids, he argues, are amongst the least skilled of hotel staff. They are expected by employers to draw upon their reservoir of domestic skills in undertaking work tasks.

The assumption that female's socialization 'naturally' suits them to the maintenance of hotel accommodation is convenient in that it enables employers to: (i) avoid giving anything other than minimal *on the job training*; and (ii) hire a group of people who bring to their work a basic training undertaken at no cost to the employer. Shamir argues that room cleaning is physically demanding and dirty work, repetitive, boring and limited in variety and scope, and undertaken at times when employees are unlikely to encounter customers. Despite this, he contends that it offers workers certain compenzations such as a relatively pleasant working environment and freedom from close supervision. The latter permits workers a limited degree of control over work rates and methods of working plus opportunities to develop strategies to cope with monotony.

The typical room-maid in the Saunders and Pullen survey was female, single, childless and aged between 25 and 44. The majority (63%) were from Europe and those who had been in post for the shortest length of time originally took up their employment because it was the only work they could obtain. Others evidenced considerable stability, with 67% of the total having worked in the industry for more than twelve months and 51% in their existing job for more than a year. Saunders and Pullen confirm Shamir's view that hotel room-maids do a physically demanding and dirty job but offer no evidence to suggest that freedom from supervision allows flexible control over work-rates and methods, or allows for socialization. Indeed, some 80%

of the sample cleaned between eleven and sixteen rooms daily, a workload regarded as unreasonable by many respondents. Again, the theme of isolation is evident here. Shamir sees absence from supervision as freeing workers from management oversight but Saunders and Pullen found that many room-maids experienced their heavy loads as all the more problematic because of an absence of management support and interest, manifest in complaints about short-staffing, the absence of help from other hotel staff and failure to provide sufficient and adequate materials for the performance of work tasks. The picture painted by Saunders and Pullen is at least implicitly confirmed by the ETAC, 1983. Their job profiles and case studies of twenty female chambermaids reveals a wider age range, 17-65 and a preponderance of single people. The average number of rooms cleaned per maid was fifteen and there is the same implication that many female take these jobs because of a lack of alternatives and find their employment a source of considerable misery. There can be little doubt that many female who undertake room-cleaning jobs do so because of a shortage of alternative employment.

Ellis (1981) found that more than 40% of school pupils were likely to be deterred from becoming room-maids because they perceived it as repetitive, unskilled and low in status. The low status of chambermaiding was felt by just under half of Saunders and Pullen's sample who suggested they were treated as less than equal by many other hotel staff. Clearly then, chambermaids rank amongst the lowest of the low in hotel work, treated as a cheap and easily replaceable resource by employers and often spumed by their fellow employees. One point on which existing evidence disagrees is in respect of access to informal rewards. The implication of Shamir's research is that customer-maid contact is limited and thus the opportunity for gaining informal rewards limited. However, Saunders and Pullen found that maids had frequent contact with customers and nearly a quarter of their sample claimed to receive tips from most guests and a further 58% from a few--though the majority only obtained between one and three pounds a week. The most commonly received fringe benefit was discount on holidays. Since Saunders and Pullen undertook their research in London hotels, at the centre of the UK tourism industry, their findings must be treated as potentially untypical, though once again the lack of research evidence highlights the problem of assessing the validity of the 'total rewards package' as an explanatory concept in understanding those influences that shape hotel employees' experiences of their work. In contrast to chambermaiding, reception work is regarded as semi-skilled.

6. Managers

The literature on the nature of managerial work in the hospitality industry is concerned principally with *hotel management.* This should be kept in mind throughout the following discussion. In the U.K. and other advanced countries, serious research into the occupation of hotel manager is a fairly recent phenomenon. Apart from early studies most research is of the 1980s. Nevertheless, taken together with U.S. evidence, there is a large measure of agreement as to the principal characteristics of management work in hotels.

Firstly, people come to hotel management careers via a range of routes. Baum (1989) in the context of the Irish Republic identified three principal sources of hotel managers: those who come to the industry with formal hotel school training; those who train for management within the industry after starting either in craft positions or being given a traineeship; and those who have an early career in another industry followed by late entry into the hotel industry. The last perhaps is most typical of owner-managers but in general there is good reason to suppose that all three routes are typical of career paths in a large number of countries.

Secondly, hotel management like other occupations and the industry itself is notoriously insular. Those who follow a formal course of training in hospitality management are generally separated from general business studies students, and hotel and catering education which normally incorporates periods of industry placement serves as a form of pre-entry socialization into the occupation of hotel management. The need for specialist training is coming under increased critical scrutiny, but has usually been justified in terms of the need for managers in the hospitality industry to possess vital technical skills, particularly in the field of food and beverage management, that allows them the opportunity to control other powerful work groups such as chefs. Such technical competence is considered as necessary is without doubt. The ETAC found that over half the managers in their sample were frequently or sometimes involved in food preparation, cooking and service. The insularity of hotel management education is reinforced by a tendency for those who commit themselves to a hotel and catering career early on to never leave the industry. In Baum's sample, two-thirds of hotel managers in Ireland had no working experience outside the hotel industry

Thirdly, and following from this, hotel management positions are gained as a result of substantial mobility. Guerrier (1987) notes that as assistant managers gain seniority they are usually given some responsibilities, the main ones in a hotel being front of house and food and beverage. Experience in both of these is usually essential to promotion. Such experience need not be gained in a single institution however. Rather it is usual for managers at this stage of their career to move frequently between hotels 'collecting' experience of both specific functions and of different types of hotel. In the three companies Guerrier examined, the career histories of managers interviewed showed a pattern of lateral moves from hotel to hotel within the same company. Similarly. Turam & Riley, 1988, found mobility a crucial feature of management career development though in their case, some 43% of career moves examined involved a change of company, with the change to general hotel manager involving a change of company in 41% of cases. High mobility amongst managers is also confirmed by the trade journal *Caterer and Hotelkeeper* in a study showing that hotel and catering managers both changed their jobs more frequently and earned less than their counterparts in nine other industrial sectors. The attainment of a General Managership of a hotel is not necessarily an end to mobility. Though Guerrier found from her small sample that the average age of attaining a General Managership was 30, many of these people were promoted from a senior assistant's position to the General Manager position in a small company hotel with little prestige. For those staying with the same company, it appears this is a cross to be borne. Promotion to General Manager is firstly to a small unit and subsequently--to use Guerrier's naval metaphor--to larger and more prestigious ships in the line. It is perhaps therefore unsurprising that many managers change company to gain a unit manager's post since mobility offers opportunities to 'short circuit' traditional patterns of promotion. Also, Guerrier noted that in the companies she studied, pay was linked to the size of hotel. If this is, as seems likely, a general feature of company owned hotels then it places a further incentive on managers to move in search of career acceleration. Certainly, little appears to constrain hotel managers' mobility. Guerrier noted that children are more likely to be the primary consideration in job moves than spouses, many of whom are in any case often involved in the running of the hotel. A more important barrier is the possibility of an end to mobility within a single company. Guerrier points out that by the time a manager who has spent his or her life with a single company reaches their mid-40s there are fewer properties to manage. Indeed, given that even general managers move with frequency, options within a single company expire quickly. Moving to another company is first option as is promotion to a head office position.

Fourthly, most senior hotel managers obtain their appointments at a relatively early age. The first part of a hotel manager's career is likely to find him or her in very junior positions, often being little more than a dogsbody. Formal qualifications do not seem to affect either position on entry or promotion prospects and career patterns. In their study of British managers, Turam & Riley in 1988, argue that vocational education and time spent working in the industry gaining experience are alternative uses of time that make little difference to prospects in long term.

Fifthly, one important characteristic of hotel management positions is the degree of latitude individual managers are given in the running of their units, a freedom reflected in the manner in which hotel management work is conducted. Nailon (1968) found that hotel managers engaged in a much larger number of activities than counterparts in other industries, saw less of their peers and were rarely involved in group situations. They spent less time alone because of the time spent in direct supervision of staff and contact with customers. Managers were usually engaged in the continuous monitoring of their unit through brief contacts with personnel and regular movement about the establishment. Subsequent research has tended to confirm this picture. Baum (1989) found management to be dominated by operational demands. Guerrier and Lockwood note that, "The traditions of hotel management emphasise the hotel manager as the person who is always around to greet guests as they arrive. The Victorian hotelier was almost like a host welcoming a guest into his own home.

The managers expressed a preference for active management and disliked the 'sitting behind a desk' aspects of their job and doing paperwork. This attitude was encouraged by cramped accommodation that made it difficult for the management team to meet and make contact. They write that managers, saw their jobs very clearly in terms of being out and about in the hotel. This very often involved working long hours -- an average of 12-14 hours a day was not seen as unusual and with very few and irregular days off, if any. Rather than seeing this as a potential source of dissatisfaction, they saw it more as perfectly normal for the industry.

The 'being there' aspects of a hotel manager's role are perhaps in normative terms an important indicator of how successful any individual is in the eyes of staff and superiors. Analyses drawing on Mintzberg's ten managerial role categories and their contribution to managerial effectiveness are instructive here. Ten managerial role categories identified: figurehead, leader, liaison, monitor, disseminator, spokesman, entrepreneur, disturbance handler, resource allocator and negotiator by Mintzberg (1973). In a small-scale study of 7 U.S. managers of a single company. Ley (1980) observed the work of management personnel and classified their activities according to Mintzberg's schema. Following from this, the ratings of these managers' effectiveness as perceived by corporate superiors was obtained. Two managers were graded highly effective, three effective and two less effective. These gradings were then compared to the role ratings. Ley argues that the highly effective managers allocated *less* time to the leadership role than the two less effective managers, and more time on entrepreneurial activities than managers with lower effectiveness ratings. In a much larger study of U.S. general managers, Arnaldo (1981) secured 194 responses involving self-classification of activities according to Mintzberg's model and a note of the time spent on each plus a rating of the importance of individual roles.

No corporate ratings of effectiveness were available here but it is worth noting that in terms of time allocated, the most important roles were leader, disseminator and monitor whilst in terms of importance they were leader, entrepreneur and monitor. It is clear then that hotel managers set great store by leadership and also on entrepreneurship—though the extent to which the latter is realized may be problematic.

Notwithstanding the likelihood of corporate perceptions of effectiveness differing from those of unit managers, the latter do appear to share a common perception of what a 'good' hotel should be and what good managers should do. In Guerrier's terms, this emphasises the importance of the occupational community's self-perception which is likely to be reinforced by the views of colleagues and subordinates. The ability of managers in the hotel industry to get involved in basic operative work is something likely to invite the respect rather than disapprobation of these groups.

Yet, as several researchers have noted, there is something absurd about this approach. Baum (1989) argues that there is little evidence to show that 'being there' styles of management are costed relative to the benefit which may accrue from them. Guerrier & Lockwood (1989a) go as far as to suggest that the culture of hotel management emphasises 'being there' as the most important aspect of hotel management and achievement of results as secondary.

Being there styles of management give rise to procedures characterized by informality of communication between management and operatives and a paternalistic and authoritarian approach to staff, although hotel managements understandably tend to dissent from these views. On the issue of paternalism/authoritarianism Guerrier and Lockwood (1989a) found that managers saw the development and care of their staff as a central part of their role but noted that they did little to convert this into direct action. In the same study, staff saw management as being rather critical, autocratic and controlling.

Worsfold (1989) found that managers were aware of participative styles of management but none of his sample had adopted such a style. This point is reinforced by Croney (1988) whose interviews with the corporate executives of hotel groups revealed claims to a philosophy of management style typically emphasising consultation, involvement and communication. In the four groups studied, there was an overall tendency to see participation as management-led, though in some instances authoritarian paternalism was ameliorated by a more co-operative approach, differing in at least most important respect--the willingness to accept the legitimacy of trade union representation, a tendency absent in two of the groups.

The attitudes of management at unit level in all groups studied evidenced a unitary outlook as opposed to a pluralistic perspective, *i.e.* a tendency to view organizations as unified bodies in which the interests of management and workforce are shared, managerial authority supreme, and conflict pathological rather than arising from a fundamental diversity of competing intents.

Ultimately in this list of the characteristics of hotel managers and hotel management there is, as ever, the issue of pay. The role of management in controlling informal rewards was discussed earlier. Management are no less susceptible to the benefits of knock-offs and fiddles than those employees whose access to such benefits they control. Like the rest of the hotel and catering workforce, their basic remuneration is relatively poor.

A survey found that the average hotel and catering manager had spent only 4.4 years with their present employer, the lowest in the data set, compared to an average of 8.3 years. Hotel managers are thus in some ways subject to many of the same pressures that the rest of the workforce experience at managers' hands.

The work is hard, often not obviously effective and rewards are, to the outsider at least, somewhat limited. Hotel management careers are easier for some than for others however.

The majority of hotel general managers are men and yet the hotel and catering industry management cadre is increasingly made up of female. According to the HCITB, 1984, report Women's path to management in the hotel and catering industry, some 55% of industry managers are female. Given that 73% of the entire industry workforce are female, the report argues that females are under-represented at managerial level.

The extent of this under-representation is highlighted by the fact that over two-thirds of students on hotel and catering management courses in the UK are female. In reality, female managers are concentrated in certain sectors and positions in the industry, evidencing once again the effects of labour market segmentation. The HCITB report calculated that female constituted 59% of managers in industrial catering and 70% in private institutions but only 29% of managers in restaurants and 39% in hotels. In general it is thus the welfare rather than commercial sector in which female are most likely to achieve a management position.

However, in the latter, female tend to be concentrated in 'staff roles' rather than 'line management'. That is, female are most likely to be found in ancillary management roles associated with, for example, sales, marketing, training and personnel (HCITB, 1984a) rather than in food and beverage management or general management. Indeed, Guerrier (1986) surveyed the 1983 World Hotel Directory and found that of the 300 major U.K. hotels included therein, only one was managed by a woman, though the number of female general managers throughout the U.K. hotel industry has subsequently seemingly increased.

The most common areas of agreement exist as to the reasons for the under-representation of female at managerial level in hotels and catering. These are:

- female's career decisions relative to traditional career paths to general management in hotels and catering;
- the attitudes and aspirations of female;
- the requirements of the role of hotel line manager vis-á-vis conventional requirements of sociability.
- organizational discrimination against female, normally in the form of male impedence of career progress, and
- gender differences in rearing and education and the orientation of girls to caring careers which involve an extension of (male defined) roles for female;

Now the remaing four issues:

Aspiration and attitudes of female: The family aspirations of many female, for example in terms of bearing and rearing children, rarely coincide with the levels of support and provision required to allow female to break from their careers without disadvantage--even when female themselves want to. Indeed, the whole edifice of work organization discriminates against female in this as in other respects. In the hotel and catering industry the problem is compounded because of the high level of mobility required in order to reach senior management. The HCITB's finding that many female hotel managers were single seems to be true of successful business female in general. However, Guerrier (1986) notes that many female opt for college courses in hotel and catering management because it represents a resolution of pressures in the form of interest in management with interest in the traditionally female field of domestic science and cookery.

In this sense, many female are arguably misled early on in the process of career choice and do not realise the extent of either the general or industry specific discrimination they will face. When they do discover the extent of discrimination and lack of opportunity, many withdraw altogether or to the point where they limit their aspirations and resign themselves to lower levels of achievement. Certainly, once female have some experience of hotel and catering management education their expectations seem to diverge from those of men.

The HCITB (1984a) reports that both male and female students had similar aspirations concerning the post they would hold five years after leaving college, but female had lower expectations of their employment prospects upon their graduation, expectations which for the most part appear to have been realised. The HCITB also administered attitudinal tests to its female respondents and found that many shared male stereotypical views as to the nature of female as lacking in confidence to push themselves, insufficiently ambitious, more influenced by their emotions (which affected their behaviour as managers), less worthy as employees because of their physiological capacity for child-bearing and not aggressive or competitive enough.

The conventional role of hotel manager. In her study of female hotel managers, Guerrier (1986) highlighted a rarely recognized problem facing all managers but of particular relevance to female--namely that much of the work of hotel management is carried out in a semi-social setting (see also Nailon, 1968: Venison, 1983). In such jobs, promotion decisions may be affected by what Guerrier calls 'extra-functional variables', for example, sex, race and education. For female, jobs where contact with the public is involved may be particularly problematic. This is not simply because male managers and clients expect female to be servile and compliant with the demands of men but they also expect them to be attractive.

As suggested earlier, physical appearance is an issue

for *male* employers and clients and can give rise to such incidents as the Berni Inns sacking of female for not fitting the company's uniforms. As far as hotel management is concerned, managers must be acceptable to the predominantly male clientele and thus female have to contend with the twin difficulties of sexism and maintaining their authority. As Guerrier summarises: "Hotel companies may prefer men to female in certain management jobs because of their greater acceptability to (predominantly male) clients, as they might prefer an older man to a younger man. And a woman who is appointed to the job of hotel manager may find it harder than a man to acquire the status and credibility she needs with clients." Guerrier argues that the vicious circle of discrimination against female managers is compounded in the case of the requirement of the visibility of the post holder because it is often antithetical to the strategy adopted by token female in organizations, that is to become socially invisible, keep a low profile and willingly accept low profile jobs and promotions.

Career paths to hotel management. As noted earlier, Guerrier (1986) found that general managers in the hotel industry tend to need mobility and experience of food and beverage and accommodation/front of house management in order to achieve their position. However, food and beverage management tends to be a male preserve and female often find themselves in departments of low status such as housekeeping, the low status definition of which often derives from nothing more than the preponderance of female in such departments. How food and beverage management has become a male preserve is difficult to establish. However, one clue is to be found in the HCITB (1984a) report on female managers which found both that more men had craft qualifications than female and more men had worked their way up to management from the lower occupational echelons. The HCITB argues that it is common to find that men who have done this have held a considerable number of positions. Female by contrast follow a more formal route involving fewer positions. What is meant by 'formal route' in this context the HCITB does not make clear but it seems not unreasonable to assume that barriers to female 'working their way up' are greater than for men because of the confinement of female to predominantly part-time, low status and nonfood and beverage jobs.

Taking the argument one step further, it could also be that colleges constitute the main supply of potential female managers. Female thus enter the industry (with formal qualifications) at an age when ambitious upwardly mobile and relatively unqualified males have already acquired several years head start Not only is it difficult for female to acquire the necessary experience even to begin to qualify for general management but they must also contend with the industry's 'old boy network' which is frequently instrumental in mobility, *i.e.* in gaining jobs within any one unit or within units in a chain.

Career moves within the industry tend to be handled informally and in a personal manner, and managers higher in the organization may sponsor individual mobility. Since the majority of managers are men it is unsurprising that they tend to sponsor men in preference to female, with the result, as Guerrier (1986) implies, that female do not acquire the mobility deemed as necessary for the attainment of senior positions. Similarly, the traditional path to hotel general management predicated on mobility does not easily facilitate the aspirations of female who also desire a family life and may require to take a break in order to raise children. It is more difficult to re-enter hotel management than many other forms of management because absence leads to a break in a career route characterized by the acquisition of experience through mobility.

Discrimination against female: Many of the discriminatory practices directed towards female have been identified under the previous headings in this discussion. Some form pan of that wider social and industrial edifice of prejudice against female that ultimately limits them in all but a small number of cases to subordinate and ancillary roles. In this category falls the absence of adequate support facilities for female seeking to bear and raise children. Not all female wish to raise children, however, nor constantly find themselves in the position of having to contemplate this course of action. All female face more general forms of discrimination that derive from the patriarchal structure of social relations in society and are mediated in the work context by the nature of the industry and organization in which they work. In the hotel industry, the stereotype of the hotel manager, the entrenched nature of career paths and the essentially male control of service provision all present female with formidable barriers to career progression. Other forms of subtle or obvious discrimination against female managers in hotels and catering not already mentioned include the nature of training.

The HCITB (1984a) report on female managers found striking differences in the in-company training of men and female. A small number of female managers had received no training at all despite the availability of programmes. Where they had undergone such training it differed considerably from that of men in that female had taken (been pushed into taking?) courses in the ancillary management functions in which they are slowly coming to dominate (e.g. sales, marketing and personnel) rather than courses in operational management. Yet, as the HCITB shows, the majority of female on hotel and catering management courses express a considerable interest in a career in operational management.

One more problem that female managers have to overcome (more often than their male counterparts) in order to be successful is that of convincing their (usually male) superiors that they are committed to the organization. Stacey (1987) cites one woman with experience of food and beverage management to the effect that 'You have to work ten times as hard to prove yourself.

Further Stacey remarks, Guests may express surprise when a woman duty manager is sent to sort out a problem. But Tom Eckstein, personnel executive with recruitment consultants LMS says the old excuse 'the customer expects a man' no longer applies.... He sees a growth in female managers in personnel and training and sales and marketing, rather than in line management. But it's partly up to female themselves to put themselves forward.... David Coubrough managing director of Portfolio, another recruitment consultant, believes that female themselves draw back from being ambitious. A salutary example is given by Joanna Foster of the Industrial Society which is thinking of organizing a course, like some it has done for other industries, for female in catering management.

Clearly this was not intended as a piece of investigative journalism. The motivations for Eckstein's comments (let alone justifications) receive no attention. Nor do Coubrough's views of female's lack of ambition receive critical attention. In fact, this article, published in the hospitality industry's professional association's house magazine, typifies only too well the problems with all discussions of female's lack of progress in terms of their own attitudes and aspirations--namely that to adopt such a stance is really to indulge in the politics of victim blaming.

Blaming female themselves for their lack of progress conveniently diverts attention from the sexism of male-dominated social institutions and the lack of effort on the part of these institutions to take affirmative action to ensure equality in the treatment of male and female employees. Similarly, as Guerrier (1986) notes, blaming female in this context ignores the fact that any real lack of aspiration or ambition is a response to the perceived lack of opportunities rather than some form of innate disposition.

REFERENCES

Burgess, J. (1982), "Perspectives on gift exchange and hospitable behaviour", *International Journal of Hospitality Management*, Vol. 1 No.1, pp. 49-57.

Cassee, E.H. (1983), "Introduction", in Cassee, E. H., Reuland, R. (Eds), *The Management of Hospitality*, Pergamon, Oxford, pp. xiii-xxii..

Cassee, E.H., Reuland, R. (1983), "Hospitality in hospitals", in Cassee, E.H., Reuland, R. (Eds), *The Management of Hospitality*, Pergamon, Oxford, pp. 143-63..

Edgar, R., Umbreit, W. (1988), "Hospitality research: re-assessing our strategy", *The Cornell Hotel and Restaurant Administration Quarterly*, Vol. 29 No.2, pp. 51-6.

Fayol, H. (1949), *General and Industrial Management*, Pitman, London.

Gray, W.S., Ligouri, S.C. (1980), *Hotel and Motel Management Operations*, Prentice-Hall, Englewood Cliffs, NJ.

Heal, F. (1990), *Hospitality in Early Modern England*, Clarendon Press, Oxford.

Hepple, J., Kipps, M., Thomson, J. (1990), "The concept of hospitality and an evaluation of its applicability to the experience of hospital patients", *International Journal of Hospitality Management*, Vol. 9 No.4, pp. 305-17.

Jones, P. (1996), "Hospitality research - where have we got to?", *International Journal of Hospitality Management*, Vol. 15.

Jones, P. (1996), "The hospitality industry", in Jones, P. (Eds), *Introduction to Hospitality Operations*, Cassell, London, pp. 1-20.

Khan, M., Olsen, M. (1988), "An overview of research in hospitality education", *The Cornell Hotel and Restaurant Administration Quarterly*, Vol. 29 No.2, pp. 54-5.

King, C. A. (1995), "What is hospitality?", *International Journal of Hospitality Management*, Vol. 14 No.3/4, pp. 219-34.

Lewis, R. (1988), "Uses and abuses of hospitality research", *The Cornell Hotel and Restaurant Administration Quarterly*, Vol. 29 No.3, pp. 11-12.

Litteljohn, D. (1990), "Hospitality research: philosophies and progress", in Teare, R., Moutinho, L., Morgan, N. (Eds), *Managing and Marketing Services in the 1990s*, Cassell, , London.

Medlik, S., Airey, D.W. (1978), *Profile of the Hotel and Catering Industry*, 2nd ed., Heinemann, London.

Middleton, V.T. (1983), "Marketing in the hospitality industry", in Cassee, E.H., Reuland, R. (Eds), *The Management of Hospitality*, Pergamon, Oxford, pp. 51-68..

Muhlmann, W.E. (1932), "Hospitality", in Seligman, E.R.A. (Eds), *Encyclopaedia of Social Sciences*, Macmillan, New York, NY.

Nailon, P. (1982), "Theory in hospitality management", *International Journal of Hospitality Management*, Vol. 1 No.3, pp. 135-43.

Odgers, P. (1988), "Gale Odgers Publications", *The Hotel, Catering and Leisure Industry: A Student's Guide*, East Sussex.

Pfeifer, Y. (1983)), "Small business management", in Cassee, E.H., Reuland, R. (Eds), *The Management of Hospitality*, Pergamon, Oxford, pp. 189-202..

Reuland, R., Choudry, J., Fagel, A. (1985), "Research in the field of hospitality", *International Journal of Hospitality Management*, Vol. 4 No.4, pp. 141-6.

Ryan, C. (1980), *An Introduction to Hotel and Catering Economics*, Stanley Thornes, Cheltenham.

Slattery, P. (1983), "Social scientific methodology and hospitality management", *International Journal of Hospitality Management*, Vol. 2 No.1, pp. 9-14..

Taylor, S., Edgar, D. (1996), "Hospitality research: the emperor's new clothes?", *International Journal of Hospitality Management*, Vol. 15 No.3, pp. 211-27.

Tideman, M. C. (1983), "External influences on the hospitality industry", in Cassee, E.H., Reuland, R. (Eds), *The Management of Hospitality*, Pergamon, Oxford, pp. 1-24.

White, A. (1970), *Palaces of the People: A Social History of Commercial Hospitality*, Taplinger, New York, NY.

Wood, R. C. (1994), "Some theoretical perspectives on hospitality", in Seaton, A.L. (Eds), *Tourism: The State of the Art*, John Wilcy & Sons Ltd, Chichester, pp. 737-42.

Glossary

ADS. Alternate Distribution System, such as Expedia and Travelocity

Attendance Building. Marketing and promotional programs designed to increase attendance at conventions, trade shows, meetings, and events.

Attraction. Any visitor service or product which tourists would enjoy visiting or using. An attraction may not be an "attractor" but can still be an attraction. To be considered an attraction, a product must be: A. Findable (clearly located on maps and street addresses, and directions provided). If tourists can't find the facility, it is not a tourist attraction. B. Hours of operation clearly denoted in any and all promotional materials (if a tourist arrives only to find the attraction closed, it is not an attraction). Examples of attractions include everything from a theme park that attracts over a million visitors a year, to a produce stand by the side of the road. General all-inclusive term travel industry marketers use to refer to products that have visitor appeal, like museums, historic sites, performing arts institutions, preservation districts, theme parks, entertainment and national sites.

Attractor. A significant tourist attraction, which compels visitation. The primary "must sees" in an area. The top reasons a tourist would choose to visit this area.

AVHRM. Association of Vacation Home Rental Managers.

Bed Tax (Transient Occupancy Tax of TOT). City or county tax added to the price of a hotel room.

Benchmarking. The process of comparing performance and processes within an industry to assess relative position against either a set industry standard or against those who are "best in class" (Synergy, 2000).

Best Practice(s). A term used to designate highest quality, excellence, or superior practices in a particular field by a tourism operator.

Blocked rooms. Hotel rooms held without a deposit.

Blocked. (1) Hotel rooms held without deposit. (2) Hotel rooms, airline tickets or other travel services held for a specific client.

Booking. Term used to refer to a completed sale by a destination, convention center, facility, hotel or supplier (i.e. convention, meeting, trade show or group business booking).

Brigade. French term used to describe all the staff working on the floor of the restaurant or the kitchen.

Business Travel. Travel for commercial, governmental or educational purposes with leisure as a secondary motivation.

Business Travel. Travel for commercial, governmental or educational purposes with leisure as a secondary motivation.

Buyer. A member of the travel trade who reserves room blocks from accommodations or coordinates the development of a travel product.

BYO. Bring Your Own. A restaurant which allows patrons to bring their own alcohol.

Carrier. Any provider of mass transportation, usually used in reference to an airline.

Chambers of Commerce. Typically, a Chamber of Commerce will specialize in local economic development that can include tourism promotion.

Charter Group. Group travel in which a previously

organized group travels together, usually on a custom itinerary.

Commissions. A percent of the total product cost paid to travel agents and other travel product distributors for selling the product to the consumer.

Consumer Show. A product showcase for the general public. Differs from a "Trade Show" as a trade show generally targets industry professionals. Consumer Shows target the consumer. Often there is a charge to get into the show.

Convention and Visitors Bureau. These organizations are local tourism marketing organizations specializing in developing conventions, meetings, conferences and visitations to a city, county or region.

Conventions and Trade Shows. Major segment of travel industry business. Trade shows differ from conventions in that they have exhibit space that provides product exhibition and sales opportunities for suppliers, as well as information gathering and buying opportunities for customers.

Conversion Study. Research study to analyze whether advertising respondents actually were converted to travelers as a result of advertising and follow-up material.

Co-op Advertising. Advertising funded by two or more destinations and /or suppliers.

Cooperative Marketing. Marketing programs involving two or more participating companies, institutions or organizations.

Cooperative Partner. An independent firm or organization which works with a tourism office by providing cash or in-kind contributions to expand the marketing impact of the tourism officeÕs program.

Country of Residence. Consists of the country where she/he has lived for most of the past year (12 months), or for a shorter period if she/he intends to return within 12 months to live there.

Cover. Each diner at a restaurant.

CRS. Central Reservation System

CTRLA. Car and Truck Rental and Leasing Association.

Cultural tourism. Travel for the purpose of learning about cultures or aspects of cultures (NEAP, 2000).

CVB. Convention and Visitors Bureau.

Day visitors. Visitors who arrive and leave the same day for leisure, recreation and holidays, visiting friends and relatives, & business and professional.

Destination Marketing Organization (DMO). A company or other entity involved in the business of increasing tourism to a destination or improving its public image. Local tourism marketing organizations, such as convention and visitors bureaus or chambers of commerce.

Destination Marketing. Marketing a city, state, country, area or region to consumers and trade.

Destination. **A hotel, resort, attraction, city, region, or state.**

Discounted Fare. Negotiated air fare for convention, trade show, meeting, group and corporate travel.

Discover America. Theme used by the Travel Industry Association and its marketing partners to market travel within the United States.

Ecotourism. "Responsible travel to natural areas that conserves the environment and improves the welfare of local people," according to The International Ecotourism Society.

Fam Tours. Organized trips for travel agents, tour operators, tour wholesalers or other members of the travel trade for the purpose of educating and "familiarizing" them with tourism destinations. By seeing the destinations where they are sending travelers, the travel trade is better prepared to answer customer questions and promote travel to the location. Also called "fams" or "familiarization tours."

Familiarization Trip. A complimentary or reduced-rate travel program for travel agents, airline or rail employees or other travel buyers, designed to acquaint participants with specific destinations or suppliers and to stimulate the sale of travel. Familiarization tours, also called fam tours, are sometimes offered to journalists as research trips for the purpose of cultivating media coverage of specific travel products.

Feeder Airport/City. An outlying city which feeds travelers to hubs or gateway cities.

FIT (Free Independent Travel). Individual travel in which a tour operator has previously arranged blocks of rooms at various destinations in advance for use by individual travelers. These travelers travel independently, not in a group, usually by rental car or public transportation.

Foreign Independent Travel or Foreign Individual Travel (FIT). An international pre-paid unescorted tour that includes several travel elements such as accommodations, rental cars and sightseeing. A FIT operator specialises in preparing FITs documents at the request of retail travel agents. FITs usually receive travel vouchers to present to on-site services as verification of pre-payment.

Frequency. The number of times an advertisement appears during a given campaign.

Fulfillment. Servicing consumers and trade who request information as a result of advertising or promotional programs. Service often includes an 800 number, sales staff and distribution of materials.

Function. Term used to for specialty catering such as weddings, meetings, birthdays, dances and product launches etc.

Gateway or Gateway City. A major airport, seaport, rail or bus center through which tourists and travelers enter from outside the region.

GDS. Global Distribution System, such as Sabre and Worldspan

GIT (Groups Independent Travel). Group travel in which individuals purchase a group package in which they will travel with others along a pre-set itinerary.

Gourmet. French term, originally and still used to describe a person who is a critic of food and beverage. Also used to describe establishments that provide sophisticated food and beverage.

Gross lettings. This refers to all room lettings, i.e. both paid & complimentary listings are included

Group Rate. Negotiated hotel rate for convention, trade show, meeting, tour or incentive group.

Group Tour and Group Leader - Group Tour. A travel agent type company which plans motor coach trips. Group Leader: A small, informal group, such as a church group, scout troop, or social group. Usually one person plans the activities for the group. Some travel shows target these planners such as GLAMER.

Head in Beds. Industry slang referring to the primary marketing objective of accommodations and most destinations. increasing the number of overnight stays.

Hospitality Industry. Another term for the travel industry.

Hospitality. A general term used in travel & tourism describing the "hospitality industry"; Refers to the general greeting, welcoming, food service, etc

Hotel Package. A package offered by a hotel, sometimes consisting of no more than a room and breakfast; sometimes, especially at resort hotels, consisting of (ground) transportation, rooms, meals, sports facilities and other components.

Hub and Spoke. Air carriers use of selected cities as

"hubs" or connected points for service on their systems to regional destinations.

Hub. An airport or city which serves as a central connecting point for aircraft, trains or buses from outlying feeder airports or cities.

Icon. A facility or landmark which is visually synonymous with a destination.

IDS. Internet Distribution System

Incentive Tour. A trip offered as a prize, usually by a company to stimulate employee sales or productivity.

Incentive Travel. Travel offered as a reward for top performance and the business that develops, markets and operates these programs.

Inclusive Tour. A tour program that includes a variety of feature for a single rate (airfare, accommodations, sightseeing, performances, etc.)

Inclusive Tour. A tour program that includes a variety of feature for a single rate (airfare, accommodations, sightseeing, performances, etc.)

Inquiry. A request for more information about an attraction or destination.

International Marketing. Marketing a destination, product or service to consumers and the trade outside the of the United States.

IPU. Interface Processing Unit

Itinerary. A travel schedule provided by a travel agent for his/her customer. A proposed or preliminary itinerary may be rather vague or specific. A final itinerary however provides all details (flight numbers, departure times, reservation confirmation numbers) and describes planned activities.

Joint venture. A form of strategic alliance or co-operative arrangement where ownership is shared and a separate enterprise formed. This may strengthen existing businesses through shared expertise, capital, removal of competition and creation of economies of scale. International tourism joint ventures between foreign organisations and local partners facilitate introduction of foreign products into local markets.

Jungle tourism. Jungle tours have become a major component of green tourism in tropical destinations. A jungle is a subclimax tropical forest consisting of a tangled growth of lianas, trees and scrub which may form an almost impenetrable barrier to the tourist. Jungle tours are a relatively recent phenomenon of Western international tourism.

Key-informant Survey. This involves interviewing people who are likely to have some insight into a problem: operating managers; sales staff; managers; suppliers; and consultants.

Keying. A social convention by which social 'reality' is transformed and seen as something else, such as the presentation of a fight as mere horseplay. In tourism, a peculiar, inverted variety of keying is frequently employed: the 'as if' situation in which participants are induced to playfully make believe that presented settings, activities or events are 'real', when as tourists they may be well aware that such occurences are contrived.

Leisure Tourist. Leisure tourists, in contrast with business travellers, travel for pleasure and thus are not under any obligations to frequent specific destinations or facilities. They tend to be price and fashion conscious, concentrate their touristic activities to specific (vacation) times, and are influenced by marketing and publicity. Leisure tourism is heavily influenced by living standards, discretionary income levels and vacation entitlements.

Leisure Travel. Travel for recreational, educational, sightseeing, relaxing and other experiential purposes.

Length of Stay. This refers to the period of time which people spend in a destination. Many definitions require that visitors to a destination stay at least 24 hours or overnight, and less than one year, to be considered a tourist. Destination areas often look for means to extend tourists' length of stay in order to increase positive economic impacts.

Limited Bar. Restricted service of alcoholic beverages at a function. For example, $1000 limit for beer, wine and soft drinks, or unlimited beer wine and soft drinks for four hours. In both cases spirits would incur additional costs.

maître*d'*. Full term is 'maître d' hôtel'. Literally 'master of the hotel'. In English we sometimes call this position the headwaiter, but the French term is frequently used.

Market Share. The percentage of business within a market category.

Market Volume. The total number of travelers within a market category.

Maximum Room Nights. This is calculated based on the total room inventory for all gazetted hotels.

Mise en place. Literally this means to 'put in place' and generally refers to pre-service preparation, including setting the tables and stocking up the stations. Also used in the kitchen, where it refers to the pre-preparation before cooking takes place.

Mission (Sales). A promotional and sales trip coordinated by a state travel office, conventional and visitors bureau or key industry member to increase product awareness, sales and to enhance image. Target audiences may include tour operators, wholesales, incentive travel planners, travel agents, meeting planners, convention and trade show managers and media. Missions often cover several international or domestic destinations and include private and public sector participants. Mission components can include receptions, entertainment representatives of the destination, presentations and pre- scheduled sales and media calls.

Motorcoach. Deluxe equipment used by most tour operators in group tour programs. Amenities include reclining seats, bathrooms, air conditioning, good lighting and refreshment availability.

Nature Tourism. Travel to unspoiled places to experience and enjoy nature.

Net Rate. The rate provided to wholesalers and tour operators that can be marked up to sell to the customer.

No Show. A customer with a reservation at a restaurant, hotel, etc. who fails to show up and does not cancel.

NTA. National Tour Association, comprised of domestic tour operators.

Occupancies. A percentage indicating the number of bed nights sold (compared to number available) in a hotel, resort, motel or destination.

Occupancy Rate. A tourism business occupancy rate refers to the number of airline seats or the units of hotel room space sold. This demand is usually measured as a percentage of available seats or space occupied for a given period of time. It is calculated by dividing the number of occupied rooms/seats by the total number available for sale during the same period.

Open Bar. unrestricted service of alcoholic beverages at a function. plated food presentation of food on plates by kitchen staff.

Outbound. Outbound tourism is defined as tourism involving residents of a country travelling to another country. Outbound tour operators offer package tours abroad. They either operate the tours themselves, or they commission the services of an inbound operator to handle local arrangements at the destination. The country from which the tourists originate is known as the generating market or country.

Package Tour. A saleable travel product offering an inclusive price with several travel elements that would otherwise be purchased separately. Usually has a predetermined price, length of time and features but can also offer options for separate purchase.

Package. A fixed price salable travel product that makes it easy for a traveler to buy and enjoy a destination or several destinations. Packages offer a mix of elements like transportation, accommodations, restaurants, entertainment, cultural activities, sightseeing and car rental.

Paid Lettings. This refers to room lettings that are paid for by hotel guests

Peaks and Valleys. The high and low end of the travel season. Travel industry marketers plan programs to build consistent year-round business and event out the "peaks and valleys."

Person Trip Visit. Every time a person travels more than 100 miles (round-trip) in a day or stays overnight away from their primary domicile, whether for business or leisure purposes, they make one "person trip visit."

Pow Wow. The largest international travel marketplace held in the United States, sponsored by the Travel Industry Association of America.

Press Trips. Organized trips for travel writers and broadcasters for the purpose of assisting them in developing stories about tourism destinations. Often, journalists travel independently, though with the assistance of a state's office of tourism of a DMO.

Press/Publicity Release. A news article or feature story written by the subject of the story for delivery and potential placement in the media.

Property. A hotel, motel, inn, lodge or other accommodation facility.

Quality. In tourism, the product is often intangible and quality is not apparent until after it is consumed. Quality has been defined as zero defects or defections, but still may be defined by the customer. The International Organisation for Standardisation defines quality as 'the totality of features and characteristics of a product or service that bear on its ability to satisfy stated or implied needs'. Others believe that quality is a combination of outcome and processes, including internal and external conditions, and is obtained when the expectations and needs of customers are met.

Rack Card. The typical tourism brochure sized 4" x 9" and used primarily in tourism racks. Also known as a "teaser."

Rack Rate. The official cost posted by a hotel, attraction or rental car, but not used by tour operators. The rate accommodations quote to the public. Group rates, convention, trade show, meeting and incentive travel rates are negotiated by the hotel and program organizers.

Reach. The percentage of people within a specific target audience reached by an advertising campaign.

Receptive Operator. Specialists in handling arrangements for incoming visitors at a destination including airport transfers, local sightseeing, restaurants, accommodations, etc. Receptive operators can be a travel agent or tour operator.

Repeat Business. Business that continues to return, thereby generating increased profits.

Reservation Systems (Automation Vendors). Computerized systems leased to travel agencies offering airline, hotel, car rental and selected tour availability and bookings. Systems are affiliated with major carriers, including American (Sabre), United (Apollo), Eastern (System One), TWA (PARS), and Delta (DATAS II) and feature flight schedules of the sponsoring and other carriers, plus additional travel products.

Resident. A person living in a given country, whether he is a national or not.

Retail Agent. A travel agent.

Retail Agent. A travel agent. **Retailer.** Another term for travel agents who sell travel products directly to consumers.

Retailer. Another term for travel agents who sell travel products directly to consumers.

Room Block. Several rooms held for a group.

Room. Double: No guarantee of two beds; Double Double: Two double beds (or two queens or kings); Twin: Two twin beds (or two doubles or queens)

Sales Mission. Where suppliers from one DMO travel together to another state of country for the purpose of collectively promoting travel to their area. Sales missions may include educational seminars for travel agents and tour operators.

Sales Seminar. An educational session in which travel agents, tour operators, tour wholesales or other members of the travel trade congregate to receive briefings about tourism destinations.

Shells. A marketing and sales promotional piece that depicts a destination, accommodation or attraction on the cover and provides space for copy to be added at a later date. Usually shells fit a #10 envelope.

Site Inspection. An assessment tour of a destination or facility by a meeting planner, convention or trade show manager, site selection committee, tour operator, wholesaler or incentive travel manager to see if it meets their needs and requirements prior to selecting a specific site for an event. After site selection, a site inspection may be utilized to make arrangements.

Spouse Program. Special activities planned for those who accompany an attendee to a convention, trade show or meeting. Note that programs today are not simply for women, but rather for men and women, spouses and friends. Programs must be creatively designed to interest intelligent and curious audiences.

Station. The preparation, or worktable allocated to dining room staff. It also serves as limited storage for crockery, cutlery and table linen in the restaurant or dining room.

Supplier. Those businesses that provide industry products like accommodations, transportation, car rentals, restaurants and attractions.

Sustainable tourism. This is, according to the World Tourism Organisation, "envisaged as leading to management of all resources in such a way that economic, social and aesthetic needs can be fulfilled with maintaining cultural integrity, essential ecological processes, biological diversity, and life support systems."

Table d'hôte menu. Set menu of two or more courses and maybe one or more choices within each course. The price is pre-set for this style of meal.

Target Audience/Market. A specific demographic, sociographic target at which marketing communications are directed.

Target Rating Points. TRPÕs are a statistical measurement which allows one to evaluate the relative impact of differing advertising campaigns.

Tariff. Rate of fare quoted and published by a travel industry supplier (i.e. hotels, tour operators, etc.) Usually an annual tariff is produced in booklet form for use in sales calls at trade shows.

TIA. Travel Industry Association of America.

TIA. Travel Industry Association of America.

TOT. Transient Occupancy Tax.

Tour Operator. Develops, markets and operates group travel programs that provide a complete travel experience for one price and includes transportation (airline, rail, motorcoach, and/or ship), accommodations, sightseeing, selected meals and an escort. Tour operators market directly to the consumer, through travel agents and are beginning to be listed on computerized reservation systems.

Tour Wholesaler. An individual or company that sells tour packages and tour product to travel agents. Tour wholesalers usually receive a 20% discount from accommodations, transportation companies and attractions and pass on a 10 to 15% discount to the retail agent.

Tourism Receipts. Tourism Receipts (TR) measures the total revenue received by Singapore from tourism activity. It includes all payments and prepayments for goods and services made by visitors, transit passengers, air & sea crew and foreign students (staying for one year or less) during their stay in Singapore. Visitors' payments to our national carriers (SIA & Silk Air) for international transport are also included.

Tourism. Leisure travel.

Tourism. The business of providing and marketing services and facilities for pleasure travellers. Thus, the concept or tourism is of direct concern to governments, carriers, and the lodging, restaurant and entertainment industries and of indirect concern to virtually every industry and business in the world.

Tourist. Temporary visitor staying at least twenty-four hours in the country visited for a purpose classified as either holiday (recreation, leisure, sport and visit to family, friends or relatives), business, official mission, convention, or health reasons.

Tourist/Visitor/Traveler. Any person who travels either for leisure or business purposes more than 100 miles (round-trip) in a day or who stays overnight away from his/her primary domicile.

Tourist/Visitor/Traveler. Any person who travels either for leisure or business purposes more than 100 miles (round-trip) in a day or who stays overnight away from his/her primary domicile.

Trade Show. A product showcase for a specific industry. Generally it is not open to the public. Differs from a "Consumer Show" in that a trade show targets the professional industry, while a consumer show targets consumers.

Transient Occupancy Tax. TOT or bed tax is a locally set tax on the cost of commercial accommodations and campgrounds.

Travel Agent. (1) An individual who arranges travel for individuals or groups. Travel agents may be generalists or specialists (cruises, adventure travel, conventions and meetings.) The agents receive a 10 to 15% commission from accommodations, transportation companies and attractions for coordinating the booking of travel. They typically coordinate travel for their customers at the same or lower cost than if the customer booked the travel on his/her own. (2) The individual who sells travel services, issues tickets and provides other travel services to the travel services to the traveller sat the retail level.

Travel Product. Refers to any product or service that is bought by or sold to consumers of trade including accommodations, attractions, events, restaurants, transportation, etc.

Travel Seasons. Travel industry business cycles including: *Peak:* Primary travel season *Off Peak:* Period when business is slowest *Shoulder:* Period between peak and off peak periods when business is stronger, but has room for growth.

Travel Trade. The collective term for tour operators, wholesalers and travel agents.

Travel. Leisure and other travel including travel for business, medical care, education, etc. All tourism is travel, but not all travel is tourism.

Traveler. (1) Definitions very, but in general a traveler is someone who leaves their own economic trade area, (usually going a distance of a minimum of fifty to one hundred miles) and stays overnight. (2) Someone who leaves his or her own economic trade area, (usually going a distance of a minimum of fifty to one hundred miles) and stays overnight.

Underdevelopment. Within development theory, the concept of underdevelopment suggests that wealthy capitalist countries have held back the development of so-called Third World countries. Tourism in Third World destinations is controlled for the economic benefit of foreign owners, reinforces dependency, lacks involvement of local decision makers, leads to negative sociocultural impacts, and results in the promotion of staged attractions to capture an international tourism market.

Urban recreation. The concept of urban recreation covers recreational activity that takes place in an urban environment in contrast to a rural setting. Participants in such activities are either urban residents themselves, day visitors from rural areas, or tourists. The major activities are shopping, visits to heritage sites, museums, movie theatres, operas, sport and music events, and indoor sports activities.

VFR. Visiting friends and relatives

Visitor Arrivals. Includes all who go through immigration clearance regardless of length of stay. This excludes the following: (a) All Malaysian citizens arriving by land, (b) Returning Singapore citizens residing abroad, (c) Non-resident air and sea crew (except for sea crew flying in to join ship), (d) All visitors arriving and leaving Singapore on the same ship/vessel and stayed in Singapore for less than 24 hours are not required to complete Disembarkation / Embarkation (D/E) cards, if passenger manifest is submitted, (e) All organised tour groups leaving Singapore for Johor Bahru, Batam and Bintan, returning on the same day are not required to complete Disembarkation / Embarkation (D/E) cards, if passenger manifest is submitted, (f) Air transit passengers

Visitor Expenditure. Includes expenditure incurred during a visitor's stay in Singapore, or prepayment by non-package tour visitors (this took effect from 1995). This excludes: (a) international air and sea fare. It is made up of the following components: (a) Shopping, (b) Accommodation, (c) Entertainment, (d) Sightseeing, (e) Food & beverage (f) Local transportation, (g) Medical/dental treatment, (h) Miscellaneous

Visitor. Any person visiting a country other than that in which he has his usual place of residence for any reason other than following an occupation remunerated from within the country visited.

Visitors Center. Travel information center located at a destination to make it easier for visitors to plan their stay; often operated by a convention and visitors bureau, chamber of commerce or tourism promotion organization.

Vouchers. Forms or coupons provided to a traveler who purchases a tour that indicate that certain tour components have been prepaid. Vouchers are then exchanged for tour components like accommodations, meals, sightseeing, theater tickets, etc. during the actual trip.

World Tourism Organisation (WTO). The World Tourism Organisation, a UN-related institution based in Madrid that collects data on tourism and lobbies on behalf of the industry.

World Travel and Tourism Council (WTTC). The WTTC is made up of chief executives from all sectors of the tourism industry, including accommodation, catering, cruises, entertainment, recreation, transportation and travel-related services. Its central goal is to work with governments to realise the full economic impact of tourism. Its millennium vision is to make tourism a strategic economic and employment priority, to move towards open and competitive markets, to pursue sustainable development, and to eliminate barriers to growth.

Xenophobia. Xenophobia is an irrational fear or contempt of strangers or foreigners. This ancient cultural and political phenomenon is also present in contemporary tourism, mainly manifesting itself in the hostile attitudes of residents towards tourists. Xenophobia should be considered in domestic and international tourism in terms of economic, social and cultural distance, which is accentuated by the type and the number of tourists and the rate of tourism development.

Yield Management. The concept of maximising the revenue by raising or lowering prices in respect to demand is known as yield management. The necessary conditions for a successful application of yield management include a fairly fixed capacity, high fixed costs, low variable costs, fluctuations in demand and similarity of inventory capacity. Yield management was popularised with the deregulation of the US airline industry and it is extensively used by this and other tourism sectors.

Yield Percentage. To demonstrate the variable effect of both average price rates and occupancy rates, tourism managers develop a comparison focusing upon the yield rates during a given period of time. Managers can increase the yield rate (see yield management) by raising rates when demand is high.

Zoning. Zoning seeks to regulate land uses by separating them based on incompatibility, or allowing like/compatible uses to co-exist. A basic principle of tourism zoning is the conservation of specific environmental features such as wetlands, archaeological and historic sites, important stands of vegetation and unusual geological features. Related to this is the maintenance of visual diversity. Also important is the achievement of successful functional groupings of resort facilities and activities, such as accommodation, commercial and cultural facilities, and recreation facilities in suitable areas. Buffer zones containing mixtures of tourism facilities and less fragile environmental preservation requirements may also be designated.

Bibliography

Aaker, D.A., Keller, K.L. (1990), "Consumer evaluations of brand extensions", *Journal of Marketing*, Vol. 54 pp. 27-41.

Aalberts, R.J., Seidman, L.H. (1996), "Sexual-harassment policies for the workplace—a tale of two companies", *Cornell Hotel and Restaurant Administration Quarterly*, Vol. 37 No.5, pp. 78-85.

Aaron, T., Dry, E. (1992), "Sexual harassment in the hospitality industry", *The Cornell Hotel and Restaurant Administration Quarterly*, Vol. 33 No.2, pp. 93-5.

Abercrombie, N., Warde, A., Soothill, K., Urry, J., Walby, S. (1994), *Contemporary British Society*, 2nd ed., Polity, Cambridge.

Adams, D.J. (1991), "Do corporate failure prediction models work?", *International Journal of Contemporary Hospitality Management*, Vol. 3 No.4, pp. 25-9.

Adkins, L. (1995), *Gendered work: Sexuality, Family and the Labour Market*, Open University Press, Buckingham

Ahmed, Z.U., Krohn, F.B. (1990), "Marketing dynamics of a hotel tax: the case of Chautauqua County, New York", Vol. 8 No.2, pp. 15-26.

Airey, D., Johnson, S. (1999), "The content of tourism degree courses in the UK", *Tourism Management*, Vol. 20 No.2, pp. 229-35.

Alberto, L.M. "Contemporary issues in hotel and restaurant law: use and occupancy of a guest's room-entry by innkeeper", Vol. 14 No.1991, pp. 1-8.

Aldrich, H.E. (1979), *Organizations and Environments*, Prentice-Hall, Englewood Cliffs, NJ.

Alexander, N., McKenna, A. (1999), "Rural tourism in the heart of England", *International Contemporary Hospitality Management*, Vol. 10 No.5, pp. 203-7.

Allen, R.E. (1994), "Hospitality group: underpromising and overdelivering", *Nation's Restaurant News*, Vol. 28 No.13, pp. 110-2.

Allison, J.H., Byron, M.A. (1996), "Aligning quality improvement with strategic goals at ANA Hotel San Francisco", *National Productivity Review*, Vol. 15 No.2, pp. 89-99.

Almanza, B.A., Jaffe, W., Lin, L. (1994), "Use of the service attribute matrix to measure consumer satisfaction", *Hospitality Research Journal*, Vol. 17 No.2, pp. 63-75.

Altman, L.A., Brothers, L.R. (1995), "Career longevity of hospitality graduates", Vol. 13 No.2, pp. 77-84.

Amoah, V., Baum, T. (1997), "Tourism education: policy versus practice", *International Journal of Contemporary Hospitality Management*, Vol. 9 No.1, pp. 5-12.

Amoah, V., Baum, T. (1997), "Tourism education: policy versus practice", *International Journal of Contemporary Hospitality Management*, Vol. 9 No.1, pp. 5-12.

Ananth, M., DeMicco, F.J., Moreo, P.J., Howey, R.M. (1992), "Marketplace lodging needs of mature travellers", *The Cornell Hotel and Restaurant Quarterly*, Vol. 33 No.4, pp. 12-24.

Anderson, G.K. (1991), "The education and training of general managers in Scotland", *International Journal of Contemporary Hospitality Management*, Vol. 3 No.2, pp. 26-9 .

Armstrong, R.W., Seng, T.B. (2000), "Corporate-customer satisfaction in the banking industry of Singapore", *International Journal of Bank Marketing*, Vol. 18 No.3, pp. 97-111.

Arnaldo, M.J (1981), "Hotel general managers: a profile", *The Cornell Hotel and Restaurant Administrative Quarterly*, Vol. 22 No.3, pp. 53-6.

Ashworth, A., Harvey, R.C. (1995), "Mass higher education: a first stage model for the United Kingdom", *Quality Assurance in Education*, Vol. 3 No.4, pp. 6.

Ashworth, P., Saxton, J. (1992), *Managing Work Experience*, Routledge, London.

Ayala, H. (1996b), "Resort ecotourism: a master plan for experience management", *Cornell Hotel and Restaurant Administration Quarterly*, Vol. 37 No.5, pp. 54-61.

Ayala, H. "The unresearched phenomenon of 'hotel circuit".

Barrows, C., Gallo, M., Mulleady, T. (1996), "AIDS in the US hospitality industry: Recommendations for education and policy formulation", International Journal of Contemporary Hospitality Management, Vol. 8 No.1.

Barrows, C.W., Hobson, J.S.P. (1993), "A model for teaching service management in hospitality", *International Journal of Contemporary Hospitality Management*, Vol. 5 No.3, pp. 32-6.

Baum, T. (1990), "Competencies for hotel management: industry expectations of education", *International Journal of Contemporary Hospitality Management*, Vol. 2 No.4, pp. 13-16.

Baum, T. (1993), "Human resources in tourism: an introduction", in Baum, T. (Eds), *Human Resource Issues in International Tourism*, Butterworth-Heinemann, Oxford, pp. 3-21.

Baum, T. (1995), *Managing Human Resources in the European Tourism and Hospitality Industry: A Strategic Approach*, Chapman & Hall, London.

Baum, T. (1996), "Unskilled work and the hospitality industry: myth or reality?", *International Journal of Hospitality Management*, Vol. 15 No.3, pp. 1-3.

Bould, A., Breeze, G., Teare, R. (1992), "Promoting service excellence through service branding", *International*

Journal of Contemporary Hospitality Management, Vol. 4 No.1 , pp. iii-vi.

Bradley, A., Ingold, A. (1993), "An investigation of yield management in Birmingham hotels", *International Journal of Contemporary Hospitality Management*, Vol. 5 No.2, pp. 13-16.

Brander-Brown, J. (1994), "Effective management control systems for the UK hotel sector", *International Journal of Contemporary Hospitality Management*, Vol. 6 No.5, pp. i-iii.

Brander-Brown, J., McDonnell, B. (1995), "The balanced score-card: short term guest or long-term resident?", *International Journal of Contemporary Hospitality Management*, Vol. 7 pp. 7-11.

Breiter, D., Tyink, S.A., Corey-Tuckwell, S. (1995), "Bergstrom Hotels: a case study in quality", *International Journal of Contemporary Hospitality Management*, Vol. 7 No.6, pp. 14-18.

Brotherton, R., Coyle, M. (1990), "Managing instability in the hospitality operations environment. Part One: variability", *International Journal of Contemporary Hospitality Management*, Vol. 2 No.3, pp. 24-32.

Brown, D. (1996), "Team rewards: lessons from the coal-face", *Team Performance Management*, Vol. 2 No.2, pp. 6-12.

Brown, M. (1996), "Environmental policy in the hotel sector: green strategy or stratagem?", International Journal of Contemporary Hospitality Management, Vol. 8 No.3.

Brownell, J. (1994), " Creating strong listening environments: a key hospitality management task", *International Journal of Contemporary Hospitality Management*, Vol. 6 No.3, pp. 3-10.

Brymer, R.A. (1991), "Employee empowerment: a guest-driven leadership strategy", *Cornell Hotel and Restaurant Administration Quarterly*, Vol. 32 No.1, pp. 56-8.

Burgess, C. (1994), "The education and training needs of the hotel financial controller", *International Journal of Contemporary Hospitality Management*, Vol. 6 No.5, pp. 9-13.

Burgess, C. (1996), "A profile of the hotel financial controller in the United Kingdom, United States and Hong Kong", International Journal of Hospitality Management, Vol. 15 No.1, pp.19-28.

Butcher, W.C. (1997), "The need for ethical leadership", Executive Speeches, Vol. 11 No.5, pp.83-6.

Callan, R.J. (1992), " Jersey's hotel grading scheme: an idiosyncratic approach", *International Journal of Contemporary Hospitality Management*, Vol. 4 No.3, pp. 30-36 .

Callan, R.J. (1992), "Quality control at Avant Hotels--the debut of BS 5750", *Service Industries Journal*, Vol. 12 No.1, pp. 17-33.

Callan, R.J. (1993), "An appraisal of UK hotel quality grading schemes", *International Journal of Contemporary Hospitality Management*, Vol. 5 No.5, pp. 10-18.

Callan, R.J. (1994), "Statutory hotel registration and grading: a review", *International Journal of Contemporary Hospitality Management*, Vol. 6 No.3, pp. 11-17.

Calver, S., Vierich, W. , Phillips, J. (1993), "Leisure in later life ", *International Journal of Contemporary Hospitality Management*, Vol. 5 No.1, pp. 4-9.

Camisón, C. (1996), "Total quality management in hospitality: An application of the EFQM model", Tourism Management, Vol. 17 No.3, pp.191-201.

Carson, D., Cromie, S., McGowan, P., Hill, J. (1995),

Marketing and Entrepreneurship in SMEs: An Innovative Approach, Prentice-Hall, London..

Caruana, A., Pitt, L.F., Morris, M.H. (1995), "Are there excellent service firms and do they perform well?", *Service Industries Journal*, Vol. 15 No.3, pp. 243-56.

Caster, D. (1995), "Letter from the editor", QED News, Vol. 2 No.2, pp.2.

Chaffee, E.E., Sherr, L.A. (1992), Quality: Transforming Postsecondary Education, (ASHE-ERIC Report 3).

Charles, K.R., Marshall, L.H. (1992), "Motivational preferences of Caribbean hotel workers: an exploratory study", *International Journal of Contemporary Hospitality Management*, Vol. 4 No.3, pp. 25-9.

Christensen, J. (1993), "The diversity dynamic: implications for organisations in 2005", *Hospitality Research Journal*, Vol. 17 No.1, pp. 69-86.

Church, I., Lincoln, G. (1998), "Quality management", in Thomas, R. (Eds),*The Management of Small Tourism and Hospitality Firms*, Cassell,, London, pp.138-55.

Clifton, W.J., Johnson, K. (1994), "A structural analysis of the European hotel sector: a simple case of déjà-vu?", *International Journal of Contemporary Hospitality Management*, Vol. 6 No.4, pp. vii-viii.

Close, A., Teare, R. (1990), "Effective management development", *International Journal of Contemporary Hospitality Management*, Vol. 2 No.4, pp. i-ii.

Conaway, R.N., Fernandez, T.L. (2000), "Ethical preferences among business leaders: implications for business schools", Business Communication Quarterly, Vol. 63 No.1, pp.23-8.

Connelly, F.M., Clandinin, D.J. (1988), Teachers as Curriculum Planners: Narratives of Experience, Teachers' College Press, New York, NY.

Cooper, C. (1993), "An analysis of the relationship between

industry and education in travel and tourism", *Teros International*, Vol. 1 No.1.

Costa, J., Teare, R. (1994), "Environmental scanning and the Portuguese hotel sector", *International Journal of Contemporary Hospitality Management*, Vol. 6 No.5, pp. iv-vii.

Counsell, S. (1991), "Fifty-seven-fifty and all that", *International Journal of Contemporary Hospitality Management*, Vol. 3 No.3, pp. iii-iv.

Crawford-Welch, S. (1991), "Marketing hospitality into the 21st century", *International Journal of Contemporary Hospitality Management*, Vol. 3 No.3, pp. 21-7.

Crawford-Welch, S., Tse, E. (1990), "Mergers, acquisitions and alliances in the European hospitality industry", *International Journal of Contemporary Hospitality Management*, Vol. 2 No.1, pp. 10-16.

Dickinson, A., Ineson, E.M. (1993), "The selection of quality operative staff in the hotel sector", *International Journal of Contemporary Hospitality Management*, Vol. 5 No.1, pp. 16-21.

Dodrill, K., Riley, M. (1992), "Hotel workers' orientations to work: the question of autonomy and scope", *International Journal of Contemporary Hospitality Management*, Vol. 4 No.1 , pp. 23-5.

Dodwell, S., Simmons, P. (1994), "Trials and tribulations in the pursuit of quality improvement", *International Journal of Contemporary Hospitality Management*, Vol. 6 No.1/2, pp. 14-18.

Dodwell, S., Simmons, P. (1994), "Trials and tribulations in the pursuit of quality improvement", *International Journal of Contemporary Hospitality Management*, Vol. 6 pp. 14-18.

Donaldson, T., Werhane, P.H., Cording, M. (2002), Ethical Issues in Business, 7th ed., Prentice Hall, New Jersey.

Doren, K., Blackman, D. (1993), "Communication systems and connectivity for the 'intelligent bedroom' of the future", *International Journal of Contemporary Hospitality Management*, Vol. 5 No.2, pp. 25-6.

DTI (1997), *Statistical Bulletin: Small and Medium-Sized Enterprise (SME) Statistics for the United Kingdom, 1996*, DTI, Sheffield..

DuFrene, D.D., Elliott-Howard, F.E., Daniel, L.G. (1990), "Development of a rating scale for determining importance of ethical issues in business," Delta Pi Epsilon Research Conference Proceedings, pp. 57-62.

Edgar, D, Nisbet, L. (1996), "A matter of chaos - some issues for hospitality businesses", International Journal of Contemporary Hospitality Management, Vol. 8 No.2.

Edgar, D.A. (1996), "The strategic gap: a multi-site, short break perspective", in Johns, N. (Eds), *Productivity Management in Hospitality and Tourism*, Cassell, London, pp. 38-54.

Edgar, D.A., Littlejohn, D.L., Allardyce, M.L. (1994), "Strategic clusters and strategic space: the case of the short break market", *International Journal of Contemporary Hospitality Management*, Vol. 6 No.5, pp. 20-26 .

Elliot, J., Johns, N. (1993), "The influence of international tourism trends on the design of leisure resorts", *International Journal of Contemporary Hospitality Management*, Vol. 5 No.2 , pp. 6-9.

Elloy, D., McCombs, T (1996), "Application of open systems theory in a manufacturing plant", *Team Performance Management*, Vol. 2 No.3, pp. 15-22.

Enghagen, L.K. (1990), "Teaching ethics in hospitality and tourism education", Hospitality Research Journal, Vol. 14 No.2, pp.467-74.

Enghagen, L.K., Hott, D.D. (1992), "Students' perceptions of ethical issues in the hospitality and tourism industry", Hospitality Research Journal, Vol. 15 No.2, pp.41-50.

Epstein, E.M. (1989), "Business ethics, corporate good citizenship and the corporate social policy process: a view from the United States", Journal of Business Ethics, No.8, pp.583-95.

Esquivel, M.A., Kleiner, B.H. (1996), "The importance of conflict in work team effectiveness", *Team Performance Management*, Vol. 2 No.3, pp. 42-8.

Evans, M., McDonagh, P., Moutinho, L. (1991), "The development of the Portuguese hotel industry: contributory factors", *International Journal of Contemporary Hospitality Management*, Vol. 3 No.2, pp. 10-13.

Fahey, L., King, W.R., Narayanan, V.K. (1983), "Environmental scanning and forecasting in strategic planning - the state of the art", in Hussey, D.E. (Eds),The Truth About Corporate Planning: International Research Into the Practice of Planning, Pergamon Press, Oxford, pp.495-509.

Fender, D., Litteljohn, D. (1992), "Forward planning in uncertain times", *International Journal of Contemporary Hospitality Management*, Vol. 4 No.3, pp. i-iv .

Fender, D.J.W. (1990), "'Getting started'—the use of simple strategic frameworks", *International Journal of Contemporary Hospitality Management*, Vol. 2 No.3, pp. iv-vi.

Festinger, L., Schachter, S., Back, K. (1950), *Social Pressures in Informal Groups: A Study of a Housing Project*, Harper and Row, New York.

Fockler, S. (1996), "All-suite hotels in the USA", Travel and Tourism Analyst, Vol. 3 pp.44-64.

Forte, R., Teare, R. (1990), "Responding to the competitive challenge of the 1990s", *International Journal of Contemporary Hospitality Management*, Vol. 2 No.3, pp. i-ii.

Friel, M. (1998), "Marketing", in Thomas, R. (Eds),*The Management of Small Tourism and Hospitality Firms*, Cassell, London, pp.117-37.

Gamble, P.R. (1990), "Culture shock, computers and the art of making decisions", *International Journal of Contemporary Hospitality Management*, Vol. 2 No.1, pp. 4-9

Gamble, P.R. (1991), "An information technology strategy for the hospitality industry of the 1990s", *International Journal of Contemporary Hospitality Management*, Vol. 3 No.1, pp. 10-16.

Gamble, P.R. (1991), "IT connectivity and pan-European hospitality marketing", *International Journal of Contemporary Hospitality Management*, Vol. 3 No.4, pp. 37-41.

Goldsmith, A., Zahari, M.S.M (1994), "Hospitality education in Malaysia: filling the skill gap", *International Journal of Contemporary Hospitality Management*, Vol. 6 No.6, pp. 27-31.

Gu, Z. (1994), "Hospitality return, risk and performance indexes: a ten-year examination", *Hospitality Research Journal*, Vol. 17 No.3, pp. 17-26.

Gunz, S., McCutcheon, J. (1998), "Are academics committed to accounting ethics education?", Journal of Business Ethics, Vol. 17 No.11, pp.1145-54.

Hair, J. Jr, Anderson, R.E., Tatham, R.L., Black, W.C. (1995), Multivariate Data Analysis with Reading, Prentice-Hall, Englewood Cliffs, NJ.

Hall, S.S.J. (1992), Ethics in Hospitality Management, Educational Institute of the American Hotel and Motel Association, East Lansing, MI.

Hallam, G., Baum, T. (1996), "Contracting out food and beverage operations in hotels: a comparative study of practice in North America and the United Kingdom", International Journal of Hospitality Management, Vol. 15 No.1, pp.41-50.

Harris, K. (1996), "International hospitality marketing on the Internet: Project 'Interweave'", International Journal of Hospitality Management, Vol. 15 No.2, pp.155-63.

Harris, P.J. (1992), "Hospitality profit planning in the practical environment: integrating cost-volume-profit analysis with spreadsheet management", *International Journal of Contemporary Hospitality Management*, Vol. 4 No.4, pp. 24-32 .

Harris, P.R., Harris, K.G. (1996), "Managing effectively through teams", *Team Performance Management*, Vol. 2 No.3, pp. 23-6.

Hartman, S., Yrle, A. (1996), "Can the hobo phenomenon help explain voluntary turnover?", International Journal of Contemporary Hospitality Management, Vol. 8 No.4.

Heymann, K. (1992), "Quality management: a ten-point model", *Cornell Hotel and Restaurant Administration Quarterly*, Vol. 33 No.5, pp. 50-60.

Higgs, M. (1996), "Overcoming the problems of cultural differences to establish success for international management teams", *Team Performance Management*, Vol. 2 No.1, pp. 36-43.

Hillman, T., Albert, J. (1999), "Total quality management and higher education: the employers' perspective", Total Quality Management, Vol. 10 No.7, pp.997-1009.

Hing, N. (1996), "An empirical analysis of the benefits and limitations for restaurant franchisees", International

Journal of Hospitality Management, Vol. 15 No.2, pp.177-87.

Hirst, M. "Creating a service-driven culture globally", *International Journal of Contemporary Hospitality Management*, Vol. 4 No.1, pp. i-iii.

Hobson, J.S.P. (1994), "Feng shui: its impacts on the Asian hospitality industry", *International Journal of Contemporary Hospitality Management*, Vol. 6 No.6, pp. 21-6 .

Hubrecht, J., Teare, R. "A strategy for partnership in total quality service ", *International Journal of Contemporary Hospitality Management*, Vol. 5 No.3, pp. i-v .

Hughes, H. (1993), "The structural theory of business demand: a comment", *International Journal of Hospitality Management*, Vol. 12 No.4, pp.309-11.

Ineson, E.M., Brown, S.H.P. (1992), "The use of biodata for hotel employee selection ", *International Journal of Contemporary Hospitality Management*, Vol. 4 No.2, pp. 8-12.

Ingold, T., Worthington, T. (1994), "Prophylaxis, not diagnosis and cure", *International Journal of Contemporary Hospitality Management*, Vol. 6 No.1/2, pp. 46-52.

Ingram, H., Teare, R., Scheuing, E., Armistead, C. (1997), "A systems model of effective teamworking", *The TQM Magazine*, Vol. 9 No.2, pp. 118-27.

Jienpetivate, M. (1995), "The management of service encounters", University of Surrey, Guildford., MSc dissertation.

Johns, N. (1992), "Quality management in the hospitality industy: Part 1. Definition and specification", *International Journal of Contemporary Hospitality Management*, Vol. 4 No.3, pp. 14-20.

Johns, N. (1993), "Productivity management through design and operation: a case study", *International Journal of Contemporary Hospitality Management*, Vol. 5 No.2, pp. 20-24.

Johns, N. (1993), "Quality management in the hospitality industry: part 3: recent developments", *International Journal of Contemporary Hospitality Management*, Vol. 5 No.1, pp. 10-15.

Johns, N., Chesterton, J. (1994), "ICL Kidsgrove: engineering a quality culture", *International Journal of Contemporary Hospitality Management*, Vol. 6 No.1/2, pp. 25-9.

Johnson, C., Buehler, M. (1993), "Applying global concepts to individual hotels at Park Inn International", *International Journal of Contemporary Hospitality Management*, Vol. 5 No.5 , pp. i-ii.

Jones, P., Iannon, A. (1993), "Measuring guest satisfaction in UK-based international hotel chains: principles and practice", *International Journal of Contemporary Hospitality Management*, Vol. 5 No.5, pp. 27-31.

Jones, P., Lockwood, A. (1995), "Hospitality operating systems", *International Journal of Contemporary Hospitality Management*, Vol. 7 No.5, pp. 17-20.

Jones, P.A. (1990), "A profile of management development and training", *International Journal of Contemporary Hospitality Management*, Vol. 2 No.2, pp. 7-12.

Kanji, G.K., Tambi, A.M. (1999), "Total quality management in UK higher education institutions", Total Quality Management, Vol. 10 No.1, pp.125-54.

Kaplan, R.S, Norton, D.P., (1992), "The balanced scorecard--measures that drive performance", *Harvard Business Review*, Vol. 70 No.1, pp. 71-9.

Karathanos, D. (1999), "Quality: is education keeping pace with business?", Journal of Education for Business, Vol. 74 No.4, pp.231-5.

Kelliher, C. (1989), " Management strategy in employee relations: some changes in the catering industry", *International Journal of Contemporary Hospitality Management*, Vol. 1 No.2, pp. 7-11.

Kelliher, C., Blackman, D. (1991), "Human resource strategies for the 1990s", *International Journal of Contemporary Hospitality Management*, Vol. 3 No.2, pp. 4-9.

Kirk, D. (1995), "Hard and soft systems: a common paradigm for operations", Vol. 7 No.5, pp. 13-16.

Kirzner, I. (1980), "The primacy of entrepreneurial discovery", in Seldon, A. (Eds), *Prime Mover of Progress: The Entrepreneur in Capitalism and Socialism*, Institute of Economic Affairs, London, pp.101-16.

Kwansa, F.A. (1994), "Acquisitions, shareholder wealth and the lodging sector: 1980-1990", *International Journal of Contemporary Hospitality Management*, Vol. 6 No.6, pp. 16-20.

Langer, G. (1996), "Traffic noise and hotel profits - is there a relationship?", Tourism Management, Vol. 17 No.4, pp.295-305.

Larsen, S., Aske, L. (1992), "On-stage in the service theatre", *International Journal of Contemporary Hospitality Management*, Vol. 4 No.4, pp. 12-15.

Litteljohn, D. (1993), "Western Europe", in Jones, P., Pizam, A. (Eds),*The International Hospitality Industry*, Pitman Publishing, London, pp.3-24.

Littlejohn, D., Slattery, P. (1991), "Macro analysis techniques: an appraisal of Europe's main hotel markets", *International Journal of Contemporary Hospitality Management*, Vol. 3 No.4, pp. 6-13.

Littlejohn, D., Watson, S. (1990), "Management development approaches for the 1990s", *International Journal of*

Contemporary Hospitality Management, Vol. 2 No.2, pp. 36-42.

Liu, M-C.B. (1995), "Information technology and management of hotel operations: an examination of the link between the effective use of IT, managerial effectiveness and improvement in business performance", University of Surrey, Guildford., MSc dissertation.

Lockwood, A. (1994), "Using service incidents to identify quality improvement points", *International Journal of Contemporary Hospitality Management*, Vol. 6 No.1/2, pp. 75-80 .

Lockwood, A., Guernier, Y. (1989), "Flexible working in the hospitality industry: current strategies and future potential", *International Journal of Contemporary Hospitality Management*, Vol. 1 No.1, pp. 11-16.

Lockwood, A., Jones, P. (1990), "Applying value engineering to rooms management ", *International Journal of Contemporary Hospitality Management*, Vol. 2 No.1, pp. 27-32.

Lowe, L.S., Kruger, A. (1991), "Motel advertising: practices and themes", *International Journal of Contemporary Hospitality Management*, Vol. 3 No.1, pp. 17-21.

Lucas, R., Laycock, J. (1991), "An interactive personnel function for managing budget hotels", *International Journal of Contemporary Hospitality Management*, Vol. 3 No.3, pp. 33-6.

Lucas, R.E. (1993), "Hospitality industry employment: emerging trends", *International Journal of Contemporary Hospitality Management*, Vol. 5 No.5, pp. 23-6.

Luckock, S. (1991), "Flexible working practices for women returners", *International Journal of Contemporary Hospitality Management*, Vol. 3 No.3, pp. 4-9.

Luke, D., Ingold, A. (1990), "Planning for industry: a study in curriculum design", *International Journal of Contemporary Hospitality Management*, Vol. 2 No.2, pp. 20-23.

Lundberg, C.C., Woods, R.H. (1990), "Modifying restaurant culture: managers as cultural leaders", *International Journal of Contemporary Hospitality Management*, Vol. 2 No.4 , pp. 4-12.

Marsh, C.J. (1997), Perspective, Key Concepts for Understanding Ccurriculum, Falmer Press, London.

Morey, R.C., Dittman (1995), "Evaluating a hotel GM's performance", *Cornell Hotel and Restaurant Administration Quarterly*, Vol. 36 No.5, pp. 30-2.

Morrison, A. (1996), "Guesthouses and small hotels", in Jones, P. (Eds),*Introduction to Hospitality Operations*, Cassell,, London, pp.73-85.

Morrison, A. (1998), "Small firm statistics: a hotel sector focus", *Service Industries Journal*, Vol. 18 No.1, pp.132-42..

Nebel, E.C. III, Braunlich, C.G., Zhang, Y. (1994), "Career paths in American luxury hotels: hotel food and beverage directors", *International Journal of Contemporary Hospitality Management*, Vol. 6 No.6, pp. 3-9.

Nebel, III, E.C., Rutherford, D., Schaffer, J.D. (1994), "Reengineering the hotel organization", *Cornell Hotel and Restaurant Administration Quarterly*, Vol. 35 No.5, pp. 88-95.

Newton, S. (1992), "Customer obsession", *Managing Service Quality*, pp. 269-74.

Nibblelink, A., Teare, R. (1991), "Hotel services for the international business traveller", *International Journal of Contemporary Hospitality Management*, Vol. 3 No.2, pp. iv-vi.

Olsen, M.D. (1991), "Structural changes: the international hospitality industry and firm", *International Journal of Contemporary Hospitality Management*, Vol. 3 No.4, pp. 21-4.

Parry, B., Collins, B. (1993), "Where is facilities management going?", *International Journal of Contemporary Hospitality Management*, Vol. 5 No.2, pp. 36-40.

Parsa, H., Khan, M. (1993), "Quick-service restaurants of the 21 st century: an analytical review of macro factors", Vol. 17 No.1, pp. 161-74.

Parsa, H.G. (1996), "Franchisor-franchisee relationships in quick-service-restaurant systems", *Cornell Hotel and Restaurant Administration Quarterly*, Vol. 37 No.3, pp. 42-9.

Partlow, C.G. (1993), "How Ritz-Carlton applies 'TQM'", *Cornell Hotel & Restaurant Administration Quarterly*, Vol. 34 No.4, pp. 16-24.

Partlow, C.G. (1996), "Human-resources practices of TQM hotels", *Cornell Hotel and Restaurant Administration Quarterly*, Vol. 37 No.5, pp. 67-77.

Paulson, D.M., Baltzer, L.E., Cole, R.S. (1990), "Methods of educating cashiers in a restaurant teaching laboratory", Vol. 13 No.2, pp. 31-44.

Pavesic, D.V. (1989), "Hospitality education 2005: curricular and programmatic trends", Vol. 13 No.1, pp. 285-88.

Pavesic, D.V. (1993), "Hospitality Education 2005: curricular and programmatic trends", *Hospitality Research Journal*, Vol. 17 No.1, pp. 285-94.

Payne, J.W. (1982), "Contingent decision behavior", *Psychological Bulletin*, Vol. 92 pp. 382-402.

Peacock, M. (1993), "A question of size", *International Journal of Contemporary Hospitality Management*, Vol. 5 No.4, pp. 29-32.

Peacock, M. (1995), "A job well done: hospitality managers and success", *International Journal of Contemporary Hospitality Management*, Vol. 7 No.2, pp. 48-51.

Peacock, R. (1995), "International tourism and hospitality training—expanding the expertise", *Australian Journal of Hospitality Management*, Vol. 2 No.1, pp. 55-9.

Pearce, D. (1989), *Tourism Development*, Longman Scientific & Technical, New York, NY.

Pearce, J.A.I., Robinson, R.B. Jr (2000), "Cultivating Guanxi as a foreign investor strategy", *Business Horizons*, Vol. 43 No.1, pp. 31-8.

Pearce, P. (1991), "Locating tourism studies in the landscape of knowledge", paper presented at New Horizons Conference, University of Calgary, Calgary, Alberta.

Pearce, R.A. (1995), Maintains the Quality of University Education, University of Buckingham, Buckingham.

Pederson, B. (1994), "Future seniors and the travel industry", Vol. 12 No.2, pp. 59-70.

Pederson, B., DeMicco, F.J. (1993), "Restaurant dining strategies: attracting nutrition conscious future seniors", Vol. 11 No.2, pp. 7-18.

Pederson, E.B. (1992), "Future seniors: is the hospitality industry ready for them?", Vol. 10 No.2, pp. 1-8.

Peppers, D., Rogers, M., Dorf, B. (1999), "Is your company ready for one-to-one marketing?", *Harvard Business Review*, Vol. 77 No.1, pp. 151-60.

Perdue, J., Woods, R.H., Ninemeier, J. (2000), "Club management competencies 2005: updated information for the classroom", *Journal of Tourism and Hospitality Education*, Vol. 14 No.2, pp. 19-32.

Perkins, J., Cummings, P. (1994), "A community economic development survey of part-time labor: implications for the hospitality industry", Vol. 17 No.3, pp. 111-18.

Perlmutter, H. (1969), "The tortuous evolution of the multinational corporation", *Columbia Journal of World Business*, January-February, pp. 9-18.

Peters, T.J., Waterman, R.H. (1982), *In Search of Excellence*, Harper & Row, New York, NY.

Petrof, J.V. (1997), "Relationship marketing: the wheel reinvented?", *Business Horizons*, Vol. 40 No.6, pp. 26-31.

Pfeifer, Y. (1983)), "Small business management", in Cassee, E.H., Reuland, R. (Eds), *The Management of Hospitality*, Pergamon, Oxford, pp. 189-202.

Phillips, P.A. (1994), " Welsh hotel: cost-volume-profit analysis and uncertainty", *International Journal of Contemporary Hospitality Management*, Vol. 6 No.3, pp. 31-6 .

Pickering, J., Greenwood, J., Hunt, D. (1971), *The Small Firm in the Hotel and Catering Industry (Committee of Inquiry on Small Firms: Research Report 14)*, HMSO, London.

Pickert, M.J., Miller, J. (1996), "Food production forecasting in six commercial foodservice operations: a pilot study", *Hospitality Research Journal*, Vol. 20 No..2, pp. 137-44.

Plummer, K. (1995), *Telling Sexual Stories: Power, Change and Social Worlds*, Routledge, London.

Pocock, B (1987), *Changing Systems Women, Work and TAFE: A Report for the Commonwealth Tertiary Education Commission*, Australian Government Publishing Service, Canberra.

Policy Studies Institute (1993), *Private Sector Experience of Competitive Tendering for Local Authority Services: Stage One*, Policy Studies Institute, London.

Pollert, A (1991), *Farewell to Flexibility*, Basil Blackwell, Oxford.

Pollitt, D., Mellors, C. (1992), "Preparing for the Single Market: The Role of Trade Associations and Professional Bodies", *European Business Review*, Vol. 92 No.2, pp. 22-5.

Poorani, A., Smith, D.R. (1994), "Franchising as a business expansion strategy in the bed and breakfast industry: creating a marketing and development advantage", Vol. 18 No.2, pp. 19-28.

Poorani, A.A. (1996), "Trade-show management: budgeting and planning or a successful event", *Cornell Hotel and Restaurant Administration Quarterly*, Vol. 37 No.4, pp. 77-84.

Powers, T.F., Riegel, C.D. (1993), "A bright future for hospitality education: providing value in the 21st century", *Hospitality Research Journal*, Vol. 17 No.1, pp. 295-308.

Prascevic, Z, Petrovic-Lazarevic, S (1992), "Application of the fuzzy set theory for optimal choice of a contractor for a project realisation", *Cybernetics and Systems*, Vol. 1 pp. 439-46.

Prascevic, Z, Petrovic-Lazarevic, S (1998), "Fuzzy multiple objective decision making in the construction industry", Monash University, Department of Management, working paper 90/98.

Pratt, R., Whitney, D. (1991), "Attentional and interpersonal characteristics of restaurant general managers in comparison with other groups of interest", Vol. 15 No.1, pp. 9-24.

Price, F. (1986), *Right First Time - Using Quality Control for Profit*, Wildwood House.

Price, P. "Customer care in licensed retailing", *International Journal of Contemporary Hospitality Management*, Vol. 1 No.2 , pp. 17-18.

Prichard, M. (1981), *Guests and Hosts*, Oxford University Press, Oxford.

Prideaux, B., Dunn, A. (1995), "Tourism and crime--how can the tourism industry respond?", *Australian Journal of Hospitality Management*, Vol. 2 No.1, pp. 7-16.

Pringle, R., Turner, M. (1998), *Europe's New Money*, Central Banking Publications, London.

Przeclawski, K. (1993), "Tourism as the subject of interdisciplinary research", in Pearce, D.G., Butler, R.W. (Eds), *Tourism Research: Critiques and Challenges*, Routledge, London and New York, NY.

Riley, M. (1992), "Labour utilization and collective agreements: an international comparison", *International Journal of Contemporary Hospitality Management*, Vol. 4 No.4, pp. 21-3.

Riley, M. (1993), "Labour turnover: time to change the paradigm?", *International Journal of Contemporary Hospitality Management*, Vol. 5 No.4, pp. i-iii.

Riley, M. (1996), *Human Resource Management: A Guide to Personnel Practice in the Hospitality and Tourism Industry*, Butterworth- Heinemann, Oxford.

Riley, M., Jauncey, S. (1990), "Examining structure in decision making in hotels", *International Journal of Contemporary Hospitality Management*, Vol. 2 No.3, pp. 11-15.

Rita, P., Moutinho, L. (1992), "Allocating a promotion budget", *International Journal of Contemporary Hospitality Management*, Vol. 4 No.3, pp. 3-8.

Ritchie, J.R.B. (1993), "Educating the tourism educators: guidelines for policy and programme development", *Teros International*, Vol. 1 No.1.

Roper, A., Carmouche, R. (1989), "Budget hotels - a case of mistaken identity?", *International Journal of Contemporary Hospitality Management*, Vol. 1 No.1, pp. 25-31.

Rothstein, L.R., Hackman, J.R., Pascual, E., Gelinas, M.V., James, R.G., Randolph, W.A. (1995), "The empowerment effort that came undone", *Harvard Business Review*, Vol. 1 pp. 20.

Schubert, W.H. (1986), Curriculum Perspective, Design, and Possibility, Macmillan, New York, NY.

Segal-Horn, S. (1995), "Core competence and international strategy in service multinationals", in Teare, R., Armistead, C. (Eds), *Service Management: New Directions, New Perspectives*, Cassell, London.

Sellah, H., Riley, M. (1994), "Measuring culinary learning processes: education and experience contrasted", *International Journal of Contemporary Hospitality Management*, Vol. 6 No.6 , pp. iii-v.

Senior, M., Morphew, R. (1990), "Examining structure in decision making in hotels ", *International Journal of Contemporary Hospitality Management*, Vol. 2 No.3, pp. 3-9.

Shonk, W., Shonk, J.H. (1988), "What business teams can learn from athletic teams", *Personnel*, Vol. 65 No.June, pp. 76..

Simmons, P., Teare, R. (1993), "Evolving a total quality culture", *International Journal of Contemporary Hospitality Management*, Vol. 5 No.3, pp. v-viii .

Sinclair, J., Arthur, A. (1994), "Inhospitable cultures and continuous improvement ", *International Journal of Contemporary Hospitality Management*, Vol. 6 No.1/2, pp. 30-6.

Sparks, B. (1993), "Guest history: is it being utilized?", *International Journal of Contemporary Hospitality Management*, Vol. 5 No.1, pp. 22-6.

Sparrow, J., Ingold, T. , Huyton, J., Baker, J. (1992), " Experienced staff and tailoring food service", *International Journal of Contemporary Hospitality Management*, Vol. 4 No.1, pp. 4-10.

Sparrow, J., Wood, G. (1994), "You're stopping me from giving quality service", *International Journal of Contemporary Hospitality Management*, Vol. 6 No.1/2, pp. 61-7.

Sparrow, J., Wood, G. (1994), "You're stopping me from giving quality service", *International Journal of Contemporary Hospitality Management*, Vol. 6 No.1, pp. 61-7.

Stainforth, D. (1996), "Teamworking, or individual working

in a team?", *Team Performance Management*, Vol. 2 No.3, pp. 37-41.

Staw, B.M. (1986), "Organizational psychology and the pursuit of the happy/productive worker", *California Management Review*, Vol. 4 No.Summer, pp. 40-53.

Stevens, B. (1997), "Hotel ethical codes: a content analysis", International Journal of Hospitality Management, Vol. 16 No.3, pp.261-71.

Stevens, B., Fleckenstein, A. (1999), "Comparative ethics: how students and human-resources directors react to real-life situations", Cornell Hotel and Restaurant Administration Quarterly, Vol. 40 No.2, pp.69-75.

Stewart, G.R., Kleiner, B.H. (1996), "The enabling power of teams and information technology", *Team Performance Management*, Vol. 2 No.2, pp. 13-18.

Storey, D.J. (1994), *Understanding the Small Business Sector*, Routledge,, London..

Strachan, P.A. (1996), "Achieving environmental excellence through effective teamwork", *Team Performance Management*, Vol. 2 pp. 25-9.

Syer, J. (1986), *Team Spirit: The Elusive Experience*, The Kingswood Press, London, pp. 13-14.

Taba, H. (1962), Curriculum Development: Theory and Practice, Harcourt Brace and World, New York, NY.

Tam, M. (1999), "Quality assurance policies in higher education in Hong Kong", Journal of Higher Education Policy and Management, Vol. 21 No.2, pp.215-21.

Taylor, S., Edgar, D. (1996), "Hospitality research: the emperor's new clothes?", International Journal of Hospitality Management, Vol. 15 No.3, pp.211-27.

Teare, R, Ingram, H., Schueing, E., Armistead, C. (1997), "Organizational teamworking frameworks: evidence from UK and US-based firms", *Journal of Service Industry Management*, Vol. 8 No.3.

Teare, R. (1991), "Developing hotels in Europe: some reflections on progress and prospects ", *International Journal of Contemporary Hospitality Management*, Vol. 3 No.4, pp. 55-9.

Teare, R., Davies, M., McGeary, B. (1989), "The operational challenge of hotel short breaks", *International Journal of Contemporary Hospitality Management*, Vol. 1 No.1, pp. 22-4.

Thomas, R. (1992), "1992 and the hospitality industry: a review of information provision", *International Journal of Contemporary Hospitality Management*, Vol. 4 No.2, pp. 3-7.

Thomas, R. (1994), "European union enterprise policy and the hospitality industry", *International Journal of Contemporary Hospitality Management*, Vol. 6 No.4, pp. 10-15.

Thomas, R., Friel, M., Jameson, S., Parsons D. (1997), *The National Survey of Small Tourism and Hospitality Firms: Annual Report 1996-97*, Centre for the Study of Small Tourism and Hospitality Firms, Leeds..

Thomas, R.M., Clermont, C., Maimbolwa-Sinyangwe, I. (1984), "Assessing the meaning of moral", Studies in Educational Evaluation, Vol. 10 No.2, pp.167-77.

Timmons, J. (1994), *New Venture Creation*, Irwin, Boston, MA..

Tofts, A. (1991), "Executive development for hospital managers", *International Journal of Contemporary Hospitality Management*, Vol. 3 No.3, pp. 16-20.

Tracey, J., Hinkin, T. (1996), "How transformational leaders lead in the hospitality industry", International Journal of Hospitality Management, Vol. 15 No.2, pp.165-76.

Tse, E., Olsen, M.D. (1990), "Business strategy and organisational structure: a case of US restaurant firms", *International Journal of Contemporary Hospitality Management*, Vol. 2 No.3 , pp. 17-23.

Twomey, K., Kleiner, B.H. (1996), "Teamwork: the essence of the successful organization", *Team Performance Management*, Vol. 2 No.1, pp. 6-8.

Uysal, M., McDonald, C.D., Marton, B.S. (1994), "Australian visitors to US national parks and natural areas", *International Journal of Contemporary Hospitality Management*, Vol. 6 No.3, pp. 18-24.

Valdez, R., Kleiner, B.H. (1996), "How to build teamwork in the defence industry", *Team Performance Management*, Vol. 2 No.2, pp. 41-8.

Vallen, G., Casado, M. (2000), "Ethical principles for the hospitality curriculum", Cornell Hotel and Restaurant Administration Quarterly, Vol. 41 No.2, pp.44-51.

Velasquez, M.G. (1998), Business Ethics, Concepts and Cases, 4th ed., Prentice Hall, Englewood Cliffs, NJ.

Vierich, W., Calver, S. (1991), "Hotels and the leisure sector: a product differentiation strategy for the 1990s", *International Journal of Contemporary Hospitality Management*, Vol. 3 No.3, pp. 10-15.

Walsh, M.E. (1993), "The Republic of Ireland", in Baum, T. (Eds), *Human Resource Issues in International Tourism*, Butterworth-Heinemann, Oxford, pp. 201-16.

Watson, S. (1991), "From a la carte to cafeteria-style management development", *International Journal of Contemporary Hospitality Management*, Vol. 3 No.4, pp. 42-6.

Watson, S., D'Annunzio-Green, N. (1996), "Implementing cultural change through human resources: the elusive organization alchemy?", International Journal of Contemporary Hospitality Management, Vol. 8 No.2.

Weaver, P.A., Oh, H.C. (1993), "Do American business travellers have different hotel service requirements?", *International Journal of Contemporary Hospitality Management*, Vol. 5 No.3 , pp. 16-21.

Webster, M. (1998), "Strategies for growth", in Thomas, R. (Eds),*The Management of Small Tourism and Hospitality Firms*, Cassell, London, pp.207-18.

Webster, M.M. (1994), "Strategic management in context at Swallow Hotels", *International Journal of Contemporary Hospitality Management*, Vol. 6 No.5, pp. 3-8.

Boatright, J.R. (2000), Ethics and the Conduct of Business, 3rd ed., Prentice Hall, Englewood Cliffs, NJ.

Wilson, F. (1996), "Great teams build themselves", *Team Performance Management*, Vol. 2 No.2, pp. 27-31.

Witt, C., Witt, S.F. (1989), "Why productivity in the hotel sector is low", *International Journal of Contemporary Hospitality Management*, Vol. 1 No.2, pp. 28-33.

Witt, C.A., Witt, S.F. (1989), "Why productivity in the hotel sector is low", *International Journal of Contemporary Hospitality Management*, Vol. 1 No.2, pp. 28-34.

Index

D

E

F

G

H

I

J

K

L

M

N

O

P

Q

W

Y

Z